COMMON ENEMIES

COMMON ENEMIES

Georgetown Basketball, Miami Football, and the Racial Transformation of College Sports

THOMAS F. SCHALLER

University of Nebraska Press • *Lincoln*

∞

Names: Schaller, Thomas F., author.
Title: Common enemies: Georgetown basketball, Miami football, and
the racial transformation of college sports / Thomas F. Schaller.
Description: Lincoln: University of Nebraska Press, [2021] | Includes
bibliographical references and index.
Identifiers: LCCN 2021021082
ISBN 9781496215710 (Hardback)
ISBN 9781496230041 (ePub)
ISBN 9781496230058 (PDF)
Subjects: LCSH: College sports—United States—History. | College
sports—Social aspects—United States. | Racism in sports—United
States—History. | Discrimination in sports—United States—History. |
Social movements—United States. | Social change—United States—
History—20th century. | Georgetown University—Basketball—
History. | Basketball players—United States—Social life and customs. |
University of Florida—Football—History. | Football players—United
States—Social life and customs. | BISAC: SOCIAL SCIENCE / Ethnic
Studies / American / African American & Black Studies | SPORTS &
RECREATION / Football
Classification: LCC GV351 .S33 2021 | DDC 796.04/30973—dc23
LC record available at https://lccn.loc.gov/2021021082

Set in Arno Pro by Laura Buis.

To Laura:
Your support, love, and patience humble me

CONTENTS

PREFACE

As a teenager and during my college undergraduate years in the 1980s, I hated Georgetown basketball and Miami football.

It's easy to convince myself today that my rooting interests were valid because I grew up in upstate New York, home to Hoyas basketball rival Syracuse University, and later attended Florida State University (FSU), one of the Hurricanes' primary football foes. I was lucky to see in person two of the most storied games in those two rivalries: the 1985 Syracuse-Georgetown game at the Carrier Dome and the 1987 FSU-Miami game at Doak Campbell Stadium. I was pleased that Syracuse won thanks to Dwayne "Pearl" Washington's shot in the waning seconds and was devastated two years later in Tallahassee when the Seminoles squandered what seemed like an insurmountable 19–3 halftime lead and thus their chance to win FSU's first national championship.

But I would be lying if I did not confess that part of my hatred toward both the Hoyas and the Hurricanes partly derived from the fact that they were, for lack of a better term, "Black programs" whose posture and performance seemed foreign to me, a white kid who grew up in an almost entirely white suburb of Albany, New York. Sure, the Syracuse Orangemen basketball and Seminole football teams also relied heavily on talented Black athletes; heck, now-retired Syracuse center Derrick Coleman and Florida

State cornerback Deion Sanders, both African American superstars, remain two of my favorite professional athletes. But only later, as I came to better understand the meaning of race in U.S. sports—which is to say, the meaning of race itself in the United States—did I fully appreciate how important and impactful those Georgetown and Miami teams were. This book is a byproduct of that awakening.

As set forth in the opening chapter, my primary argument in the book is straightforward. During the pivotal 1980s, Georgetown basketball and Miami football helped pioneer the emergence of what sportswriter Bill Rhoden calls the "black style" of play in major-college televised sports. Neither team originated this style, nor did either practice it exclusively. But the Hoyas and Hurricanes are rightly remembered for accelerating both the on-field and off-field changes that led to the deeper, cultural integration of Division I men's basketball and football following the preceding, literal integration of major-college sports.

That hard-fought battle by Black athletes and coaches during the postwar period to integrate major-college sports, especially at universities in the segregated South, is my focus in chapter 2. In it I chronicle the key actors and moments of this sometimes glorious but more often painful transformation. What's most fascinating is that, though both Georgetown basketball and Miami football played their own, small roles in the integration of college sports, the Hoyas and the 'Canes were relatively lackluster, even obscure programs during this formative era.

That obscurity is what made these two programs, their universities, and their surrounding cities such unlikely incubators for the second-wave racial revolution within college sports that took place during the 1980s, the subject of chapter 3. In the years leading up to the emergence of the Hoyas and the Hurricanes as national powerhouses, Washington and Miami experienced rapid, tumultuous, and sometimes violent racial transformations. Though different in important aspects, the 1968 riots in Washington and the 1980 riots in Miami were important historical backdrops to the respective emergence of the Hoyas and the Hurricanes.

Chapter 4 chronicles the 1983–84 college athletic season during which the Hurricanes and the Hoyas won their first national championships. Those two titles cannot be properly understood without examining the years of fits-and-starts progress for both programs prior to that fateful season. Accordingly, I also recount key moments for each program that set the stage for Miami and Georgetown to burst onto the national stage in such dramatic fashion in the early 1980s.

The fifth chapter offers deeper biographical portraits of the two coaches and two athletes who in many ways defined those 1980s Hoyas and Hurricanes teams: Georgetown's John Thompson and Patrick Ewing, and Miami's Jimmy Johnson and Michael Irvin. Other players, coaches, and administrators contributed significantly to forging and sustaining these two sporting dynasties. But beyond leading their teams to some of their greatest sporting achievements, these four men were notable for developing each program's uniquely racialized identity.

In chapter 6, I examine the lasting cultural and commercial imprints left by Georgetown basketball and Miami football. In particular, I discuss how the nascent Black style of play forever changed how players and teams in major-college men's sports are marketed and sold to alumni, sports fans, and consumers. From Spike Lee movies to South Florida rap albums, Georgetown and Miami quickly morphed from mere sports programs into cultural icons with far-reaching influence, especially within the African American and, later, Latino communities. From "Hoya Paranoia" to "The U," Georgetown and Miami commodified the Black style, thereby aiding its transformation into the now-familiar experience forged at the intersection of sports, popular culture, and mass-market branding.

Finally, in the concluding chapter I widen the lens to assess the impact of Black and other minority college athletes and coaches on today's sports, culture, and politics. I specifically address how those athletes and coaches changed eligibility standards for student athletes; how the continuing efforts to diversify coaching staffs and administrative ranks are succeeding in some ways, yet failing in others; how contemporary minority athletes are fighting back against the corporate exploitation of their likenesses for profit; and how today's amateur athletes are using sports to change public awareness and attitudes on issues of race.

Writing a book is, first and foremost, a learning experience for the author. Obviously, that experience involves inquiry into the book's subject matter. But in my three previous books and doctoral dissertation, I also learned what I presume many other authors do, namely, how challenging it is to find the resources and time to write a book, including how (and how not) to balance completion of such a large endeavor against other, often more important professional and personal goals. In that regard this book is no different.

What *is* different about writing *Common Enemies* is that it changed how I think about both sports and race. That is, it changed me not only as a writer but also as a fan. I look at—and root for—different athletes, coaches, universities, and professional sports teams, and for different reasons, than those I did before starting this project. My great regret is that I arrived at this new perspective too late to enjoy in real time those legendary Georgetown and Miami teams of my youth.

ACKNOWLEDGMENTS

No book is a solo endeavor. I want to thank many people for their contributions.

I start with my editor, Rob Taylor of the University of Nebraska Press, who took a chance on a political scientist with limited, long-ago experience as a freelance sportswriter when he assigned me to write a book about politics and race in college sports. His editorial guidance was exceeded only by his faith in me.

I also want to recognize the many people at University of Maryland, Baltimore County (UMBC), where I teach, who provided institutional support for this project: my department chair, Carolyn Forestiere; former College of Arts, Humanities, and Social Sciences dean Scott Casper and current acting dean Kimberly Moffitt; and UMBC president Freeman Hrabowski. My political science colleagues Tyson King-Meadows and William Blake, both of whom know quite a bit about race and sports, also provided encouragement. UMBC historian Derek Musgrove, a native of my adopted hometown of Washington DC, offered his insights; he also connected me with visiting scholar Theresa Runstedtler, author of an outstanding Jack Johnson biography, who provided helpful comments.

A number of brilliant sports historians and observers contributed their voices to the book. My deepest thanks to Alejandro

Danois, Todd Boyd, Billy Corben, Dan Le Batard, Chuck Todd, and Dave Zirin. Conversations with sports historians Amy Bass, Jeff Pearlman, and former *Salon* colleague and fantastic sportswriter King Kaufman, yielded useful tips on how to research and write a sports book. My thanks also to copanelists and audience members who made suggestions after an early presentation about the book at the 2018 annual meeting of the North American Society for Sport History (NASSH) in Winnipeg, Manitoba.

To ensure the book would appeal to a general readership, I tapped into a vital and reliable resource: a number of my close, long-time friends, some of whom are also academics but all of whom are sports junkies. My eternal thanks to Sean Aday, Kirk Bowman, Mike Cocchi, Bill Koleszar, Sean Martin, Dan Piazza, Jeff Stanger, Chris Thompson, Jonathan Weiler, and my brother-in-law Steve Smith for their comments and input.

COMMON ENEMIES

[1]

Rise of the Black Style

Intimidation is part of life. The strong get
stronger and the weak get weaker.
—PATRICK EWING, Georgetown University center, 1981–85

We were the [Muhammad] Alis of that era. Not only
were we going to beat you up, we were going to
talk to you while we beat you up.
—BENNIE BLADES, University of Miami defensive back, 1984–87

Columnists called them "wilding" rogues and thugs. Fans wore
T-shirts and held signs aloft at games mocking them as illit-
erates, convicts, even apes. In tones and language that would be
nearly unimaginable today, spectators and even sportswriters in
the 1980s continued to use thinly veiled racist terms to derogate
and demean Black college athletes. Legal segregation and overt
discrimination against minority student athletes were mostly relics
of the recent past, but subtler forms of discrimination persisted.
Despite notable progress, Black athletes were still not fully assim-
ilated into an intercollegiate sporting experience dominated by
white athletes, coaches, administrators, alumni, and fans. It fell
to a new generation of Black athletes to lead the social and cultural transformation of major-college sports.

1

Georgetown University basketball and University of Miami football spearheaded this racial revolution in televised men's team sports during the 1980s. The Georgetown Hoyas and Miami Hurricanes changed the way Black athletes competed and performed on the field. The two programs forced universities to reconsider how minority players and coaches were treated, discussed by fans, and covered by the media. By attracting legions of new fans, Black and white alike, African American players transformed sports apparel and marketing and helped turn college basketball and football into multibillion-dollar industries. Specifically, the Hoyas and Hurricanes infused the basketball hardcourts and football gridirons with a new and highly controversial "black style" of play, a term coined by award-winning *New York Times* sports columnist William Rhoden in his 2006 book *Forty Million Dollar Slaves*. "The introduction of African American athletes to the mainstream marked the beginning of a tremendous influx of black football and basketball players to previously segregated Southern schools," Rhoden wrote. "It also marked the beginning of an intense struggle to control the extent to which African American 'style' was expressed through sports."[1]

The 1980s were the critical, transitional decade for college sports. Mostly gone were the patently racist practices common during the postwar period. Those uglier days included threats of violence against Black athletes during games; the refusal by many programs and even entire conferences to integrate their teams or so much as compete against integrated opponents; and the systematic on-campus segregation of minority athletes even at integrated universities. Black athletes were spat on and verbally harassed by opposing players and coaches. They endured substandard housing accommodations and transportation. Coaches and athletic directors often reprimanded Black athletes who protested these abuses. In some cases Black athletes were banned from competition by their own universities.

By 1980 Division I team sports were fully integrated, even in the deepest corners of the long-segregated Deep South. Black athletes constituted a growing share of the starting basketball and football lineups at many top-ranked programs. A small, nascent cohort of Black head coaches and assistant coaches led college teams. As rosters became more inclusive, so did rooters. College football and basketball programs attracted new and increasingly diverse audiences that transcended geographic fan bases and racial barriers. Despite these changes, Africans Americans still represented a tiny share of students and alumni from institutions other than historically Black colleges and universities (HBCUs). More than 90 percent of athletic directors, sports information directors, and other athletic administrators were white.[2] And sports boosters—the alumni who packed football tailgating parking lots and pricey suites at college basketball games—remained overwhelmingly white.

Although the National Collegiate Athletic Association (NCAA) and the courts had cleared many of the legal and structural hurdles for Black college athletes, in the 1980s they faced enduring obstacles. Born too late for the Civil Rights Movement and anti–Vietnam War protests, this generation of athletes began to challenge persistent on- and off-field sporting norms: how players comported themselves during games, how the media covered the achievements and exploits of Black athletes, and how the NCAA and its member conferences treated Black student athletes. Racial conflicts in college sports shifted from the court system to the courts of public opinion.

The decade was a particularly ripe moment for a racial revolution in televised college sports. At the same time that college football gridirons and basketball hardcourts came to rely on Black talent, lucrative broadcast television contracts and sporting apparel endorsements made Division I college basketball and football increasingly profitable industries. The major conferences inked long-term broadcast contracts with the national networks, and the 1979 launch of the innovative all-sports cable channel ESPN promised higher revenues and greater exposure. A pivotal 1984 Supreme Court ruling gave individual universities and conference the power to negotiate television deals directly with the networks, without approval from the National Collegiate Athletic Association.

In early 1980 *Sports Illustrated*'s Curry Kirkpatrick forecast a number of reasons why the 1980s promised change for major-college basketball. "More black players performing at the big state universities in the South. Additional conferences springing up with accompanying TV exposure, especially in the East. Bigger and better arenas across the land. Players sophisticated enough as freshmen"—the NCAA had recently eliminated its ban on freshmen participation—"to handle conditions on the road," wrote Kirkpatrick.[3] In his 1987 book *Breaking the Ice*, about the racial transformation of college football's long-segregated Southwest Conference (SWC), sports historian Richard Pennington reached a similar conclusion about the racial transformation also happening in Division I football. "Since blacks are no longer barred from competing, the game is bigger, faster, and far better than before," Pennington wrote. "Had blacks been allowed to enroll in SWC institutions and play football in the days of rugby-like balls, leather helmets and high-top shoes, they would have dominated then, too. Clearly, a revolution has occurred in the SWC football and if the campus hero no longer has blond hair and blue eyes, so be it."[4] With a more inclusive appeal, college basketball and football faced the prospect of attaining national reach on a scale that athletic directors and media executives long hoped for.

The 1980s were also ready-made for racial clashes between "good-guy" white athletes and bombastic "bad-boy" Black opponents. In the preceding years contests suffused with racial subplots drew huge audiences. Four years after the much-hyped 1975 heavyweight championship bout between Muhammad Ali and "great white hope" Chuck Wepner, the 1979 NCAA men's basketball title game pitting Michigan State's Magic Johnson against Indiana State's Larry Bird became—and to this day remains—the highest rated televised college basketball game in history. The successes of Black players and teams flipped the script on historic imbalances between whites and minorities. Audiences tuned in to watch sporting clashes between the new Black Goliaths and white Davids.

Rise of the Black Style

The rapid racial integration of college sports provided a unique opportunity to university presidents, conference officials, television executives and corporate sponsors. To capitalize, they needed to expand broadcast college sports' following among both Black and white spectators. The good news for Black athletes was that these developments presented new opportunities and a greater, if still limited degree of control over their student-athlete experiences. Suddenly, network executives found themselves in expensive bidding wars for the right to broadcast Division I men's college basketball and football games. Sports apparel companies, including Nike and Adidas, likewise competed to ink lucrative sponsorship deals with prominent coaches and notable athletic programs. In theory, a college sports industry increasingly dependent on Black and other minority student athletes to deliver their product should have given these athletes greater agency and leverage.

The bad news was that new opportunities and greater visibility for Black athletes forced university leaders and athletic administrators to respond, and sometimes they responded rashly. To capitalize on the rising value of televised college sports, university and athletic-conference leaders asserted greater control over the administration and marketing of their student athletes. Not surprisingly, the growing profitability of major-college sports attracted greater scrutiny and even backlash. Alumni, academics, public officials, sports boosters, and the media called for more oversight. Athletic officials found themselves addressing questions that previously went unanswered, if not unasked. What are the appropriate rules for recruiting student athletes? To what academic standards should they be held? What tradeoffs should be made between athletes' academic and sporting calendars? What apparel sponsorships and television contracts should universities sign?

To claim their share of the sports-industrial complex's burgeoning fame and fortune, Black athletes and coaches also had to act. Sometimes, that meant acting up. "The Black style" refers in part to the heightened competitiveness that Black and other minority athletes brought to sports. But as Bill Rhoden argued, the Black style also includes the performative aspects of participation, from sporting apparel to demonstrative victory celebrations to intimidating trash-talk. "The gestures that make up the black style—the chest bumps, high fives, shakes and shimmies—are more profound than simple mannerisms," Rhoden explained. "Style is a specialized form of black expression, a consequence of being 'outside of,' or 'other.'"[5] The Black style went beyond mere performance. It was a not-so-subtle reminder to white overseers that the profitability of major-college televised sports depended on Black participation.

Naturally, the Black style appealed to newly attentive African American spectators. But the Black style also piqued new interest among white audiences. Many white sports fans tuned in to root *against* the perfect foils: the Black and other minority athletes defeating—and sometimes demeaning—their opponents. Inevitably, certain players and programs morphed from mere opponents into useful villains. And no two teams in the 1980s welcomed the role of antagonist more than the basketball Hoyas and the football Hurricanes.

Georgetown and Miami practiced a proudly racialized style of play. They taunted opponents. They celebrated scores and victories with in-your-face swagger. "Intimidation is part of life. The strong get stronger and the weak get weaker," quipped Georgetown's All-American center Patrick Ewing.[6] "We were the [Muhammad] Alis of that era," recalled Bennie Blades, star defensive back for the 1980s Hurricanes squads. "Not only were we going to beat you up, we were going to talk to you while we beat you up."[7] The Hoyas and Hurricanes relished playing the menacing role of Darth Vader in their respective sports.

Both programs also left deep imprints on sporting culture beyond the courts and playing fields. Coaches at Georgetown and Miami changed the tenor of postgame media appearances and the language that journalists and broadcasters used to describe athletes. Black and minority athletes at both schools made sports apparel fashionable for younger fans, particularly young, urban African American males. The two universities' logos and colors quickly spread across urban landscapes as African Americans who had never set foot on either campus began flashing Miami's orange-and-green and Georgetown's gray-and-blue gear. Players consorted with and were glorified by hip-hop artists, including 2 Live Crew and N.W.A. The Hoyas and the 'Canes were fashionable because they made the bad-boy image look good. Popular culture took notice.

Perhaps most importantly, Georgetown basketball and Miami football won. The programs may have attracted fans and critics purely by dint of their defiant, chest-thumping style of play. Had they fielded middling teams, however, far fewer spectators and commentators would have paid them any mind. But in fact, the two schools dominated the decade.

The Hoyas won four of the first six Big East Conference tournaments, and six of the ten tournaments during the 1980s. In nine of the decade's years, the Hoyas finished the regular season ranked in the top twenty.[8] They played in the NCAA tournament all ten seasons, and reached at least the Elite Eight round in six of those ten years. Georgetown played in the championship game three times and won it once during the four-year span from 1982 to 1985 that coincided with center Patrick Ewing's career. Eric "Sleepy" Floyd, Reggie Williams, and Charles Smith joined Ewing in earning All-American honors during the decade.[9] After Georgetown's 1984 championship, *Sports Illustrated*'s cover featured coach John Thompson and Ewing bracketing a grinning President Ronald Reagan.

The Hurricanes played in a postseason bowl game in eight of the decade's ten seasons—the same number of bowl appearances as in the program's previous fifty years.[10] During a remarkable seven-year run from the 1983 through the 1989 seasons, Miami lost just eleven games en route to winning three national championships. (It won a fourth to start the 1990s.) During one mid-decade stretch, Miami won thirty-six consecutive regular-season games, a figure equal to more than three full seasons of competition. The Hurricanes also held the No. 1 national ranking for more weeks than any other college football program during the 1980s. Fourteen players received first-team All-American honors from at least one rating organization, including Eddie Brown, Willie Smith, Jerome Brown, Bennie Blades, Cleveland Gary, and Vinny Testaverde, who in 1987 became the first Miami player to win the Heisman Trophy (awarded to the sport's top player), cementing the school's reputation as "Quarterback U."[11]

The two programs' most lasting impact was not the titles and trophies they won, but how they infused and eventually normalized the Black style in college team sports. In the process Georgetown and Miami transcended sports to become racial Rorschach tests for the sporting media and for white and Black spectators alike. The Hoyas and 'Canes were as difficult to ignore between games as they were during them. In Georgetown and Miami, many sports fans recognized themselves and their values—or their mirror opposites.

The Hoyas and Hurricanes made the rare leap from media and cultural touchstones into true brands because they ratcheted up the stakes of the traditional rivalries that governed collegiate-sports fandom. Historically, perennial rivalries pitted the teams, administrators, boosters, and alumni of one university against its in-state, regional, and conference foes. You hated the University of California, Los Angeles (UCLA) because you or your family went to or worked at the University of Southern California (USC), and vice versa. It was as simple as that. Although they were neither the first nor the last programs to do so, Georgetown and Miami helped dissolve these geographic bounds. Wittingly or not, they did so by tapping into reflex so hardwired into the American DNA it was codified in the original Constitution: the tribalism of race.

It's remarkable how unlikely these two universities were to lead a cultural and racial revolution in college sports. Georgetown was a sleepy Jesuit college nestled in a tony corner of northwest Washington; its sports reputation for most of the twentieth century, insofar as it had one, was built around sailing, rowing, and track and field. Prior to John Thompson's arrival as the Hoyas' coach, the team hadn't made the postseason national basketball tournament since 1943. That year's "Kiddie Korps" team made it to the title game and lost. The program's most recognizable alums, including future Illinois congressman Henry Hyde and future

National Football League (NFL) commissioner Paul Tagliabue, were known more for their post-Georgetown careers that for what they achieved on the court during their playing days. The university terminated its football program in 1951 and did not revive it again until 1970 (and then only at the Division III level).

Situated in exclusive Coral Gables, the University of Miami's football program enjoyed a bit more success prior to its 1980s renaissance than Georgetown's long-dormant basketball team. With rosters featuring quarterback George Mira, running back Chuck Foreman, and ferocious defensive lineman Ted Hendricks, the 'Canes had a brief football heyday during the 1950s and 1960s under coach Andy Gustafson. But the private university's football fortunes plummeted so far that in 1976 the university's board of governors came within one vote of abandoning its football program altogether. Less than seven years later, the Hurricanes were national champions.

Pivotal new coaching hires set the stage for Miami's and Georgetown's revivals. The Hoyas tapped Thompson in 1972 to coach Georgetown basketball. In 1979 the Hurricanes hired Howard Schnellenberger, followed by Jimmy Johnson and Dennis Erickson, as their head football coaches. These four men recruited dozens of superstar Black and Latino players during the 1980s, including two of the most prominent figures in their respective programs' sporting renaissances: Hoyas center Patrick Ewing and Hurricanes wide receiver Michael Irvin. Top prep athlete prospects from minority communities across America who might otherwise have never heard of Georgetown or Miami suddenly pined to play for the Hoyas and 'Canes.

Jimmy Johnson was Miami's path-breaking hire, and he and Georgetown's John Thompson left lasting imprints on their schools and collegiate sports more broadly. One white and the other Black, Johnson and Thompson were particularly aware of the degree to which race contributed to their respective teams' national reputations. After leaving Miami in 1989 to coach the NFL's Dallas Cowboys, Johnson talked about the Hurricanes' racialized image during his coaching days in Coral Gables:

We had a lot of black players out front. I think a lot of the resentment came that way. The black players knew that, and the black players knew how I felt. I don't know that there was racism involved in the resentment, but there was some ignorance involved—people who have had few dealings with other ethnic groups. I mean real relationships, not getting somebody to clean your house.[12]

Of Thompson, his university president, the Rev. Timothy Healy, said: "This is a man from the Washington area who is taking kids who don't have two coins to rub together and is literally teaching some of them how to use a knife and fork. He knows just what he's doing. And we at Georgetown support him in what he's doing."[13] For his part, Thompson, the 6-foot-10-inch former center from Providence College and the Boston Celtics, was as central to his team's racial identity as his players. Years later, rapper Chuck D of Public Enemy described the racial potency of those 1980s Hoyas squads this way: "Not only was this a team full of black players who would definitely take it to you [but] you had a big-ass black man as a coach who wasn't taking no shit. That was big."[14]

The Hoyas and Hurricanes would never have had the temerity to change college athletics without the support and encouragement of their coaches. By defending their players, Thompson and Johnson provided them safe harbor to express themselves. "Ever since John Thompson recruited Patrick Ewing three years ago, Georgetown has become the team some fans love to hate," *New York Times* sportswriter George Vecsey proclaimed in March 1984, a week before the Hoyas won the national championship.[15] "The emotion is not because of Georgetown's considerable ability and discipline but because of its image of hostility and aggressiveness." As for the loyalty Johnson inspired from his Black players, *Miami Herald* columnist Dan Le Batard said that Randy Shannon—hired by Miami in December 2006—only technically has the technical distinction of being the Hurricanes' first Black coach: "Jimmy Johnson was the University of Miami's first black coach."[16]

In America, sports and race have always been tightly, if sometimes uncomfortably, entwined. From Jack Johnson to Jackie

Robinson to Serena Williams, a clear pattern repeats itself. Black athletes who dare to challenge the sporting status quo are vilified initially but later, if grudgingly, accepted. The 1980s generation of barrier-busting college athletes took this process a step further. Georgetown's and Miami's aggressive style of play angered many fans and commentators, especially at first. Tribal reflexes are difficult to suppress. Yet the Black style was not only accepted but eventually imitated by other athletes, Black and white. Opponents wanted to beat them, but also be like them. Love them or hate them, the Hoyas and Hurricanes captivated opponents, fans, and the media.

Indeed, these two programs shaped much of what followed in Division I football and basketball: Florida State football's 1988 preseason rap video and the flamboyant antics of cornerback "Neon" Deion Sanders; the brash, in-your-face 1990 and 1991 University of Nevada, Las Vegas (UNLV) basketball teams featuring superstar Larry Johnson and the "menacing" Moses Scurry; and, of course, the baggy shorts and black socks donned by the "Fab Five" freshmen who led the University of Michigan's basketball team to back-to-back NCAA championship games in 1992 and 1993. Added to that all-Black list are the rebellious on- and off-field stunts of the Oklahoma Sooners' white linebacker Brian Bosworth. Bosworth was an early pioneer in white athletes' appropriation of Black affect in collegiate sports. He taunted opponents and flaunted NCAA rules. Bosworth's celebrity made broadcast media and NCAA executives realize that white appropriation of the Black style meant bigger radio and TV ratings, which in turn meant more profits. It is impossible to imagine modern sports without the touchdown celebrations and dramatic dunks, the finger-pointing and trash-talking that have become staples of broadcast college basketball and football. Even fans who tended to side with Duke over Michigan in basketball or rooted for Notre Dame rather than Florida State in football were drawn to the Black style.

Fast forward to today and the lasting impacts of the 1980s transformation on major-college sports are clear. The popular and highly profitable NCAA March Madness basketball tournament and the new College Football Playoff championship would not be the cultural showcases they are today if the seats in the playing arenas and on couches across America were filled almost exclusively by white spectators. Today, African American viewership—13 percent for NCAA major bowl games, 14 percent for the Division I men's March Madness basketball tournament—is comparable to the Black shares of the national population[17] and bachelors degrees earned.[18] "African-Americans are a very important part of our constituency," ESPN president John Skipper said in February 2016. "They watch a lot of sports. And I believe that we have to be their home, and they have to believe that we represent their interests."[19]

Simply put, Georgetown basketball and Miami football helped expand and integrate spectatorship in ways that all the visionary college presidents and athletic directors together could not. They broadened the reach of college sports by attracting new white and nonwhite viewers alike. Some fans tuned in to root for these Black athletes, others to root against them. Either way, the Hoyas, 'Canes, and two subsequent generations of imitators helped make college sports popular and highly lucrative cultural institutions. The NCAA and its allied television and radio networks operate comfortably in the black thanks in no small measure to the Black and other minority athletes who revolutionized college basketball and football. What's perhaps most remarkable about the changes wrought by the two programs is that student athletes—mere amateurs without salaries or any formalized, collective power—were able to exert such a profound impact. "It was incredibly difficult in the 1980s for players to feel they had any maneuverability," sportswriter Dave Zirin explained. "They would look backward and see there was no space to say or do anything. They certainly didn't have a union. They were highly dependent upon word-of-mouth from coaches, and highly dependent on what then were year-to-year scholarships."[20]

The expansion of Division I basketball and football beyond its traditional followership did not occur overnight. Nor was it the result of efforts by any single player, coach, team, or university.

During the 1980s, however, Georgetown basketball and Miami football led the racial transformation of major-college broadcast sports. The Hoyas and Hurricanes shook college sports from its cozy, predominantly white confines and helped broadcast networks and advertisers reach national audiences. They did so, knowingly or not, by capitalizing on the polarizing power of American racial identities.

Never far removed from the national discourse, race continues to intersect with politics in NFL players' protests over police brutality. Despite league salary caps that allow professional team owners to pay below-market prices for their rosters, critics of the Colin Kaepernick–led protests revived the curious complaint that Black athletes (including Kaepernick) are a pack of "whiny, overpaid millionaires" who should be silently grateful for their success. The legal and structural reforms of the postwar era led to the cultural and social revolutions of the 1980s, which in turn opened the door to the proprietary and political fights still raging in college sports. Although they exercise greater influence today, modern Black athletes, coaches, general managers, and owners remain minority stakeholders in both senses of that word.

Broadcast college sports today are big business. Sports fandom has broadened with the steady integration of higher education. Millions of spectators tune into the showcase College Football Playoff and March Madness tournament. Multidecade broadcast contracts run into the tens of billions of dollars. Every Division I basketball and football conference and their hundreds of member universities depend on the exposure and revenues generated annually by these contracts. The sale of jerseys, hats, sneakers, and countless additional sports-themed paraphernalia embossed with team colors and logos is lucrative for apparel vendors, the memorabilia industry, and, of course, the universities that hold the trademark rights.

Georgetown and Miami are not the dominant programs they once were, but they helped forge the corporate and cultural juggernauts of major-college men's televised sports. Many notable athletes and coaches from the 1980s heyday of both programs remain prominent in today's national sporting landscape. The Hoyas hired Patrick Ewing in 2017 to be their new head basketball coach. Michael Irvin is a weekly fixture on ESPN's and NFL Network's televised pro football coverage. Former Hurricanes coach Jimmy Johnson is a paid, in-demand television analyst, as was Hoyas coach John Thompson before his death in 2020. Former Hurricanes linebacker Dwayne "The Rock" Johnson is a blockbuster movie star.

How did these two formerly unheralded programs lead such a transformation? One answer is that Georgetown and Miami rose to national prominence at the very moment the cultural mainstreaming of African American life—from the successes of *The Cosby Show* to the hip-hop innovations of Grandmaster Flash—converged with around-the-clock cable sports programming and big-money collegiate conference competition. A shorter answer is that the Hoyas and Hurricanes infused televised college sports with a new, impossible-to-ignore Black style of play—and won.

One Style, Two Variants

No other men's college teams dominated the 1980s like Georgetown and Miami. Both teams were proud purveyors of the Black style. Yet each program practiced its own variant of that style. Georgetown held no monopoly on rough play, but the Hoyas' signature was a brusque, physical form of basketball rarely witnessed in the college game in previous eras. With towering centers Ewing and later Alonzo Mourning, the Hoyas sought to project their physical dominance. Formed in 1979, the Big East Conference in which Georgetown, Syracuse, and St. John's were charter members quickly developed a reputation for physicality that perfectly suited Thompson's Hoyas. In the early 1980s tensions between Big East teams often boiled over. A few player skirmishes led to fisticuffs, and relationships among the conference's coaching staffs frequently soured. "Thompson coaches aggressively, and his team is an extension of him on the court," *New York Times* sportswriter Peter Alfano observed. "The Hoyas play an almost bullying style that can intimidate opponents and challenge the spirit of the rules which pertain to contact."[21]

Rough play was a signature of Georgetown games. Opponents routinely pushed and fouled Ewing hard in an effort to rattle the All-American. The quick-tempered Ewing answered these aggressions with glowering facial expressions, verbal retorts, and occasionally his fists. After losing to the Hoyas three times by an average of more than 20 points during Ewing's 1981–82 freshman season, conference rival St. John's was determined not to be pushed around the following year. In a 76–67 victory over the Hoyas in early January 1983, Redmen forward Kevin Williams lured Ewing into two altercations that whipped both teams and the Madison Square Garden crowd into a frenzy. Williams suffered a swollen lip courtesy of a Ewing punch, but Williams's needling tactics during the game achieved their intended effect. Ewing missed 10 of 14 shots from the field and the Hoyas lost a winnable game.

During his postgame comments, Thompson warned Big East referees that if they permitted smaller players to harass Ewing with impunity, he would advise his superstar sophomore to turn professional at season's end.[22] Critics chirped that a skinny Ewing would suffer worse beatings from centers in the pro game, something the National Basketball Association (NBA) veteran Thompson surely knew to be true. But Thompson also knew he got the attention of league officials and profit-minded network executives who didn't want to risk two seasons' worth of lower ratings and ad revenues if Ewing turned pro early. Before the rise of one-year-and-done superstars, Ewing was a media meal ticket. "Had Ewing chosen to play for Jim Calhoun, Tom Davis or Rick Pitino at Northeastern, Boston College and Boston University, respectively, it takes no stretch of the imagination to state that those fans and media members would have been more accepting of his posture and style of play, the bullseye on his back much less visible and savored," argued sports historian Alejandro Danois.[23]

Ewing was frequently targeted for verbal and even racial abuse by opposing spectators, especially white fans. Responding to reports that Ewing had struggled to meet the academic standards required for admission to Georgetown, opposing fans routinely held up signs at games with phrases like "The Missing Link" to taunt and demean the 7-foot center. In a 1983 game against the Villanova Wildcats at Philadelphia's Palestra arena, Wildcats supporters threw a banana on the court during the pregame introduction of Georgetown's starting lineup. One Villanova fan hoisted a bedsheet proclaiming, "Ewing Is An Ape," and others donned T-shirts declaring, "Ewing Kant Read Dis." Infuriated, Hoyas coach John Thompson pulled his players from the court in protest until the signs were removed. "It is cheap, racist stuff," bemoaned Georgetown's president, the Rev. Timothy Healy. "No one on the face of the earth can tell me if Patrick were a 7-foot high white man that people would still carry these signs around. I'm a white man and I know it."[24] Thompson occasionally complained to Big East Conference officials, but decided to handle matters mostly on his own. "Coach Thompson tried to shield myself and the rest of the team from some of the negative things that were being said," recalls Ewing.[25]

Thompson cut an imposing figure. The former Providence College and Boston Celtics center stood literally head-and-shoulders above his fellow Big East coaches, Lou Carnesecca of St. John's and Villanova's Rollie Massimino. Having coached at a Washington prep school before taking the Georgetown job, Thompson knew how to recruit players from tough, urban neighborhoods. He drew heavily from the talented stocks of nearby Washington and Baltimore public schools that served economically disadvantaged, overwhelmingly African American communities. (The Jamaica-born Ewing was an exception; he attended a Boston private school on scholarship.) Aside from a white reserve or two, Thompson's Hoyas teams were entirely composed of Black players. Thompson's growing reputation as the nation's most successful Division I Black coach surely advantaged him in the recruiting wars.

Thompson was extremely protective of his team's racial identity. He knew opponents and critics hated his Hoyas precisely because of their image and he welcomed their enmity. In 1981–82, only the Big East's third season, Thompson became the first Black coach to reach the Division I men's championship game. Two years later, he was the first Black coach to win a major championship in any college team sport. Thompson and his players instantly became role models for Black America. "African-American adults pulled for the Hoyas because Thompson played out the Black-Man-of-Power role the way many of them wished they had the authority and courage to do in the workplace," argued Curtis Bunn of the *Atlanta Black Star*, on the occasion of the thirty-year anniversary of Ewing's four-year reign at Georgetown. "Thompson orchestrated and executed things his way, without the consideration—and often to the intentional ire—of white people. But always with sound reasoning."[26] Although he and his players kept their chins up, racial abuse took its inevitable toll. "Ignorance has no color," Thompson said in March 1983, almost exactly a year after the heartbreaking championship-game loss to the University of North Carolina (UNC) and a year prior to the Hoya's redemptive 1984 title win over Houston. "The point isn't that this season has been degrading to a black man. It has been degrading to any man. On the airplane last week, I asked Patrick [Ewing] again how he was holding up. He told me, 'I've grown accustomed to it. I got so much of it in high school.' That made me saddest of all."[27]

Not every attack against Thompson's Hoyas was racially motivated, of course. The team's on-court successes made Georgetown a target for conference opponents and other national contenders, most of which also featured lineups chock-full of Black players. But overlaying the normal tensions of competitive athletics was a unique racial antipathy directed at Georgetown. Because his team and players were depicted as antagonists, Thompson could to some degree be forgiven his frequent refusal to make his players available to reporters. His reflexive defensiveness—"Hoya paranoia," as the media called it—was often justified. "Nothing is simple about John Thompson, a smart and sensitive and very large man who, besides knowing how to recruit and coach, has an outsider's sense of self-protective paranoia," *New York Times* columnist George Vecsey wrote a few days after the ugly fracas between Kevin Williams and Patrick Ewing in the 1983 St. John's-Georgetown game.[28]

Nor would Georgetown be bullied by conference officials or media executives. Then *Washington Post* sportswriter John Feinstein saw first-hand how Thompson-helmed Georgetown blossomed from an unknown program into a national powerhouse and the added scrutiny the Hoyas attracted. As early as 1984, Feinstein reported that Thompson and athletic director Frank Rienzo took flak because they ran their program differently. "These differences include often hard-line negotiations for game contracts with other schools that, among other things, virtually wipe out local rivalries. The differences extend to relationships with television networks, radio stations, magazine and newspaper reporters," Feinstein observed. "Some players and coaches complain that the Hoyas are too aggressive on the court, all of which leads in general to an image of being difficult to deal with, and resulting in the phrase 'Hoya Paranoia.'"[29] Georgetown's aggressive posture was a direct extension of Thompson's pugilistic personality.

Thompson sought to dismantle pervasive, negative stereotypes about Black athletes. He insisted they be students, not merely athletes, and role models to their campus peers and the broader community. Instead of scrimmaging, reviewing game film, or doing wind sprints, Thompson held impromptu "mental practices" a few times each season during which players sat in the bleachers for as long as two hours discussing current events. He hired an academic adviser, Mary Fenlon, solely dedicated to the players' scholastic performance. Fenlon traveled with the team and even sat on the bench alongside the players during games. As star center Dikembe Mutombo learned the hard way, Thompson's no-excuses militarism also applied to his players in the classroom. Mutombo once skipped class for a dental emergency, but failed to alert Thompson or anyone in the program about his tooth ache. When Mutombo showed up for practice that afternoon, he found a one-way ticket to Kinshasa, his hometown in the Republic of the Congo (now the Democratic Republic of the Congo), waiting for him inside his locker. Mutombo approached Thompson in a panic. Thompson said he was sending Mutombo home to his father and possible service in dictator Mobutu Sese Seko's army. "I could not believe it," Mutombo later recalled. "I thought it was the end of my education." Thompson chided his player for not scheduling the appointment around his classwork, but forgave him.[30]

Thompson silenced some of his detractors and critics of how he presented himself as a Black man by adopting and even exaggerating traditionally white norms. What appeared as stridency was, in fact, Thompson practicing his own militarized version of the Black style. Jeff Bullis, a star white forward for the Hoyas in the late 1970s, described the racial dynamics of Thompson's military-inspired coaching philosophy. "On this team the black-white thing just doesn't come up until some reporter starts asking questions. It's hard to explain how close we are, but we're closer, I think, than any of the teams we've played," explained Bullis. "That's how Mr. Thompson wants it, and that's the kind of people Mr. Thompson recruits. We're like a military unit that has gone through a lot of fire together. Mr. Thompson is the fire. He's very tough, but if you can take it, he'll make a man out of you." Bullis's references to Thompson as "Mr." rather than "Coach" are telling.

Thompson wanted sportswriters and other coaches to associate him and his teams with military-style discipline because he understood what critics meant when they described players as "undisciplined." Said Thompson:

> Undisciplined, that means n———. They're all big and fast and can leap like kangaroos and eat watermelon in the locker room, but they can't play as a team and they choke under pressure. It's the idea that a black man doesn't have the intelligence or the character to practice self-control. In basketball it's been a self-fulfilling prophecy. White men run the game. A white coach recruits a good black player. He knows the kid's got talent, but he also knows—or thinks he knows—that because he's black he's undisciplined. So he doesn't try to give the player any discipline. He puts him in the freelance, one-on-one, hot-dog role, and turns to the little white guard for discipline. Other black kids see this and they think this is how they are expected to play, and so the image is perpetuated.[31]

At a press conference the day before his Hoyas won the 1984 national championship, a reporter asked Thompson how he felt about his team being described in militaristic terms. Thompson said he loved it. "You'll never hear one of our players criticize a player on another team," he explained. "If you do, you come to me, and then I'll really become militaristic."[32] Five days later when President Ronald Reagan hosted the champion Hoyas at a celebratory event on the White House lawn, the president's staff had clearly prepped Reagan well. "I understand there's been some criticism, Coach Thompson, that maybe your coaching was a little too stringent or almost military," Reagan remarked. "I wouldn't let that bother me at all. It's results that pay off." Thompson took the remark as a compliment: "If the worst thing that could ever be said about us is that we're military, I feel very honored."[33] Thompson's Black style served twin purposes: to build cohesive and disciplined players on his mostly Black teams, and to shatter the racist tropes so often applied to Black athletes. If that meant imposing a harsh discipline on his players, so be it.

In the 1984 Big East Conference final against rival Syracuse, Georgetown won the title in an overtime classic. The very physical game is remembered for—and some say was marred by—a fight between Hoyas forward Michael Graham and Orangemen forward Andre Hawkins. After the game the media questioned Thompson about his team's intimidating posture and rough play. Thompson gave it right back to the media, saying there were times during the season when he brought Ewing to postgame press conferences but certain reporters seemed too scared to pose questions to his towering center. *Sports Illustrated*'s Curry Kirkpatrick described Thompson's remarks this way:

> That happened to be Thompson at his gruff, meanspirited, iconoclastic and odd-humored best. And though his methods may be questionable, his intentions seem laudable. He's a surpassingly bright, deep, discerning and articulate fellow who genuinely cares about his players' academic attainments—their graduation rate is very high. Nonetheless, on occasion Thompson plays the tough-guy role to the hilt, complete with such witty repartee as "get outta my face." More often than not, his team, along with its

Rise of the Black Style

leather-jackets-and-chains image, appears to slip into precisely the same character. But, of course, that's the point.[34]

Indeed, that was *exactly* the point: Thompson projected strength and even mean-spiritedness as part of his defiant, militant application of the Black style. He was more than happy to absorb criticism if it meant deflecting attention away from his players. Colonels, not corporals, shoulder the burdens of responsibility.

In the 1980s Georgetown was a national power and natural antagonist. Hoyas games were must-see television for sports fans and a hot topic for discussion in the sports media. With their blue-and-gray uniforms—a color scheme the university had adopted to recognize both sides of the Civil War[35]—and nearly all-Black roster of superstar players, the Hoyas' evil-empire image agitated many white fans and delighted their Black supporters. Georgetown was a basketball juggernaut and a potent racial icon.

Like Georgetown, the Miami Hurricanes were collegiate bad boys who stood defiantly on the Black side of the racial color line. Miami used physical and psychological taunts and a variety of pregame and in-game tactics designed to intimidate and even embarrass opponents. The Hurricanes celebrated touchdowns and turnovers in inventive, often excessive ways. Referees penalized the Hurricanes for their showmanship on the field. Sportswriters criticized Miami for breaking historical norms of sportsmanship. But lost yardage on the field and media criticisms off the field were offset by gains where they mattered most—on the scoreboard.

The most amazing part of the Hurricanes story is that Miami almost dropped football in 1976, seven years before it won its first national championship. Five years after Miami's fateful hiring of Howard Schnellenberger, Miami beat the vaunted Nebraska Cornhuskers, one of the most dominant teams in the history of college football, to win the school's first national title. The Hurricanes were already being shoe-horned into the role of bad boys. "The media could have jumped on the bandwagon and hype[d] up the Cinderella story [of] a team almost losing its program to national championship. It could have looked at all the kids from an area torn apart by racial tensions and how the school was able to unite the people of all races: white, black, Hispanic," lamented *Bleacher Report* correspondent Anakin Cane. "The media could have jumped at an opportunity to promote these kids coming from drug-infested communities, one-parent families, welfare culture, and the projects. Instead, the media fed the hatred for years to come. Terms such as Thug U and Convict U came into college football's lexicon."[36]

That critique is accurate, if a bit premature. Miami's bad-boy image actually blossomed under the stewardship of coach Jimmy Johnson, the man hired to replaced Schnellenberger after the latter quit to take what turned out to be a failed deal with the United States Football League's expansion into Miami. Johnson was more bombastic and expressive than the buttoned-down Schnellenberger. The Black style that Johnson embraced, however, differed from Thompson's militaristic mien. Johnson believed in a player-centric, permissive, and flamboyant style. In his autobiography Johnson, a psychology major in college, offered his sociopsychological explanation for why many of his urban Black athletes acted the way they did:

> We had some players who came from very deprived backgrounds. That in no way hindered their quality as men and as citizens. It did, in some cases, leave them with insecurities they had to work out and overcome. If you've grown up in the hard environments of Pahokee or Homestead, and suddenly find yourself walking the well-to-do environs of the University of Miami campus in Coral Gables, there is some adjustment to be made. And so to mask nervousness, anxiety, and insecurity, some of our players behaved quite the opposite way on the football field: cool, supremely confident, joyful. The exulted in their success and they were demonstrative about it.
>
> Confidence is necessary to play football. Different players have different ways of building confidence. . . . If I stymied and handcuffed the players who needed to be demonstrative, I would stymie and handcuff their confidence. Because of a lot of our players' backgrounds, we had to be somewhat flamboyant.[37]

Johnson told his players not to repress their personalities. "He never put any bars on us," running back Cleveland Gary said. "He never told us how to act, how to behave."[38] Johnson coached and mentored Black athletes from economically disadvantaged environments in south Florida similar to the Baltimore and Washington neighborhoods where Thompson recruited many of his players. But Johnson's confidence-based theory of the Black style contrasted sharply with Thompson's disciplinarian approach.

Johnson's approach often backfired. Under Johnson's and later Dennis Erickson's stewardships, Miami racked up repeated sanctions for its on- and off-field discipline. In addition to the NCAA's adoption of the so-called "Miami rule" regarding celebratory on-field antics, from the mid-1980s into the 1990s a veritable parade of Hurricanes players were penalized for scholastic or legal problems. Of course, as white coaches Johnson and Dennis Erickson enjoyed greater lateral to be rogue stewards of their program than Thompson did at Georgetown.

Miami's behavior, like Georgetown's, drew the ire of opposing players, coaches and the media. White fans and critics in particular scorned the Hurricanes for their style of play. These criticisms only bonded the players, coaches and university with their fans and the city of Miami. Sportswriter Dan Le Batard attended Miami as an undergraduate and upon graduation became the *Miami Herald's* young beat writer covering Hurricanes football. "The '80s and early '90s were renegade rebellion. [Notre Dame star] Tim Brown said he had genuine fear that those teams would beat him up in the parking lot after games. They were scary good and scary," Le Batard recalled of those formative-era Miami teams. "The early years were so 'us-against-the-world' in ways that transcended the athletic cliché of invented doubters and critics. Those teams were so crazy that it made the bond stronger with the city."[39]

Hurricanes players and coaches were keenly aware of how integral the Black style was for the reputation of "The U," the shorthand players began to use for their football program. They also recognized that they were practicing a form of sports psychological warfare others had invented. Long before the collegians of the 1980s were born, pioneering African American athletes from Satchel Paige to Jack Tatum to Muhammad Ali mastered the same psychological tactics. The athletic struggle between white protagonists and Black antagonists did not begin with University of Miami football in the 1980s.

The 1987 Fiesta Bowl between No. 2 Penn State and No. 1 Miami to determine the national champion is remembered as a notably racialized contest. Billed as the "Game of the Century," the matchup pitted two undefeated teams in the first true national title game under the NCAA's new bowl-matchup format.[40] As if that were insufficient hype for the game, the media portrayed the contest as nothing less than an existential battle of light versus dark. On one side stood the understated Penn State student athletes with no last names on their jerseys; on the other stood the finger-pointing Miami show-offs who supposedly never cracked a book. "The general feeling was that Miami was just a bunch of rogues," recalled television analyst Beano Cook. "They made Penn State good because everyone wanted to say Miami is evil, and so it became good versus evil."

The polarized depictions of the two teams were exaggerations. Even many Penn State players, who had heard all year about the Hurricanes' reputation for swagger, knew the truth was more complicated. "If you're told a lie for long enough, you start to believe it," Nittany Lions defensive tackle Bob White said. "They were talented, but they bullied people by running their mouths." His teammate, linebacker Trey Bauer, dismissed the 'Canes, saying that they "didn't seem very smart" to him. But Bauer also admitted that the media exaggerated the supposed duality between the teams. "They made us out to be a bunch of choirboys, but that wasn't the case, either," he said. "It wasn't like we were locked in the library 24/7."[41] *Sports Illustrated* columnist Rick Reilly also threw cold water on Penn State's squeaky-clean image. "The Nittany Lions come in as Goody Two Cleats, but they have yet to back down from a fight," Reilly wrote in a pregame analysis. "In fact, this year's squad had more personal fouls called on it than any other that Paterno has coached."[42]

Rise of the Black Style

At a ceremonial dinner in Tempe, Arizona, a few days before the game, players on both squads were scheduled to perform comedic skits to skewer each other. Penn State punter John Bruno went a bit too far with a tasteless joke that offended Miami's players and coaches. Attempting to mock the Hurricanes' self-styled "family" image, Bruno claimed Penn State was the real family because "the white players let the black players eat at the training table once a week."[43] During their own skit moments later, Hurricanes players staged a walkout. (Some Miami players later confessed that Bruno's comments were not the trigger because they had planned all along to walk out.) "We caught all the criticism," Johnson carped to the Associated Press months later. "And if a Miami player had said those things and Penn State had walked out, we would have been criticized for making racial remarks." Miami was hardly innocent of stoking pregame controversy. In the days leading up to game, wide receiver Michael Irvin and other players on Miami's offense mocked Penn State's defensive secondary as "smurfs" too small to cover them. All-American defensive lineman Jerome Brown was more insulting. "I think they're nothing," he said.[44] Johnson's team drew the lion's share of criticism in the days leading up to the Fiesta Bowl because Miami was the easier team for fans and the media to hate.

In an eerily prescient statement, Johnson chafed at the double standard that applied to his Hurricanes but not to other national powerhouses like Penn State, then coached by the legendary Joe Paterno and two decades away from the Jerry Sandusky pedophilia scandal becoming public. "Paterno told me he's had plenty of problems in State College, but nobody knows about them," said Johnson, referring to nonstop media reports about Hurricanes players' drug use, petty thefts, and low graduation rates. "If I get a parking ticket, everybody in Miami knows about it."[45] A quarter century later, Sports Illustrated published its list of the twenty-five most-hated teams in all of sports, college and professional. The magazine ranked the 1986 Hurricanes first.[46]

Penn State upset Miami, 14–10, to win the Fiesta Bowl and claim its second national title in five years. Sandusky, Penn State's defensive coordinator, devised a brilliant defensive scheme to shut down a Hurricanes offense that averaged 38 points per game during the 1986 regular season. Miami dominated except on the scoreboard, racking up 445 total offensive yards to just 162 for Penn State. And those defensives "smurfs" Irvin mocked? They intercepted Heisman Trophy winner Vinnie Testaverde five times. At the time the 1987 Fiesta Bowl was the most watched college football game in history.[47] Like the famed 1979 Bird-Magic basketball title game, the matchup with the racial undertones pitting the bad-boy Hurricanes against the good-guy Nittany Lions appealed to television viewers.

After a middling first year for Johnson in which his team finished 8-5, his 1985 and 1986 teams excelled. Miami lost only three games in those two seasons. However, the 'Canes lost their first three bowl games of the Johnson era, falling to UCLA and then Tennessee before losing the national championship to Penn State in the Fiesta Bowl. After the 1986 campaign, Johnson lost to graduation three of the 1987 NFL draft's first nine selections. The departure of Heisman Trophy winner and NFL overall No. 1 pick Vinny Testaverde left Johnson with a big hole at the quarterback position. But in Johnson's fourth season, Miami won the national title again. The Hurricanes ran the table, capping an undefeated 12-0 campaign with a 20–14 Orange Bowl victory over Oklahoma. The next year—Johnson's last as coach—only a failed two-point conversion prevented Miami from again finishing the year as undefeated national champions.

After Johnson left Coral Gables to take his friend Jerry Jones's offer to coach the Dallas Cowboys, Hurricanes assistant Dennis Erickson took over as head coach. Erickson promptly led the 1989 Hurricanes to victory over Alabama in the 1990 Sugar Bowl and the team's third national championship in seven years. The next year, the 1990 Miami team, already out of contention to repeat as champs following regular-season losses to Brigham Young University (BYU) and Notre Dame, faced the Texas Longhorns in the 1991 Cotton Bowl. "At the time, Miami was nationally known and popular for a raucous style of play that included taunting, exuberant celebrations, and a steady flow of 'commentary' that drove opponents to distraction," wrote Bill Rhoden, citing this game as the low point for the Black style of play. "The Hurricanes' games were a combination of performance and pro-wrestling match: The players danced, postured, and gestured after big plays . . . Miami whipped the Longhorns' collective asses without mercy and with great pleasure. But what was intriguing was the manner—the 'What's My Name' style—in which Miami won."[48]

Defensive lineman Rusty Medearis later explained that pressure from alumni players prompted the Hurricanes' demonstrative Cotton Bowl performance. Following those embarrassing losses to BYU and Notre Dame, former players privately questioned the 1990 team's swagger. In person and by phone, 'Cane alumni—some of them at that point notable NFL stars—let current players know that they worried the program had gone soft. "People were saying, 'Where's the dancing? Where's the intimidation?'" Medearis told a reporter. "We kind of felt a little bit humiliated. You think, 'We lose two games and there's got to be somebody to pay.' So we went to the Cotton Bowl and we were dancing before we got out of the locker room. We overdid it."[49]

The sporting media expressed collective disgust with Miami's performance in the Cotton Bowl, in which the Hurricanes players drew sixteen penalties, many of them for unsportsmanlike conduct, totaling more than 200 yards. The NCAA responded with a new set of unsportsmanlike-conduct rules and accompanying penalties. Bruce Feldman recounted in *'Cane Mutiny* how the NCAA sent football schools during the ensuing offseason a videotape with examples of unacceptable forms of conduct. The first twelve of the thirty-seven examples in the video showed Miami players. The behaviors depicted would now be penalized 15 yards. "In layman's terms, it became known as 'the Miami rule,'" wrote Feldman.[50] The NCAA made it clear to Miami and the rest of college football that it believed the Hurricanes had gone too far.

But the Hurricanes were not the only ones. After the Cotton Bowl, a few members of the sports media used racist language that today would trigger public apologies and possibly firings. "I am not without some gratitude for Miami collecting dangerous young thugs and giving them a place to be angry," wrote Bernie Lincicome in the *Chicago Tribune*. "Better in Coral Gables than on public transportation." The *Boston Globe*'s Will McDonough was equally offensive: "Sooner or later, the street would take over, and it did in the Cotton Bowl in Dallas Tuesday, when the University of Miami players delivered college football's version of wilding." The Hurricanes' behavior was garish and rule-breaking. But no sportswriters compared the Boston Celtics' bruising, white-dominated roster to urban thugs on a wilding rampage after the Celtics turned the 1984 NBA championship series against the Los Angeles Lakers into a foul-plagued rumble.

The uproar over Miami's Cotton Bowl performance occurred when the Big East Conference was deciding whether to invite the Hurricanes, a conference independent, to join its new football league. The Big East eventually added Miami, but the 'Canes arrived under a dark cloud of scrutiny. "Just as the Hurricanes have commanded attention with their extraordinary stream of talent, they have also attracted scrutiny for a belligerent approach to football that has been labeled everything from entertaining to vulgar," *New York Times* sportswriter Malcolm Moran observed. "The current generation of Miami players has been put on notice . . . that the in-your-face style of their play, a fervently displayed element of Hurricane football that many believe has been essential in its success, will now operate under specific boundaries beginning with, but not limited to, the chalk markings that surround the field."[51]

The Miami teams in the decade following that 1991 Cotton Bowl were good but not as dominant as those during the previous ten seasons. Maybe the Hurricanes slipped a bit because of poor coaching hires after Dennis Erickson left Coral Gables to take a job with the NFL's Seattle Seahawks. Surely the rise of in-state rivals Florida and Florida State made it impossible for Miami to hoard the Sunshine State's top recruits. Perhaps the Hurricanes' taunting tactics lost their advantage as more players, Black and white, began to copy Miami's aggressive style. Or maybe Miami lost some of its edge following the reprimands that the NCAA

Rise of the Black Style

and the media issued against the 'Canes after that infamous 1991 Cotton Bowl game. Whatever the case, the genie was out of the bottle: Miami's bombastic and unapologetic style of play in the 1980s had already changed major-college televised football forever.

Ascent of the Black Style

During the 1980s Georgetown University basketball and University of Miami football led a cultural revolution in televised college sports by popularizing a Black style of play that used fear and intimidation as weapons of psychological warfare against opponents. Reinforcing good-versus-evil stereotypes and storylines, the Black style practiced by each program enticed prep recruits, thrilled spectators, infuriated detractors, sold tickets and jerseys, influenced pop culture from apparel to rap music, and delighted television executives and corporate sponsors. This performative style attracted minority spectators and fans, thereby broadening the appeal of what had long been a white-dominated collegiate sports experience. What the Hoyas and Hurricanes innovated, other teams quickly imitated. Both schools forged their images through a combination of competitive exploits and culturally impactful moments off the fields and courts of play. The Hoyas and 'Canes were pioneers.

The two variants of the Black style practiced by Georgetown and Miami during the 1980s differed in important ways. Georgetown's organizational ideal was that of a military unit; Miami emphasized family and community. The Hoyas generally embraced traditional norms; the Hurricanes flaunted them. Georgetown's communication style tended toward the stoic and restrained; Miami's mien was loud and bombastic. John Thompson preached self-control as a player's most important trait; Jimmy Johnson preferred self-expression as the ideal ethic. The Black style is not monochromatic.

Today, that style so thoroughly pervades college and pro sports that it is taken as a given. Although unsportsmanlike penalties and technical fouls persist, players in major-college sports, the NFL, and the NBA enjoy far wider latitude today to demonstrate after big dunks, crushing hits, and touchdowns. Perhaps the greatest testament to the Black style's reach is that it is no longer bound by race. From Brian Bosworth to Baker Mayfield, from Jason "White Chocolate" Williams to Chris "Birdman" Andersen, the Black style is so mainstreamed it has ceased to be proprietarily Black.

Despite howls from opponents and critics—and in no small measure because their detractors were legion—Georgetown, Miami and a growing list of imitators began to attract new fans, sponsors, and audiences during the 1980s. Suddenly, young minorities who had never set foot on the manicured lawns of Georgetown, Coral Gables, or any other college expressed their shared racial identity with Black and Latino college athletes. These fans showed their solidarity simply by rooting for the Hoyas and Hurricanes as a form of protest against white-dominated culture. Many went further, appropriating the two teams' colors and logos by donning Georgetown and Miami jerseys, sneakers, jackets, and hats. With a soundtrack provided by rap music pioneers including N.W.A. and 2 Live Crew, Georgetown and Miami emerged as icons at the intersection of sports, popular culture, and racial politics in the 1980s. These two programs and their many imitators also drew white spectators and viewers to follow Division I basketball and football to root against them.

The Black style was ascendant, its remarkable rise led by a handful of elite Black athletes in their late teens and early twenties. Powered by the polarizing influence of race, rivalries long limited to conference and in-state antagonisms increasingly became nationalized. Televised college sports have not been the same since.

[2]

Campus Color Barriers

The complicity of many northern schools in [keeping their
Black athletes from participating against segregated white teams]
is not surprising, since the few black students enrolled there
were treated like second-class citizens and excluded
from some campus activities.

—CHARLES H. MARTIN, *Benching Jim Crow*

The roots of the revolt of the black athlete spring from the same
seed that produced the sit-ins, the freedom rides and
the rebellions in Watts, Detroit and Newark.

—HARRY EDWARDS, *The Revolt of the Black Athlete*

Racial progress in America has always been slow and painful, and it has never been guaranteed. Consider the fate of the so-called "Indiana University 10." With three games remaining in Indiana University's (IU's) 1969 football season, head coach John Pont kicked all ten Black players off the team after they boycotted practice that week in protest of what they deemed to be their unequal treatment. Although the players retained their scholarships and graduated, their playing careers ended abruptly and without the university addressing their complaints. The IU 10 left Bloomington dejected and bitter. It took almost a half century, but in 2015 five of the eight living members of the "IU 10" at last reconciled with their alma mater. That year, university president Michael McRobbie and athletic director Fred Glass organized an event to commemorate and publicly reconcile with the players. The university reinstated them as lettermen on the 1969 team, promised to create a permanent display about their protests inside Memorial Stadium's Henke Hall of Champions, made all ten players lifetime members of the IU Alumni Association, and created a for-credit course that examines the historical impact of their boycott and dismissal. "The IU 10 have placed ourselves in the history of Indiana, in a good place," Mike Adams, one of the five members of the IU 10 who returned to Bloomington for the 2015 event, said. "We'll finally get our recognition for our input in human rights."[1]

The civil rights movement that forever altered American life also changed collegiate sports. As the IU 10 episode demonstrates, however, the racial integration of college basketball and football during the postwar decades was a fits-and-starts struggle that required immense courage from a small group of minority athletes. Progress during that fight for integration was intermittent and often generated backlash. Small victories won by players were typically offset by personal setbacks and institutional casualties. Slower still were efforts to integrate the ranks of assistant coaches, head coaches, and athletic administrators, not to mention sportswriters, columnists, and media executives.

The 1980s were a racial turning point for Division I basketball and football. Spectatorship among African Americans and whites exploded. The decade kickstarted the long and still ongoing efforts to expand opportunities for minorities, from playing rosters to presidential suites. Key games and episodes fundamentally altered the racial dynamics of college sports for players, coaches, administrators, the media, and fans. To make way for a new generation of black and other minority athletes in the 1980s, college athletics first needed to strip away its segregationist and exclusionary past. This chapter chronicles the poignant yet painful process of integrating major-college basketball and football during the postwar period.

Postwar Integration Battles

Young Black athletes, some of whom served in uniform during World War II, returned to an America as segregated as the one they left behind for the battlefields of Europe, North Africa, and the Far East. Segregation rules that governed public housing, transportation, and services also applied to intercollegiate sports at many universities outside the historically Black college circuit. The race ceilings in major-college basketball and football would be difficult to break. As so often is the case for pioneers in social movements, a handful of key athletes broke through first and suffered the consequences.

Starting with Oregon's victory in the eight-team inaugural 1939 tournament, NCAA Division I men's basketball championship teams had all-white rosters for the first eleven years. Throughout the 1940s, all-white teams representing segregated schools like the University of Kentucky and the University of Kansas (KU) dominated play. Equally if not more prestigious at the time, the twelve-team National Invitation Tournament (NIT) also remained segregated until both tournaments finally integrated starting with the 1949–50 season. Fittingly, the City College of New York (CCNY)—an integrated urban school that started two Black players and three Jews that year—won both tournaments. In a notable second-round NIT game at Madison Square Garden pitting CCNY against defending NCAA champion Kentucky, the Wildcat starters refused to shake hands with their CCNY counterparts. "This was 16 years before Texas Western started five blacks in the NCAA title game and beat Kentucky, but any New Yorker inside the Garden, or within earshot of a radio, understood the implications of a lineup of Jews and blacks facing the white-laced Wildcats," wrote Ian Powers in a 2013 commemorative essay about the 1950 CCNY team for the *New York Daily News*.[2] CCNY humiliated Kentucky, 89–50, handing coach Adolph Rupp and the Wildcats the worst loss in the program's history.

College basketball changed rapidly in the 1950s. Two towering Black centers, All-Americans Bill Russell of the University of

San Francisco (USF) and Wilt Chamberlain of the University of Kansas, forced university officials, boosters, and the media to recognize the power of integration to transform the college game. Russell and Chamberlain led mixed-race teams to three consecutive national championship games in the mid-1950s. Russell and his USF Dons won the 1955 and 1956 titles, and Chamberlain's Kansas Jayhawks fell 1 point short in a triple-overtime loss to the University of North Carolina in the 1957 title game.

The teams Russell and Chamberlain led were majority white, but clearly excelled thanks to the contributions of Black athletes. Russell and Chamberlain faced manifold hardships and unvarnished racism. In addition to encountering the challenges of segregated housing and dining facilities, they were frequent targets for racist epithets, verbal taunts, and even physical threats. These persecutions were hardly limited to contests against southern teams or games held in southern venues. Nor were nameless, faceless spectators the sole persecutors of Black athletes, some of whom suffered verbal and physical attacks from opposing players and coaches. The achievements of Russell, Chamberlain, Elgin Baylor, Oscar Robertson, and other postwar Black stars threatened the segregated programs and conferences, especially the southern universities that stood to benefit most from tapping into their region's rich pool of talented African American athletes.

The most highly recruited prep star in the country during his senior year playing for Philadelphia's Overbrook High School, the 7-foot Wilt Chamberlain immediately made his presence known by scoring 52 points in the Jayhawks' first game of his sophomore year. At the time the NCAA barred freshmen from varsity play, but Chamberlain was so talented that his freshman team beat the KU varsity team in an intrasquad scrimmage. Partly in response to Chamberlain's dominant sophomore season, the NCAA adopted a new rule the following summer to widen the 3-second lane under the basket. Despite his stardom and dominance—and also because of it—Chamberlain became a target for racial abuse.

In his fascinating, if disturbing, account of Chamberlain's first varsity season for the University of Kansas, author Gregory Kaliss

Campus Color Barriers

chronicles the indignities Chamberlain endured. As KU plowed through the 1957 NCAA tournament toward their eventual triple-overtime defeat against UNC in the title game, Chamberlain and the Jayhawks' only other Black player, Maurice King, were routinely insulted by opposing coaches and physically attacked by opposing players. Kansas played two regional games in Dallas, the first against hometown Southern Methodist University (SMU) and the second against Oklahoma City College (OCC). During the KU-SMU game, fans called the Black players "jigaboo," "spook," and "n——," and threw objects at them on the court. In the second game, matters turned even uglier when OCC players deliberately attempted to injure Chamberlain and King. The OCC coach threatened the referees for failing to more frequently whistle "that big n——" Chamberlain for fouls.[3]

At the same time Russell and Chamberlain were transforming college basketball, speedy Black running backs and wide receivers were turning heads in college football. In Jim Brown and Ernie Davis, Syracuse University produced two of the top running backs of the late 1950s and early 1960s. In 1961 Davis became the first African American to win the Heisman Trophy. The University of Southern California soon eclipsed Syracuse by producing two Black Heisman winners in just four years: Mike Garrett in 1965 and O. J. Simpson in 1968.

Despite the talented pool of Black athletes in their own backyard, southern universities and conferences refused to integrate their football programs. The Southeastern Conference (SEC) and now defunct Southwest Conference (SWC) maintained all-white rosters well into the 1970s. Some of the teams in these two conferences refused to compete against integrated opponents, even if retaining their segregationist policies meant rejecting lucrative invitations to bowl games or year-end basketball tournaments. The Louisiana State University football program, for example, didn't play a single game against an integrated opponent from 1942 to 1970.[4] Rather than compete against integrated basketball teams, Mississippi State refused automatic bids to the NCAA tournament after winning SEC conference championships in 1959, 1961, and

1962.[5] As Charles H. Martin explained in his fascinating account of the conflict-filled desegregation of college sports, *Benching Jim Crow*, integrated northern schools that honored the so-called "gentleman's agreement" perpetuated segregation. "According to this informal but widely accepted policy, northern schools would act as gracious hosts or thoughtful visitors by withholding any black player on their squads when competing against a southern college, eliminating the need for an explicit request from the southerners," Martin wrote. "The complicity of many northern schools in this arrangement is not surprising, since the few black students enrolled there were treated like second-class citizens and excluded from some campus activities."[6] As for southern schools, the political and social risks of integrating their rosters or so much as competing against mixed-race teams outweighed the lure of additional revenues and national recognition.

Racial incidents were hardly confined to Dixie. In 1969 the University of Wyoming made national headlines by banning Black football players who dared to demand fair treatment for themselves and racial justice generally. The Wyoming Cowboys were a dominant team in the late 1960s. Coached by Lloyd Eaton, they won thirty-one of thirty-six games en route to three straight Western Athletic Conference championships from 1966 to 1968, including an undefeated 1967 regular season. Although the state of Wyoming was heavily white at the time (as it is now), the Cowboys in the 1960s fielded integrated teams. Wyoming's Black players made significant contributions, especially John Griffin, the team's leading receiver. After a 4-0 start in 1969, the twelfth-ranked Cowboys were set to play at home against Brigham Young University, run by the Mormon Church, which prohibited Black men from serving in the priesthood. The day before the game, Wyoming's fourteen Black players arrived at Eaton's office wearing black armbands in protest of the Mormons' discriminatory policies. Eaton promptly kicked the "Black 14" off the squad, causing a stir that eventually ended his coaching career.[7] This incident, like the one involving the "IU 10," shows how coaches and university administrators often punished, rather than praised, Black players who sought racial justice.

On and off the field, the tensions of campus integration proceeded along two parallel fronts. Following the rather slow pace of racial progress in the 1950s, by the early 1960s colleges and universities began to diversify their student bodies. Progress on the playing fields often outpaced integration in college classrooms. On some campuses the playing rosters in track, basketball, and football were already more racially diverse than the student body as a whole, a pattern that persists at many schools to this day. Segregation's lingering effects meant that only a small number of African American students graduated from colleges and universities other than HBCUs. The fortunate few Black or minority students who successfully matriculated at majority-white colleges often came from bourgeois families.

The four-year college experience was also foreign to a significant majority of working-class white Americans of this era. Not until President Lyndon Johnson signed the 1965 Higher Education Act did states create public university systems capable of delivering large-scale, affordable college programs for middle-class aspirants of all races. If university attendance remained an elite privilege for pre–baby boom white Americans, for all but a handful of African Americans a four-year degree must have seemed as attainable as the moon. Indeed, the most storied Division I men's basketball and football programs of the 1960s and 1970s—respectively, those at UCLA and the University of Alabama—provide fitting examples of the challenges posed by campus integration for students in general and student athletes in particular.

In the mid-1960s, when UCLA's basketball teams began a twelve-year run during which they won a record ten NCAA titles, they were typically about a third nonwhite. Black athletes recruited by legendary "Wizard of Westwood" head coach John Wooden included future NBA stars Lew Alcindor (later Kareem Abdul-Jabbar), Lucius Allen, Henry Bibby, David Greenwood, Walt Hazzard, Marques Johnson, Curtis Rowe, Sidney Wicks, and Keith (later Jammal) Wilkes. Most of these UCLA stars earned All-American honors and many enjoyed long, successful careers in the NBA. Abdul-Jabbar and Wilkes are inducted members of the

Naismith Memorial Basketball Hall of Fame, and Abdul-Jabbar retired with—and still holds—the NBA's career scoring record.

Along with perhaps only Wilt Chamberlain, Abdul-Jabbar—then still known as Lew Alcindor—was in a very small, special class of Black athletes. Like Chamberlain, by the time Alcindor completed his senior year at New York City's Power Memorial High School he was the nation's most coveted college basketball recruit. Like Chamberlain, Alcindor was so dominant during his first season (1966–67) that his freshman team beat the his university's varsity in scrimmage games. Like Chamberlain, Alcindor scored more than 50 points—56 to be exact—in his first varsity game (at the start of the 1967–68 season). UCLA would go on to an undefeated national championship season. Further, NCAA decided to adopt a new policy in response to Alcindor's skill (like it had with Chamberlain). The so-called "Alcindor rule" banned dunking, because Alcindor's powerful dunks so intimidated opponents.[8] And unfortunately, like Chamberlain a decade earlier, Alcindor endured his share of racial slights.

Meanwhile, the racial integration of the UCLA student body, especially for African American students, came nowhere close to that of the university's one-third Black basketball teams during this era. This threshold may have been unreasonable for the campus as whole, given that California's 1970 population was 7 percent African American.[9] Yet, to this day campus racial parity for African Americans at UCLA remains elusive. "African Americans remain over-represented on certain athletic teams and under-represented within the larger student body," Lane Demas, author of *Integrating the Gridiron: Black Civil Rights and American College Football*, explained. "For example, in the last century [UCLA] offered remarkable examples of racial integration via athletics, from Jackie Robinson to Lew Alcindor. We certainly celebrate these, especially vis-à-vis segregation at southern institutions. But casual fans may not know that the number of Black students at UCLA has dropped precipitously in the wake of Proposition 209. In 2006 only 2 percent of the freshmen class was African American, yet the school's highly-visible football and basketball teams continue to feature a much larger proportion of black students."[10] (Proposition 209, passed by California voters in 1996, prohibited state institutions from considering race or gender in employment or admissions decisions.)

Two thousand miles away in Tuscaloosa, the University of Alabama resisted classroom integration with the same ferocity exhibited on the field by its all-white championship football teams. By the mid-1960s, however, the Alabama Crimson Tide and other SEC teams realized their programs were suffering from segregationist campus policies. As recounted in George Roy's documentary *Against the Tide*, legendary 'Bama head coach Paul "Bear" Bryant was itching to break the color barrier, but understood the dangers of taking the lead. Bryant frequently quipped that, although he wouldn't be the *first* SEC coach to integrate his football team, he darn sure wouldn't be the *third*. To demonstrate the impact of segregation to resistant white Alabamans, Bryant colluded with University of Southern California Trojans head coach John McKay to schedule a home-and-away series with the Trojans' integrated program. In the first game, played in Tuscaloosa in September 1970, the visiting Trojans demolished the Tide, 42–21. In defeat Bryant claimed a larger victory; long-hesitant alumni and boosters suddenly begged him to integrate. Bryant's 1971 squad, which featured Alabama's first Black player, avenged the 1970 team's defeat, beating USC 17–10 at the Los Angeles Coliseum.[11]

Fittingly, athletes led the revolution that tore down these racial barriers. In *Bowled Over*, his book about the history of college football, former Notre Dame football star Michael Oriard chronicled a series of protests by players, most of them Black, designed to challenge the widespread racism and discrimination within major college football programs and athletic departments. In addition to the aforementioned episodes at Indiana University and the University of Wyoming, from 1967 to 1969 a series of boycotts and protests occurred at Arizona State, the University of California, Columbia University, the University of Kansas, Iowa State, the University of Maryland, Oregon State, the University of Pennsylvania, Princeton University, the University of Washington,

Washington State, and the University of Wisconsin. "Football was under siege at campuses around the country," wrote Oriard.[12]

San Jose State University (SJSU) and its prominent track team also emerged as a flashpoint for Black student-athlete protest in the late 1960s. Following the 1964 Olympic Games, prospective Black Olympians openly considered boycotting the 1968 Mexico City games. UCLA's Lew Alcindor ultimately did, but many other Black athletes chose to compete. After finishing first and third in the 200-meter dash, African American track stars Tommie Smith and John Carlos raised their black-gloved fists during their Mexico City medal ceremony in support of the Olympic Project for Human Rights (OPHR). The defiant, iconic image of Smith and Carlos on the medal stand sparked a furious response from the American public and angered the International Olympic Committee.

The OPHR was an outgrowth of protests on the SJSU campus the previous year led by Harry Edwards and Kenneth Noel, who formed the United Black Students for Action (UBSA) to raise public awareness about racist policies practiced by universities. In 1967 Tommie Smith and fifty-nine other SJSU student athletes joined UBSA leaders in pledging that Black athletes would boycott intercollegiate sporting events until their concerns were addressed. Their plan worked. After SJSU administrators were forced to cancel the opening football game of the season, the university acceded to most of the UBSA's demands, including the integration of campus housing and the fraternity systems. SJSU also eliminated the so-called "2 percent rule" that effectively capped the number of Black students admitted.[13] Edwards, who emerged as one of the nation's leading experts on sports and race, minced few words in his pathbreaking 1969 book, *The Revolt of the Black Athlete*. Situating the protests of Black athletes squarely within the larger struggle for racial and social justice during the tumultuous 1960s, Edwards wrote: "The roots of the revolt of the black athlete spring from the same seed that produced the sit-ins, the freedom rides and the rebellions in Watts, Detroit and Newark. The athletic revolt springs from a disgust and dissatisfaction with the same racist germ that infected the warped minds responsible for the bomb murders of four black girls as they prayed in a Birmingham, Alabama, church and that conceived and carried out the murders of Malcolm X, Martin Luther King, and Medgar Evers, among a multitude of others."[14]

The fight for racial equality in college athletics was also a component of the broader generational protests dominating college campuses during the Vietnam era. Student opposition to the war and the rise of campus feminism presented new threats to the entrenched white male leadership at many universities. According to Oriard, football came in for particular criticism as an expression of establishmentarian, even jingoistic American attitudes. "The 1960s created 'conservative' football fans—not just 'traditionalists,' who had always been part of the game, but political conservatives for whom football seemed a bulwark against political and social change," wrote Oriard. "In the 1960s football became marked for the radical Left as fascist and imperialist and for the radical Right as superpatriotic."[15] Following protests waged against everything from athletes' grooming standards to the lack of Black assistant coaches to the persistent practice of "stacking" Black players into less prominent positions, Black football players were disciplined, and in some cases even kicked off teams. "In all of these cases, boosters and alumni sided overwhelmingly with the coach," Oriard noted.[16] War protestors and gender equity advocates criticized college athletics as an escapist diversion for privileged sons from establishment, white families.

Given the racial composition of universities at the time, Vietnam-era campus protestors were overwhelmingly white. To their credit, many white athletes courageously defied their coaches and athletic directors to join fellow students in demanding racial reforms from campus, state, and national leaders. But a closer look at the era's protests and rallies reveals the faces of minority students, many of them student athletes. These Black and Latino athletes, male and female, typically did not attract the same level of media and public attention that professional athletes of the same period did. The 1967 press conference in Cleveland in support of

Muhammad Ali's refusal to be drafted into U.S. military service that featured Ali, Jim Brown, Bill Russell, and the young collegian Lew Alcindor, garnered more national attention than countless campus protests led by Black student athletes. But that small cohort of college athletes contributed in its own way.

Sportswriter Dave Zirin, who has written extensively about the intersection of race, politics, and sports, discussed the importance of that generation's Black athletes. "[Ali] really became the forerunner of what became known as the revolt of the black athlete in the 1960s. So, then you get this whole period where the best athletes in the United States are African-American, and they're political," Zirin said in a 2013 interview. "So, if you were a sports fan at this time, you were forced by necessity to confront all of these issues. That, to me, speaks to the power of sport, because it forces people sometimes to confront ideas and situations that they would otherwise be mentally segregated from."[17] Though sometimes drowned out by larger and more vital protests against systematic segregation and racial violence, the actions of minority student athletes fueled their generation's fight for political and racial justice. It's only fitting that the racial integration of major college sports began with those most directly affected by segregation's and racism's lingering effects: minority athletes themselves.

From Amateurs to Professionals

By the end of the 1970s, collegiate sports outside of the HBCUs had become fully integrated, even at the holdout schools of the Deep South. "The racial transformation of American sports during the 1970s and 1980s was truly revolutionary," wrote sports historian Richard O. Davies. "By 1980, the typical major college football team was composed of about 50 percent blacks, and college basketball had substantially more on average. No one blinked any more when a professional or college basketball team started five African Americans."[18] Davies overstated the degree of integration in major-college football. Despite being located in South Carolina, the second-Blackest state, Clemson's 1980 national championship football team was about 60 percent white. As late as the

1984 Orange Bowl, the starting lineups for Miami and Nebraska were majority white. In fact, Nebraska started a remarkable ten white players and just one Black player on defense in that game. But it's undeniable that rosters were more integrated in 1980 than they had been even a decade earlier.

As with professional sports, the racial integration of college sports beyond the HBCUs was mostly limited to the playing fields. Coaching and administrative ranks at the start of the 1980s were almost uniformly white, and so were the alumni bleacher sections. These racial barriers continued to be particularly daunting in the South. Not until 1985 did the University of Arkansas—then in the SWC, now in the SEC—hire Nolan Richardson as the first African American head coach of a major college football or basketball program in the South. The most integrated realm of American higher education may have been athletics, but pathbreaking racial advances were largely confined to rosters.

Because the white-dominated collegiate experience excluded most minorities, their rooting interests and spectator opportunities before the 1980s tended to be localized. After all, a city's fans need not have a diploma to cheer alongside their neighbors for the local professional baseball, football, or basketball franchises. Especially in the years before the cable television boom and the launching of ESPN, fandom was geographically circumscribed. People cheered for their hometown teams because, even if they could not attend games in person, they could at least follow their teams on the radio or watch them on local or regional TV broadcasts. Home teams, of course, did not necessarily make Black fans feel at home. The seating policies, availability of concessions and bathrooms, and related aspects of the spectator experience in stadiums and arenas—many of them built with public monies and tax incentives—retained the stench of racial segregation.

Worse, during the civil rights era African Americans—more than half of whom lived in the South—had no professional franchises to root for in any of the former Confederate states. Prior to the 1960s, the closest thing to a regional home team in the South was baseball's St. Louis Cardinals, the favorite of many white southerners.

Many Black sports fans in the South, of course, rooted instead for barrier-busting teams like Jackie Robinson's Brooklyn Dodgers or Larry Doby's Cleveland Indians. The professional sports invasion of the South finally began in 1960, when the St. Louis Cardinals, Dallas Cowboys, and Houston Oilers joined the NFL. Six years later, the NFL added the Miami Dolphins, and baseball's Braves relocated from Milwaukee to Atlanta. Today, eleven cities across five former Confederate states are home to twenty-five professional teams in the four major sports, including four National Hockey League franchises. However, prior to the region's pro-sports expansion, African Americans, long denied entry to southern universities, had neither college nor professional home teams to support.

Professional teams during the postwar decades were hardly paragons of racial integration and equal opportunity. Although professional rosters in the 1960s were integrated, managers continued to segregate on the field. Coaches routinely "stacked" Black players into peripheral positions, thus retaining for white pro athletes the more prominent and the better-paying assignments, like quarterback or catcher, that were supposedly suitable only for athletes who possessed natural leadership skills. Pioneering Black and Latino ballplayers on integrated pro rosters endured racial slights and segregated facilities when traveling for road games and often in their teams' hometowns, too. As David Maraniss recounted in his 2006 biography of Roberto Clemente, even the beloved Pittsburgh Pirates superstar—a Puerto Rican-born hero who led his underdog team to two World Series titles—faced many of the daily prejudices that the rest of Steel City's minority community did.[19] Bobby Mitchell was one of the three original Black players on the last NFL team to integrate, the 1962 Washington Redskins, owned by avowed racist George Preston Marshall. Washington eateries often refused to serve Mitchell, and newspaper editors avoided publishing profiles or features about him in their pages.[20] Even for a city's most popular Black and Latino players, pro sports was no paradise.

As for the front offices, professional franchises were exclusively owned and operated by a few wealthy white men and women.

Not until Black Entertainment Television (BET) founder Robert Johnson bought the NBA's Charlotte Bobcats in 2002 did a professional team in the four major leagues have a majority-stake Black owner. Elsewhere, leadership and management in professional sports remained vestiges of the segregationist era. Well into the early 1980s, Black coaches and even assistant coaches in the four major sports were few enough to be counted on a single hand, and there were almost no nonwhite general managers or even partial owners of pro franchises. Even the players' unions, which had significant pluralities if not majorities of nonwhite members, tended to elevate white members to leadership positions.

Elected president of the NBA Players' Association in 1965, just five years after finishing a brilliant career at the University of Cincinnati, Oscar Robertson was a minority pioneer in labor management. Robertson's case, however, was an exception to the hard color line that bifurcated sports labor and management. Compared to the much thicker barriers that minority coaches, managers, and union leaders confronted, the courageous paths blazed by baseball's Jackie Robinson, basketball's Chuck Cooper, football's Kenny Washington, and hockey's Willie O'Ree seem almost quaint. And although most adult Americans today can identify Robinson as the man who integrated Major League Baseball, few who aren't baseball junkies can identify Baltimore Oriole Frank Robinson as MLB's first Black manager, and only the most avid baseball historians know that the Atlanta Braves' Bill Lucas in 1977 became baseball's first Black general manager.

Despite these slights and deterrents, hometown pride at least provided Black fans some reason to root for local pro teams. In effect, African Americans grew up on the urban "campuses" where their beloved hometown teams played, and they were therefore "alumni" by birthright. College sports fandom at this time was a very different proposition. Sprawling land-grant universities requiring large tracts of available, cheap property tend to be located outside urban population centers where Black citizens—especially in the North, following the great migration—are densely concentrated. Compared to downtown stadiums accessible by public transportation, predominantly white and often rural college towns were remote in both a physical and a psychic sense for urban African American fans, particularly those without automobiles or resources to travel. Campus celebrations during game weekends were sponsored by homecoming committees, alumni chapters, Greek organizations, and other scholastic clubs to which few African Americans or minorities belonged, if they were eligible to join at all. Even for white audiences, the limitations of intrastate school rivalries prevented college football and basketball from developing national audiences.

No matter how frustrating it was for African American sports fans to witness the slow integration of their favorite pro teams, major-college athletics was far less accessible. College sports prior to the 1980s held little rooting interest for African Americans, except for those with a personal connection to specific athletes or universities. It took two full generations of athletes, coaches, and administrators to break down the historical and cultural obstacles that separated college sports from its potential base of support among African American viewers, spectators, and boosters. The Black athletes and coaches who soldiered through this period of discrimination and harassment bequeathed to the 1980s generation of collegians a more integrated, albeit imperfect, competitive environment. The pioneering efforts of postwar athletes primed college sports for a new, radical era of change. Without their courageous efforts, the racial revolution in collegiate sports led by Georgetown and Miami during the 1980s could not have happened.

Rules, Reforms, and Recasting Black Athleticism in the 1980s

By the 1980s the overtly racist policies and practices that Black and other minority athletes from earlier generations faced began to fade. Nevertheless, Black athletes playing major-college televised sports in the 1980s continued to operate within an unwelcoming political and economic environment. By the end of the decade and despite some progress in new minority hires, coaching and administrative leadership had changed little. At Division

I-A football programs in 1990 fewer than 4 percent of athletic directors and head coaches, and a bit more than one in five assistant coaches, were Black.[21] Not until 1991 did the NCAA finally create its Minority Opportunities and Interests Committee to track how many African Americans were interviewed and hired for coaching and sports administration jobs. To this day, some evidence suggests that the channeling of Black college football coaches into specialty positions, like running backs or defensive backs coaching jobs, slows their progress to gain offensive and defensive coordinator jobs that are the gateway hires to being chosen as head coaches.[22]

Racist tropes about athletes did not suddenly disappear in the 1980s. The "dumb jock" is a longstanding stereotype derived from the false belief that athletic excellence rarely coincides with intellectual capacity—or worse, that physical superiority implies mental inferiority. Oddly enough, this trope is a "somewhat recent and very North American belief," as sports historian Jon Entine explained: "For much of modern history, physical and mental activity were inextricably linked but with a *positive* bias." The notion that powerful bodies implied powerful minds prevailed from the ancient Greeks through the Renaissance.[23]

Once competitive college and pro sports became integrated, the dumb jock stereotype took on a new, racialized twist. Fueled by lazy theories of race genetics and slave breeding, people who embraced the new variant of this old trope argued that the undeniable successes of Black athletes implied their intellectual inferiority. Two ugly episodes during the 1980s raised eyebrows and forced executives to end the careers of powerful white figures who perpetuated this stereotype. What made the Al Campanis and Jimmy "The Greek" Snyder incidents so outrageous was that they laid bare the racialized version of the dumb jock stereotype.

Los Angeles Dodgers general manager Al Campanis appeared on ABC's *Nightline* with host Ted Koppel on April 6, 1987, to discuss the approaching fortieth anniversary of Jackie Robinson's integration of Major League Baseball. Koppel asked Campanis, who had played alongside Robinson, why there were still so few

Black managers and no general managers of MLB teams. Campanis claimed that African Americans might "not have the necessities" to serve in these positions. When Koppel afforded him a chance to correct or clarify his comments, Campanis refused. Two days later, the Dodgers fired him.

The Snyder episode occurred less than a year later. On January 15, 1988, the longtime CBS sports analyst and famed handicapper let slip during a televised interview on a Washington DC sports program his real feelings about why Black athletes excelled in competitive sports. "The black is a better athlete to begin with, because he's been bred to be that way. Because of his high thighs and big thighs that goes [*sic*] up into his back. And they can jump higher and run faster because of their bigger thighs," Snyder claimed. He attributed this advantage in America to the forced breeding by white slave owners of the biggest Black men with the biggest Black women. He further declared that if Blacks overtook coaching roles as well, there was "not going to be anything left for the white people." Snyder had been a fixture on the network's popular Sunday morning NFL *Today* program since 1976. Despite his attempts to backtrack, CBS fired Snyder the next day.

Georgetown's John Thompson used the Snyder episode as an occasion to hold one of his famed "mental practices." In these sessions Thompson didn't run the team through its physical and strategic paces, but instead sat players down in the bleachers to talk about current events (see chapter 1). Mark Tillmon, who played for the Hoyas in the late 1980s, explained what happened that day at practice:

> I'll never forget the incident where Jimmy "the Greek" [Snyder] was saying that African-American players were bred to be great athletes. And we had something that was called a mental practice. Coach Thompson sat us all down. When we got to one of those practices, he could talk for hours. . . . We had this mental practice day when we talked about that. So we sat there listening.
>
> He asked each one of us about what we thought about what Jimmy "the Greek" said. He got to me, I said, "I don't know. Pretty

much, I don't care." That's what I said. The words that he used on me that day . . . [ellipsis in original]. He laid into me so bad and he said, "You MFS around here always just want to read your own press clippings. They could be bombing the MF world and you don't know it. Why don't you have an opinion about something? Just because you have an opinion doesn't make you wrong, and it probably doesn't make you right. But have an opinion. Don't ever let somebody ask you something and you don't have an opinion." That never left me.[24]

Snyder offered some mitigating statements later in the interview. He attributed Black domination of basketball to dedication and effort, suggesting that Blacks "practice and they play, and practice and play" and thus were not "lazy like the white athlete."[25] Only Snyder knows whether he realized he had stepped over the line and was scrambling to walk back his earlier comments.

The Campanis and Snyder incidents were outrageous. More subtle variations of media stereotyping continued mostly unchecked, however. Michael Wilbon of the *Washington Post* was one of the few Black sports columnists at a major national newspaper in the 1980s. Wilbon used the 1988 Snyder controversy to decry white commentators' frequent and veiled invocations of racist, brain versus brawn stereotypes. In 1988, in an almost unprecedented act of public shaming, Wilbon called out a specific white TV analyst by name:

CBS college basketball analyst Billy Packer, week in, week out, is as bad as anyone on television in perpetuating stereotypes. Turn away from the TV set and listen to Packer. "What an athletic move!" means a black player made the shot. "What a smart, gutty decision that was!" means a white player hit it.

Packer, during the Pan American Games, all but called a black USA player Aunt Jemima. A CBS employee later sat with Packer and tried to explain that some of what he was saying was insulting to blacks.

Wilbon argued that sports audiences rarely if ever heard white guards at that time described by TV analysts as great athletes.

Instead, players like the University of Kentucky's Rex Chapman or the Boston Celtics' Danny Ainge were lauded for their brains and grit. "If you buy into the theory that blacks are in some way physically superior, you leave open the door for those who propose that white athletes are smarter or work harder," Wilbon wrote at the close of his column. "And if you don't have the sense not to say these things on network TV, then you ought to wise up, shut up or find another job."[26]

A year later, *Boston Globe* sportswriter Derrick Z. Jackson put Wilbon's thesis to the test. In televised broadcasts of seven NFL playoff games in 1988, Jackson categorized commentators' statements as referring to either "brains" or "brawn" mentions and their criticisms as referring to a player as either a "dunce" (pejorative brain comment) or "weakling" (pejorative brawn comment). Although Black athletes constituted 60 percent of NFL starters, they received 87 percent of all brawn comments and 90 percent of dunce mentions; by compare, white starters (40 percent of the total) were the subjects of 67 percent of brain comments and 86 percent of weakling pejoratives. Jackson found similar results in five NCAA basketball games, confirming a pattern discovered a decade earlier in a published experiment of viewer ratings of the media's depiction of white and Black NFL players.[27] Black athletes were described as physically superior but mentally weaker and white athletes as the reverse.

In *Darwin's Athletes: How Sport Has Damaged Black America and Preserved the Myth of Race*, John Hoberman surveyed the long and sordid history of biological racism in sports and sports science. That history is an outgrowth of the nefarious experiments measuring heads and body musculature conducted by pseudoscientific scholars bent on proving physiological differences among the races. Black excellence in sports bolstered the faulty and fraught premise that if the races differed physically, they therefore must also differ intellectually. "The investigation of racial athletic aptitude inspires fear in whites and blacks alike because it suggests other, more intimate racial differences pertaining to intellectual and emotional capacity," Hoberman concluded. "The anxiety level within both groups persists because scientists and the general public share the habit of concealing much of what they really think about racial anatomy and physiology, and this silence allows racial folklore and pseudo-science to flourish unchecked, satisfying the fantasy needs of both blacks and whites."[28]

Racist tropes about the differences between Black and white athletes operate on two, mutually reinforcing levels. As discussed, on the first level sports analysts often characterize Black athletes using different language and labels than those they apply to white athletes. But a compounding, second level stems from white analysts' historical domination of the sports commentariat itself. The near total lack of Black faces and voices on mainstream sports radio and TV as recently as the 1980s meant that few minorities enjoyed large enough media platforms to counter pervasive racial stereotypes broadcast on television or radio.

Of course, the lack of Black commentators was itself born from the brain-versus-brawn expectations applied to minority athletes. Although some commentators come from purely media backgrounds, former athletes and coaches routinely transition into sports media careers. Is it any surprise that the expectations that led to the stacking of minorities on the field would carry over into the press galleries and broadcast booths? "Broadcasting jobs often go to ex-head coaches, almost all of whom are white, and to ex-players who starred in controlling positions, where blacks seldom play," Phillip M. House wrote in his 1989 book *Necessities: Racial Barriers in American Sports*. "Blacks complain that major sports media have not invested in time to groom them, to give them speech training, to teach the nuances of working on-camera."[29]

Racialized depictions of athletes also littered on-air descriptions of players' sportsmanship. Trash-talking is an essential part of competitive sports on almost every level. Players run their mouths or gesture in an effort to gain whatever psychological advantages they can. Football players talk smack across the line of scrimmage before the ball is snapped, basketball players intimidate opponents by celebrating thundering dunks or in-your-face blocked shots. Media judgments of these behaviors can be inconsistent, however. In *Playing While White,* sports historian David Leonard compared the reactions to flamboyant, irreverent and trash-talking displays by white and Black sports stars. University of Mississippi white shooting guard Marshall Henderson, for example, repeatedly taunted and mocked opponents, mugged for cameras and fans, and acted out during Ole Miss basketball games. "When Henderson taunted fans, talked trash, or simulated smoking weed after draining a three, he was praised for the 'joy' and 'passion' he played with each and every night," wrote Leonard. "When Henderson threw ice into the stands of his school's student section following a bad call, his actions resulted in few consequences." Leonard concluded that trash-talking and related antics by white players, be they legends like Larry Bird or louses like Johnny Manziel, tend to be treated as more curiosity than curse. Black athletes are often held to a different, higher standard.[30]

No collegian during the 1980s better fit the bill of the rebellious, rule-breaking white hero than Brian Bosworth. The Oklahoma All-American linebacker coupled bone-rattling tackles and quarterback sacks with myriad sideline and between-game antics as "The Boz," his marketing alter ego. Bosworth attracted a national fan base by buzzing his hair short along his temples and painting it bright colors. He ran his mouth incessantly, even comparing the burnt orange of rival University of Texas to the color of his vomit. Although some of the stories he told about himself were embellished, if not fictitious, Bosworth's self-marketing savvy was evident. Bosworth figures prominently in Michael Weinreb's book about the emergence of the celebrity athlete during the 1980s, *Bigger Than the Game.* "The Boz had little regard for the rules and regulations of the NCAA, since he figured they and the school were benefitting from his image, including a poster of Bosworth that sold thousands of copies," Weinreb recounted. "This was Reagan's America, and The Boz was an unrepentant capitalist, an opportunist seeking out stardom. He would later admit to joining forces with an agent . . . to craft his image."[31]

One can hardly blame Bosworth for capitalizing on his shrewdly cultivated Boz persona. It helped, of course, that Bosworth was

Campus Color Barriers

white. Not unlike pop singers from Elvis to Madonna to Vanilla Ice, Bosworth put a white face on appropriated Black mannerisms and sold that combination to a hungry public. For example, Bosworth claimed to be the first white Sooner with an earring and, for good measure, boasted that he didn't even need anesthetic during the piercing. His shaved-sides haircut was eerily similar to the high fade favored by young Black men and popularized in the mid-1980s by rappers like Big Daddy Kane. "By the time the mid-80s rolled around, a reworked, edgier version of the fade was emerging thanks to Black barbers," wrote Princess Gabbara in an *Ebony* essay chronicling the history of the fade. "It would soon become a standard in hip-hop culture during its golden era."[32] However much Bosworth borrowed from Black culture to create his image, it hardly mattered to his young white male followers. As depicted in Thaddeus Matula's 30 for 30 ESPN documentary "Brian and The Boz," they flocked to barbershops to get their temples shaved and painted on the sides like their hero.

Bosworth used his big mouth and bigger media following to criticize the rival Miami Hurricanes. An unranked Miami came to Norman in 1985 and beat the undefeated, third-ranked Sooners on their home field, 27–14—the lone blemish on the Sooners' national championship run that season. The following year, top-ranked Oklahoma traveled to the Orange Bowl for a much-anticipated rematch against the second-ranked Hurricanes. Bosworth was still simmering about the previous year's defeat. At a press conference the week before the rematch, he said: "I hate Miami's football program. I live in Texas, and I hate everything about Texas. But there's no one thing I hate in Texas as much as I hate Miami's football program."[33] He also equated the Hurricanes to convicts, calling Miami the "University of San Quentin."

Miami head coach Jimmy Johnson didn't appreciate the racist comments, and made his displeasure known in his autobiography. "The Boz, who happened to be white, was being touted in the media as a new-wave role model and just about the coolest guy ever to hit college football—entire suburban peewee football teams were getting 'The Boz' haircuts, and weren't they cute?" wrote Johnson. But Johnson reminded his readers that Bosworth was eventually banned from the Sooners' bowl game that year because of suspected steroid use and then made "an ass of himself" by wearing a "National Communists Against Athletes" T-shirt while sitting out the bowl game to protest the NCAA's punishment. "Some role model," Johnson quipped.[34]

Ironically, Bosworth's celebrity status as a white player appropriating the Black style proved that the racial transformation of college sports underway during the 1980s was now unstoppable. Black players were increasingly slotted into positions formerly reserved exclusively for white athletes. A small but growing number of Black sportswriters and columnists now dotted the otherwise white-dominated mainstream sports media. Division I football and basketball programs began to interview and hire minorities to fill head coach, or at least assistant coach, positions. And an increasing number of white players like Brian Bosworth were suddenly adopting the Black style. The scene was set to broaden the fan base of major-college televised sports.

White Davids, Black Goliaths

Pioneering minority student athletes of the postwar era broadened competition on the college playing field and secured fairer treatment for athletes off the field. To reach fans, however, required something more. A series of pivotal episodes during the 1960s and 1970s gave spectators of color reason to start paying closer attention to major-college basketball and football.

Those moments include the defeat of the University of Kentucky's all-white basketball team in the 1966 NCAA title game by coach Don Haskins' Texas Western squad featuring five Black starters, and USC's 1970 drubbing of Bear Bryant's all-white Alabama squad before a stunned crowd of Crimson Tide fans in Tuscaloosa. But one game stands out from all others in its immediate and lasting racial impact: the 1979 NCAA Division I championship game featuring the nation's two best players that year, Indiana State's white star, Larry "the Hick from French Lick" Bird, and the Michigan State Spartans' sensational Black playmaker Earvin "Magic" Johnson.

By the late 1970s, Black college basketball players had emerged as stars of the sport. UCLA's Lew Alcindor and Keith Wilkes, Indiana's Scott May and Quinn Buckner, Marquette's Butch Lee, and Kentucky's Jack Givens were Black superstars who led their respective teams to NCAA titles prior to 1979. But Magic Johnson was more than just the next Black college basketball star; Magic was a celebrity. Meanwhile, a few hundred miles away, Larry Bird was making plenty of his own headlines despite being almost Magic's opposite. Although other players knew him to be a trash-talker on the court, off the court Bird was a shy person who avoided the spotlight. Sportswriters praised him, but Bird preferred not to make a fuss or tout himself. Whether he realized it or not, Bird perfectly embodied the white anticelebrity. He was a sporting ambassador for the so-called "silent majority" that conservative white politicians from Richard Nixon to Donald Trump have claimed to champion. On the surface the 1979 title game pitted two Midwest schools, one from a top conference and the other from a mid-major conference, and their two star players. But the larger storyline was the game pitting a new and flashy urban America against a quiet, traditional middle America. The game rates as one of the great "white David" versus "Black Goliath" matchups in the history of televised sports.

Michigan State beat Indiana State, 75–64. Johnson's game-high 24 points and his superior Spartans squad were too much for Indiana State and Bird, who suffered one of the worst shooting performances of his career. As CBS television analyst Seth Davis recounts in his splendid book about the 1979 season, *When March Went Mad*, the subtle and sometimes not-so-subtle racial undercurrents of the Magic-Bird final elevated both players' profiles. It also drew new Black *and* white viewers to their television sets even if those viewers' rooting interests were conditioned by fresh memories of the nation's racial discord during the preceding decades.[35] The boost in viewership triggered by the epic Magic-Bird contest helped athletic directors, university presidents, and television executives turn college basketball into a boom industry, and catapulted an ESPN-led explosion in broadcast college sports. Remarkably, the telecast of the 1979 NCAA title game still holds the record as the highest-rated televised basketball game, even surpassing NBA playoff games.

The 1979 Magic-Bird game did not break the racial seal on major-college team sports, but it did forecast the more fully integrated future to come. By the 1980s Black and other minority athletes ceased to be pioneering curiosities and token representatives. Racial disparities in admissions and disparate treatment of minority athletes continued. State and federal courts would increasingly be drawn into continuing campus disputes over resource provision, player safety, graduation rates and the exploitation of scholarship athletes. These battles continue and are evident in policy debates over everything from concussion risks to athlete compensation. The lasting legacy of the Magic-Bird showdown is how it drew Black and white spectators toward televised collegiate sports. The game proved what should have been evident from the career arcs of Black athletes from Jack Johnson to Jackie Robinson: racialized clashes on the collegiate hardcourts and gridirons draw big audiences.

Three months prior the Magic-Bird title game, the University of Miami hired Howard Schnellenberger as its new football coach. Schnellenberger was the Hurricanes' seventh head coach in the previous nine, mostly dismal seasons. A thousand miles away in Washington, John Thompson was attracting his first wave of national attention after completing his seventh season as the Georgetown Hoyas' head basketball coach. The Big East basketball conference had just formed. The programs led by these two men began making national headlines, and soon thereafter became racial lightning rods in their respective sports. In fact, during the 1980s Miami and Georgetown each participated in its own memorable version of a racialized Ali-Wepner or Magic-Bird showdown: Miami's 1988 game against Notre Dame and Georgetown's 1989 NCAA tournament opening-round matchup against Princeton.

Along with the 1987 Fiesta Bowl against Penn State, the most racially loaded episode in Miami football history was the "Catholics vs. Convicts" game against rival Notre Dame on October 15, 1988. The two teams hated each other. Their mutual antipathy started three seasons earlier when the Hurricanes crushed the Fighting Irish, 58–7, at the Orange Bowl. The loss was the final game of Irish head coach Gerry Faust's disastrous five-year tenure and Notre Dame's worst defeat in forty-one years. The 'Canes scored almost every way possible, mixing rushing and passing touchdowns with an interception and a blocked punt returned for two more scores. Miami's Jimmy Johnson was criticized for running up the score. He defended himself by explaining that he had replaced his starters with second- and even third-stringers whom Notre Dame still couldn't stop. Two seasons later, with Lou Holtz coaching the 1987 Irish squad, the Hurricanes shut out Notre Dame, 24–0, en route to winning the program's second national title.

As the 1988 game at Notre Dame Stadium approached, Irish coaches, players, and students harbored intense anger for the Hurricanes. Ranked fourth, Notre Dame promised to be much more competitive at home against the top-ranked and defending champion Hurricanes than it had been previously. With the media billing the match-up as the latest "game of the century," Irish fans wanted to avenge their two humiliating defeats.

Recognizing how big the game would be, two enterprising Notre Dame students decided to capitalize on the fervor. In violation of school policy and copyright laws, they sold thousands of T-shirts to fans with official Notre Dame logos and the phrase "Catholics v. Convicts" emblazoned on them. The slogan's clear implication was that a religiously righteous Irish squad faced a mob of Miami criminals. "The first time I saw the shirt I kind of laughed because I knew we weren't angels," Fighting Irish linebacker Chris Zorich later confessed. To Hurricanes players, coaches, and fans, the Catholics-versus-convicts juxtaposition was patently racist. Richard Pierce, American Studies professor at Notre Dame said, "I think when you see the word 'convict,' the image that comes to mind is 'blacks.' The terminology tapped into something that was American."[36]

The "Catholics vs. Convicts" T-shirt was not the only creative souvenir hawked on campus that week. The slogan on one shirt declared, "You Can't Spell Scum without UM." Another invoked a popular late-night TV segment. On the front was "Hate Night With David Letterman," and on the back were the "Top 10" reasons to hate Miami, with "Jimmy Johnson" listed as No. 1.[37] Another T-shirt described Miami's head coach as a "Pork Face Satan." The tone on these other shirts was nasty, but not patently offensive. On the other hand, a banner draped from Flanner Tower was eerily similar to the racist taunt directed at Patrick Ewing by Villanova students a few years earlier, asking: "Can You Read This? Miami Can't." As *Sports Illustrated* columnist Rick Telander reported at the time, all of this venom spewed forth despite the fact that, in the days and weeks leading up to the game, Notre Dame administrators, head coach Lou Holtz, and his team's tri-captains begged Irish students to keep it clean. "Did you fall for those signs and T-shirts that sprouted in South Bend during game week comparing Notre Dame to the Sistine Chapel and the University of Miami to the River Styx house of detention?" Telander wrote, following the Irish win. "If you did, then you probably feel now that all is right with the world and that God is in his place."[38]

What's ironic about the racial invective hurled by Notre Dame students is that Irish Americans were once an ethnic minority dismissed by white Protestants as less than fully American. According to race theorists, the ambiguous category of American whiteness has repeatedly broadened to include non–Anglo-Saxon ethnic groups—Germans, Italians, and the Irish a century ago, eastern Europeans, and even some Latinos more recently. Assimilation takes time, however. The othering of Irish Catholic Americans—for their Irishness, their Catholicism, and often for both—was commonplace in the early decades of the twentieth century. "Notre Dame and its teams and students were labeled a number of disparaging things at the turn of the century, into the 1920s," explained historians C. Richard King and Charles Fruehling Springwood in *Beyond the Cheers: Race as Spectacle in College Sport.* "The press typically referred to Notre Dame variously as the 'Catholics,' 'the Papists,' or the 'Horrible Hibernians.'"

Irish Americans steadily gained acceptance within the broader white culture that had previously cast them out. King and Springwood cited the mainstreaming of St. Patrick's Day as a notable example. "Achieving this Americanness was an arduous process, and Notre Dame offers many Americans a shining example of how a circumscribed racial identity, Irish, was whitened as Irishness became not only an ethnic domain but literally everyone's 'favorite' charming ethnicity," they wrote. "Perhaps the single most important means through which Notre Dame created these new identities was its football team, which went from being the poor Catholic boys' team to being, in reality, the national team of college football, simultaneously loved and hated by fans more than any other team."[39] Such is the nature of racial assimilation that formerly vilified ethnic minorities—so long as they are white—can steadily evolve from outcasts to insiders. If any team in America should have appreciated the way in which the Hurricanes used their football prowess as a way to gain acceptance for Black and Latino minorities, a Notre Dame program once mocked as the "Dirty Irish" and "Dumb Micks" was it.

For his part, Jimmy Johnson cited the 58–7 blowout of Notre Dame as the moment the 'Canes established their bad-boy reputation. After that 1985 dismantling of the Irish, "we had started to get more and more negativity with our players," Johnson wrote in his 1993 autobiography, *Turning the Thing Around.* "They were very, very good and they knew they were good, and they were aggressive, enthusiastic, sometimes loud and boisterous, and without question, by general America's definition, cocky. This caused negative reactions on a lot of fronts, not only from the media but from our college administration."[40] Hated or loved, the Hurricanes now had a reputation. In a span of five years, Johnson had turned what might have been a flash-in-the-pan champion into the most dominant team in college football. Along the way, he also recrafted the program's image. Howard Schnellenberger's courtly jackets, pipe, and bushy mustache gave way to Johnson's tight-fitting polo shirts, hair-sprayed bangs, and player-friendly temperament.

The Irish won the closely contested 1988 game, 31–30. As in Miami's 1984 Orange Bowl victory to win its first national title and its crucial 1987 defeat of Florida State en route to its second championship, the game came down to a failed 2-point conversion on a pass attempt into the right corner of the end zone. This time the cleat was on the other foot; Miami's offense was on the field and watched its comeback fall short when Notre Dame cornerback Pat Terrell batted away Hurricanes quarterback Steve Walsh's pass. Walsh recalls that the Irish defense stuffed Miami's rushing attack that day, forcing him to pass more. "Normally we . . . wanted to run the ball for 125 yards and throw for 275. We couldn't run it very well," said Walsh. "So we were a little out of our element."[41] Although Walsh passed for 424 yards in one of his best college performances, his incomplete pass on the 2-point conversion is the game's most enduring moment.

As the final seconds ticked away, Notre Dame's players and fans erupted in joy. The Irish had avenged their 1985 and 1987 defeats and kept alive what turned out to be Notre Dame's successful run to the championship. It's no surprise that Irish alumni polled in 2005 rated the "Catholics v. Convicts" game the greatest win the school's history.[42] Nevertheless, the Irish victory that Saturday and their national title forever carry the taint of racism. Only a handful of students made and sold those infamous "Catholics vs. Convicts" T-shirts. University officials caught and punished them. But thousands of Irish students and adult fans bought and wore them, or laughed aloud at illiteracy- and criminality-themed signs.

Demand for the T-shirts continued for the next two years, in fact. Shrewd entrepreneurs sold "Catholics vs. Convicts II" and "Catholics vs. Convicts III" shirts for the 1989 and 1990 Notre Dame–Miami matchups, making sure to avoid confiscation by not infringing on any copyrights nor selling them on campus property. Sellers even took out space to advertise the shirts in the campus newspaper and the Notre Dame booster magazine.

Irish legend Paul Hornung held one of the 1990 T-shirts in front of his chest and smiled shamelessly for a keepsake photo.[43] "To understand Miami/Notre Dame is to understand the cultural dichotomies of the '80s," the *Undefeated's* Justin Tinsely wrote in an essay thirty years after that decade-defining college football rivalry. "President Ronald Reagan's blueprint to 'Make America Great Again' divided an already divided country that was neck-deep in recession. Crack cocaine flooded poor neighborhoods, setting off an epidemic that ripped apart black America. Inner-city plight was the backdrop for political campaigning and news-casts thirsty to capitalize on pain (but not the source). Race was still the straw stirring America's proverbial drink. Sports were a big part of the cocktail."[44]

Georgetown's opening-round 1989 NCAA tourney matchup with the Princeton Tigers was another iconic game with clear racial overtones. Ranked second nationally and the top seed in the tournament's East Region, the 1988–89 Hoyas were the run-away favorite to dispatch the pesky Ivy League champion Tigers, the region's No. 16 seed. The NCAA tourney field had recently expanded to sixty-four teams, and no No. 16 seed had ever upset a No. 1 seed. (Not until 2018 did the University of Maryland, Baltimore County, become the first No. 16 team do so.) Vegas book-makers rated Princeton a 23-point underdog. ESPN basketball analyst Dick Vitale was so certain Princeton would lose that he promised to wear a Tigers cheerleading outfit for Princeton's next game if the team won. Even John Thompson's height advantage over most opposing coaches—magnified when he walked mid-court at the Providence Civic Center to shake hands with the Tigers' Lilliputian coach Pete Carril before the game—reinforced how lopsided the game was expected to be.

Though not as dramatic, the size differential between the play-ers was equally evident. The Tigers' tallest starter was Kit Mueller, their 6-foot-7-inch center and leading scorer. Mueller's opposite was Alonzo Mourning, the 6-foot-10-inch, long-armed Hoyas fresh-man. Nor was there any reprieve for Mueller if Mourning came out of the game, because Mourning's backup was 7-foot-2-inch fellow freshman Dikembe Mutombo. (Mutombo didn't play in the Princeton game, but that season he and Mourning, combined, blocked an average of 7.3 shots per game.[45]) To prepare Mueller to face the Hoyas' twin towers, Tigers assistant coach Jan van Breda Kolff devised a creative solution. "Everyone tried to pass this off as, Oh, it's just another game; we can play with these guys," Mueller recalled. "Then I was at a side basket with [coach] van Breda Kolff, and he was holding up a broom to simulate Mourning's reach. Yeah, it's just another game—the absurdity of that."[46]

Surrounding the Hoyas' two freshman centers was a deep roster of Georgetown juniors and seniors with plenty of Big East and NCAA tournament experience. Starting two freshmen and two sophomores, Princeton had far less big-game experience and no nationally televised games that season. Because Princeton's freshmen decided to get crew cuts before the tournament, the Tigers looked more like the starting lineup from the popular 1986 movie *Hoosiers* than a Division I team ready to face a national powerhouse. Simply put, the Hoyas held every possible advantage. They were the bigger, faster, and more veteran team.

They were also Blacker, of course. Princeton's roster included just two Black players, one of whom started. Every Georgetown player was Black. A quarter century later, Mourning shared his recollections of the game in an essay for the *Players' Tribune*. He described the contest the same way the ESPN broadcast team did during the pregame, as David versus Goliath. But Mourning's description of the matchup's "cultural implications" was his polite way of saying it was really white David taking on Black Goliath:

> We could not have been any more different from Princeton. It was 1989, and Georgetown was right in the middle of hip-hop culture—Starter jackets, name-checks in rap songs. People talked about the cultural implications of that game, and sure, sometimes we felt some cultural tension. But you know what's so funny? People thought Georgetown was a black school. It was just an Ivy League school with a black basketball team.[47]

His teammate Jared Jackson was blunter. "I hate to put the race spin on it, but it's so obvious—all black guys against the majority white team, Princeton," Jackson said. "And the styles of play stood out as well. We were not only an African-American team, but we played athletic, we pressured the ball. It was a completely different form of system we faced." Ironically, John Thompson's older, namesake son had just completed four seasons at Princeton as one of Pete Carril's few Black players.

Princeton's senior forward, Bob Scrabis, later downplayed the race angle. "The racial side of it, that's a media creation, or just our society looking at it that way, but for basketball players and competitors, it was more about their style against our style," he said.[48] The "style" to which Jackson and Scrabis refer was Princeton's signature slow-paced, pass-heavy offense that relied on deceptive backdoor cuts. Carril's system was particularly dangerous for teams that played a smothering, man-to-man defense in which defenders jumped into the passing lanes to steal the ball in order to create easy, fast-break baskets—precisely the defensive style Georgetown used. Despite Coach Thompson's warnings all week at practice to be wary of Princeton, some Hoyas later admitted that they did not take the Tigers seriously enough. That arrogance extended to Thompson himself. According to his son John, whose direct experience playing for Carril made him the perfect scout, the elder Thompson never consulted his namesake on how to prepare for the Tigers.[49]

Princeton put Georgetown on notice from the opening tip. The Tigers scored the first 4 points, led the entire first half and took a 29–21 lead into intermission. Sure enough, Princeton's deliberate offense and backdoor cuts befuddled and frustrated the Hoyas. Ninety miles away at ESPN's studios in Bristol, Connecticut, executives were giddy. During the era before all tournament games were broadcast, ESPN chose Princeton-Georgetown as one of its five live broadcast games in the opening round. According to Sports Illustrated's Sean Gregory in a 2014 commemorative article, "The Game that Saved March Madness," ESPN asked the NCAA to schedule the game in prime time. The NCAA did, and the decision paid off handsomely. By halftime, fans around the country began calling their friends to tell them to turn on their TV sets. They also started calling Bristol. "You didn't have Twitter and Facebook," noted ESPN's John Saunders, who cohosted with Dick Vitale the network's studio coverage from Bristol that night. "What you did have was people calling the control room, the switchboard lighting up, people running into the studio going, 'Do you believe this?'"[50]

The second half began the same as the first: Princeton's Matt Lapin, a DC native who attended Thompson's Georgetown summer camps as a kid, delivered a backdoor bounce pass to Jerry Doyle for a layup. The Tigers had their biggest lead of the night, 10 points. The crowd, which had already turned against the Hoyas, roared its approval. Georgetown steadily chipped away at Princeton's lead during a nail-biting second half. The Hoyas looked tight, especially senior point guard and Big East player-of-the-year Charles Smith, who faced the grim prospect of ending his career in nightmarish fashion. Despite averaging nearly 19 points per game, Smith shot just 2-for-12 from the field, missed all five of his 3-point attempts, and committed three turnovers.[51]

With less than a minute to play and the score tied, Princeton's Bob Scrabis fouled Alonzo Mourning as he tried to score after rebounding a missed shot by teammate Mark Tillmon. Mourning made the first of two free throws, but Scrabis rebounded Mourning's failed second attempt. With fifteen seconds to play and the Hoyas up 50–49, Princeton took a timeout to design a play to win the game. The Tigers got the ball to Scrabis and set two screens for him at the top of the key. Scrabis got free, squared to the basket, and rose to shoot. But Mourning reached out and swatted away Scrabis's shot. The ball went out of bounds. The Tigers attempted another shot at the buzzer but Mourning blocked that one, too. Mourning's monster performance—21 points, 13 rebounds, 7 blocked shots—saved the Hoyas from epic embarrassment. The fans at the Providence Civic Center booed the result. Princeton lost the game, but won viewers' hearts and the Hoyas' respect.

They also earned the eternal gratitude of broadcast executives and small-conference executives. In 1989 the NCAA was considering whether to strip small-conference champions of their automatic tournament bids. The Ivy League's three previous entrants, for example, had lost in their opening-round games by a combined 40 points. Sean Gregory argued that Princeton's near upset of Georgetown had two lasting effects on the tournament. First, the lure of potential upsets meant small-conference champions would forever retain their guaranteed spots in the tournament field. Second, CBS quickly realized it had to strike a multimillion-dollar deal with the NCAA for the rights to broadcast *every* tournament game.[52] Every game between sixteenth-seeded and first-seeded teams pits a longshot against a prohibitive favorite. But the added racial undertones of that 1989 opening-round game between Princeton and Georgetown contributed to the Cinderella lore that became the perennial selling point for the tournament, the networks that broadcast it, and the sponsors who shell out billions to advertise during the games. The Princeton-Georgetown game may not have saved March Madness, but it changed the tournament forever.

Americans love underdog stories and are hardwired by history to follow stories with racial subplots. It is no surprise, then, that Americans exhibit a special fascination with games that intersect these two phenomena: racialized David versus Goliath matchups. These contests are compelling because the historical script is flipped and the white athletes—be they Larry Bird, Irish Catholics, or brainy Ivy League overachievers—play the role of David.

The Hoyas, the 'Canes, and the Racial Tradition in College Sports

The physical exploits and cultural contributions of Black athletes transformed American sports. In the ring and on the racetrack, Jack Johnson and Jesse Owens put the lie to scientific canards about racial and genetic inferiority. Generations of Black athletes from Paul Robeson to Wilma Rudolph to Jim Brown challenged the way sporting and other public institutions treated them as athletes and citizens. A subset of Black athletes stood alongside minority artists, writers, and politicians who played outsized roles in civil rights battles over everything from desegregation to community policing.

College sports and the athletes who play them are part of that history. The political contributions of athletes resonate because athletic successes are so difficult to dismiss. A racist might chalk up a Latina congresswoman's rise to a racially gerrymandered district, attribute a Black graduate's four-year degree to affirmative action, or dismiss a minority novelist's literary recognition to an award committee's political correctness. But athletic accomplishments—a touchdown scored, a ball dunked—are difficult to discount and impossible to ignore. Unfortunately, the athletic successes of Black athletes thus fuel some of the most nefarious, brain-over-brawn racist stereotypes. Indeed, few stereotypes are as enduring as the "dumb Black jock" whose physical superiority implies a deficient intellect or character. "When African Americans began to register an increasing number of victories on the playing fields during the first decades of the twentieth century, mainstream commentators abandoned the athletic creed that linked physical prowess, manly character, and the best feature of American civilization [long applied to white athletes]," noted sports historian Patrick B. Miller. "The recognition successful black athletes actually received from many educators and journalists explained away their prowess by stressing black anatomical and physiological advantages or legacies from an African past."[53] For those who subscribe to such stereotypes, the "Africanness" of these athletes implies inferiority.

A related trope involves classifying Black athletes by situating them on an imposed "good-bad" behavioral continuum. The "good" Black athlete draws praise if he or she is understated rather than demonstrative, team-centric rather than selfish, apolitical rather than outspoken. By contrast, the "bad" Black athlete invites derision from management and the media. Those who exert power in sports—coaches, administrators, and especially the media—define and enforce the good-bad continuum. Historically, of course, the arbiters of who fell where along that continuum were almost uniformly white.

The story of outfielder Dick Allen, one of the Philadelphia Phillies' first Black players, offers an instructive case study from the 1960s. Allen was a promising young player but he refused to adopt the subservient, "Stepin Fechit" role—to borrow an analogy later used by pioneering sports sociologist Harry Edwards—expected of him. Though Allen referred to himself as "Dick," as his family always had, Philadelphia's white media ignored Allen's protests and called him "Richie" anyway. Phillies fans booed Allen from his very first home game in 1964, and during his time in Philly they threw batteries and other objects at him, or called him names like "chocolate drop." When Allen complained about this treatment, the media depicted him as a malcontent and militant. For daring to take a swing in the dugout at white teammate Frank Thomas after Thomas called Allen "Muhammad Clay" and "Richie X," Allen's own manager, Gene Mauch, scapegoated Allen and turned Thomas into the innocent victim. Fans, the media, coaches and even teammates had decided where "Richie" Allen belonged on the continuum. He was the prototypical "bad" Black athlete.[54]

Black sports administrators and sportswriters challenged these stereotypes. Historically, their voices were few and easily drowned out. Although the share of media jobs held by African Americans has increased dramatically in the past two decades, the sports media in the 1980s was almost exclusively white. In *Smashing Barriers*, Richard Lapchick reported that *as recently as 2000* there were no Black sports columnists at 90 percent of the nation's 1,600 daily newspapers. "Fans build stereotypes of athletes from the media coverage of the athletes and the games," Lapchick, who now heads the University of Central Florida's Institute for Diversity and Ethics in Sports, explained. "Fans, who are mostly white, observe sport through a media filter that is created by an overwhelming number of white men."[55]

Surely the implicit if not explicit biases of the predominantly white sports commentariat influenced how major-college Black basketball and football athletes were covered in the 1980s, a decade when Black columnists were so few that they could be assembled in one room. The pernicious "dumb Black jock" stereotype in college sports has endured partly because student athletes are expected to meet standards for academic admission and scholastic progress—requirements from which professional athletes are exempt. "The black athlete in the predominantly white school was and is first, foremost, and sometimes only, an athletic commodity," Harry Edwards wrote. "He is constantly reminded of this one fact, sometimes subtly and informally, at other times harshly and overtly, but at all times unequivocally. The black athlete is expected to 'sleep, eat and drink' athletics."[56]

Given the expectations for their behavior and the consequences of acting against type, consider how unlikely it was in the 1980s for amateur Black athletes in their teens and early twenties to wield any power to transform college sports. Yet that is exactly what several hundred basketball and football players at Georgetown and Miami did. As the players and coaches readily admit, neither program would have been able to lead this sporting revolution if not for the pioneering efforts of the minority athletes in the four decades following World War II who paved the way for an integrated and more inclusive collegiate sporting experience. Their pathbreaking experiences were a necessary precursor to the revolution about to unfold on two of the most unlikely campuses in America.

[3]

Unlikely Incubators

We were aware of what a basketball team can do for
a university in terms of positive publicity.

—CHARLES DEACON, head of the Georgetown search
committee that hired John Thompson

For years, Miami had the dubious distinction of being a
place where good teams went for a vacation.

—CRAIG T. SMITH, University of Miami alumnus
and author of *Game of My Life*

The University of Miami and Georgetown University are
private colleges with notable commonalities. Both universities were founded by visionary men who earmarked neglected
sections of land on the periphery of large, East Coast cities to
build their campuses. Both schools struggled to remain solvent
in their early years. Both boast notable graduates. In addition to
president Bill Clinton, Hoyas alumni include technology millionaire and Washington sports franchise owner Ted Leonsis,
former NFL commissioner Paul Tagliabue, and Oscar-nominated
actor Bradley Cooper. Miami claims actor Ray Liotta, singer
Gloria Estefan, and *Meet the Press* host Chuck Todd among its
famous alums.

The colleges differ in important ways, too. Founded in the eighteenth century, Georgetown is a Jesuit school recognized for its emphasis on diplomacy, law, and public affairs. The main campus is nestled in a tony perch along the banks of the Potomac River in the city's Northwest section, the city's whitest and most affluent quadrant. Once the terminal point for barges towed by mules from western Maryland via the Chesapeake and Ohio Canal, Georgetown at the start of the twentieth century was an outlier community favored by the city's African American majority. In fact, its cemetery on the neighborhood's northern edge was one of the few places within city limits where Blacks were eligible for burial. As in other neighborhoods across the city, steady gentrification drove Georgetown's housing prices up and longtime residents out. A mixed community of college students and M Street shop owners, modern Georgetown is home to some of Washington's most exclusive residences and upscale boutiques. The Four Seasons hotel and Café Milano restaurant are preferred hangouts for visiting celebrities, wealthy socialites, and political powerbrokers who run the city.

In 1789, the first year of George Washington's presidency, Jesuit bishop John Carroll founded Georgetown as a university with a companion prep school feeder. A century later, the university adopted its blue-gray colors as a symbolic gesture designed to bridge the divide between the Union and Confederate states after the Civil War. Initially run by a small core of religious instructors, Georgetown today is an international magnet school with a first-rate and mostly secular faculty. Priding itself on producing future leaders and diplomats, Georgetown matriculates more graduate students in its law, business, foreign service, and medical programs combined than it does undergraduates. The university's main quad is bracketed by the Lauinger Library and the Healy Building. In a circle outside Healy the statue of a seated John Carroll greets visitors. At some point before they graduate, students make a traditional, if tricky, climb up into the founder's lap to pose for keepsake photos.

Miami is a secular university less than a century old that boasts well-regarded programs in medicine and physical therapy. The main campus is located in Miami's neighboring city of Coral Gables, a bustling commercial and residential appendage built from a low-lying strip of South Florida citrus groves. Incorporated in 1925, Coral Gables is a planned city built by developer George Merrick in Spanish-style architecture amid the orange farms he inherited from his father. It boasts a Miracle Mile commercial district and the famed Venetian Pool, a public swimming facility designed by the architect Merrick hired to create Coral Gables' original landmarks. The Miami-Dade County city is home to only a small African American population relative to countywide and state-wide shares, and most of the county's Latino population lives in other Miami neighborhoods. A sleepy haven for affluent sun-worshippers, Coral Gables stands apart from so much of what then and now constitutes the crowded, multicultural urban axis formed by Miami and Ft. Lauderdale along the southeastern tip of the Florida coast.

The University of Miami was founded in 1925, the same year the city was incorporated. Coral Gables' other famed institution, The Biltmore Hotel, opened a few miles away along the city's storied beachfront a year later. The university's main campus today matriculates about seventeen thousand students. Almost half of the University of Miami's undergraduates are out-of-state residents. Approximately eight percent of students are African American, and nearly a quarter are Latino. Miami's most notable president is Donna Shalala, Health and Human Services Secretary in the Clinton Administration and former U.S. representative from Florida's Miami-based twenty-seventh Congressional District. The Hurricanes mascot is Sebastian the Ibis, a bird the university champions as both a symbol for knowledge and a fowl so hearty that it is the "last sign of wildlife to take shelter before a hurricane and the first to reappear after the storm."[1]

Whatever their similarities and differences, the sporting histories of Georgetown and Miami are alike in an important way. Nobody in the mid-1970s predicted that these two schools would become incubators for the racial transformation of major college sports. Both Washington and Miami have turbulent racial histories. Both universities underwent the painful process of integration, including some very early twentieth-century moments of racial reconciliation. The pre-1980s sports history of both programs before the pivotal coaching hires of Georgetown's John Thompson and Miami's Howard Schnellenberger often fell far short of glory. There were few if any reasons to believe that these two teams at these two universities in these two cities would trigger a racial revolution in college sports during the 1980s.

Chocolate City Becomes a Boom Town

For most of its history, Washington was a southern swampland in search of a modern urban identity separate from the federal government it hosts. The enduring nucleus of the city's federal footprint is the National Mall and its familiar symbols of American power and history, including federal government buildings, wartime and presidential monuments, and the national network of galleries and Smithsonian museums. But much else has changed.

Washington has always been a highly segregated city comprising two very different populations. The first are the mostly Black natives of the self-described "Chocolate City" who, until the late twentieth century, were a majority of DC residents. The second are the overwhelmingly white outsiders who descend on the nation's capital seeking power and influence. The city's geographic fabric is woven from a number of distinct demographic strands. The Northwest quadrant contains the affluent, mostly non-native, and majority-white communities of Kalorama, the West End, and Georgetown—each the byproduct of decades of transplanted gentrification. The Dupont Circle and adjacent Logan Circle neighborhoods are home to young professionals and a burgeoning gay community that today is larger than San Francisco's and almost as culturally significant. A small but fast-growing sliver of the city's Latino population is clustered in neighborhoods including Columbia Heights, Adams Morgan, and Mt. Pleasant. Most of the city's African American population lives in the two eastern quadrants. The Southeast quadrant remains the poorest and most crime-plagued, and it still presents city officials with the most sociological and urban-planning challenges.

By 1980 the city's African American population had already declined for a full decade from its 71 percent peak in 1970.[2] Whether or not its residents knew it, the 1980s triggered major gentrification that eventually turned African Americans into a statistical minority. That transformation was hard to imagine a mere dozen years after the riots that devastated the city following the April 4, 1968, assassination of Rev. Martin Luther King Jr.

King was gunned down in Memphis at 7:05 p.m. He died an hour later. As early reports of the shooting filtered into Washington by radio and television, many Black Washingtonians congregated at the intersection of 14th and U Streets Northwest. Because local offices of the Student Non-Violent Coordinating Community (SNCC), the Southern Christian Leadership Conference (SCLC), and the National Association for the Advancement of Colored People (NAACP) were all within a few blocks of the intersection, it served as the unofficial headquarters for the city's African American political community. H. Rap Brown famously declared violence to be "as American as apple pie" at the SNCC's office two blocks north of 14th and U.

An hour after King's death was confirmed, President Lyndon Johnson delivered a three-minute address on national television. Johnson praised King and called for calm, but his appeals were too little, too late. The gathering crowd at 14th and U quickly turned from anguish to anger. By chance, former SNCC chair Stokely Carmichael was in town for an event at nearby Howard University, his alma mater. After conferring with SNCC colleagues, Carmichael advised local businesses to close immediately. The decision satisfied Walter Fauntroy, DC City Council vice chair and head of the city's chapter of the SCLC, the organization he helped build with King, his friend and colleague.[3] Neither the president's call for calm nor similar entreaties from Black leaders on the ground could stop the three days of rioting that followed.

In *Most of 14th Street Is Gone*, historian J. Samuel Walker recounted the destruction that rioters visited upon businesses and other buildings, particularly those concentrated along 14th Street and 7th Street NW and H Street NE. Led mostly by young Black men, rioters looted and burned supermarkets and other, mostly white-owned businesses. After conferring with Mayor Walter Washington, President Johnson ordered more than fifteen thousand federal troops and national guardsmen to secure the city and enforce nightly curfews. Local and national law enforcement used more than five thousand cannisters of tear gas and arrested nearly eight thousand people, more than half of them for curfew violations. More than a thousand residents were injured and thirteen were killed. Miraculously, given the scale of the riots and the massive deployment of forces, metropolitan police killed only three citizens; federal troops killed none. Including the expenses for law enforcement, the riots cost an estimated $27 million. More than 1,300 businesses and 600 buildings were damaged, and half of those buildings were later razed.[4]

According to Walker, two explanations for the Washington riots emerged. The first was that political agitators led by Carmichael incited locals to loot and burn the city. But Carmichael was in the city by chance and already under federal surveillance before King was assassinated. Authorities ultimately concluded that he did not incite rioters. In fact, on the second day of the riots DC police publicly absolved "racial agitators" of blame. The second explanation for the riots was that they resulted from the same sociopolitical inequities that the Johnson-appointed Kerner Commission cited five weeks earlier in the conclusions of its investigation of the 1967 riots in Detroit and elsewhere. In Walker's words: "The riots in Washington were consistent with well-established patterns for domestic disorders throughout American history. Those who participated acted on rational motives. They resorted to violence because legitimate grievances were not otherwise being effectively remedied. . . . In Washington, as in other urban area disorders of the 1960s, the favorite targets were often the police and white shop owners, whom many city-dwellers viewed with intense animosity."[5] The proof for the second, deeper explanation was evident beyond Washington, as riots erupted in more than

160 cities. Clearly, political agitators were not responsible for so many riots in so many cities all in the same week.

In *A Nation on Fire*, Clay Risen revisited the nationwide riots in the days following King's assassination. Risen described the long-term political impact the riots had on race relations generally, and African American livelihoods in particular. "A race war did in fact come to America" the day King was shot, Risen concluded, "but a cold war, not a hot one." For African Americans in the nation's capital, that ongoing cold war meant the unnecessary perpetuation of inequalities that existed before King's death and the ensuing riots. Risen noted: "Blacks in Washington, most strikingly, have not seen a significant increase in income, educational attainment, or job prospects in the forty years since. The urban crisis did not begin the night King was killed. But the long echo of the riots that followed is a critical reason why America abandoned any effort to end it."[6] African Americans responded with understandable anger to a white racist's assassination of the nation's most prominent and inspirational Black leader. They have been paying a hefty political and economic price since.

Georgetown's campus was safety removed from the rioting. There, a young and idealistic senior from Arkansas named Bill Clinton was approaching graduation and working part time on Capitol Hill for his home state senator and idol, William Fulbright. According to Clinton biographer David Maraniss, Clinton felt compelled to do something in response to the riots. He and Carol Staley, a hometown friend from Hope Springs High School who happened to be visiting, slapped a Red Cross sticker on Clinton's white convertible and delivered food and supplies in the city. "From their protected place high on the hill above the city, Georgetown students were in no physical danger during the riots that week," wrote Maraniss. "There was nonetheless a certain wartime feel to the campus. Hundreds of National Guard troops spent their nights sleeping on the floor of McDonough Gym. In the afternoons packs of students clambered up to the Gothic rooftops and watched giant plumes of smoke drift over the faraway embattled streets."[7] The riots were the first in a series of episodes that forced the university to reconsider its relationship with the city and even prompted it to hire its first Black basketball coach.

Georgetown's head coach John Thompson experienced the city's racial struggles at first hand. He was raised in the Southeast quadrant. Segregated public facilities, especially schools, exacerbated the city's deep and persistent inequalities. Although Washington was capital of the country during the Civil War and today is typically regarded as part of the northeastern urban corridor, it is south of the Mason-Dixon Line. Well into the twentieth century, Washington shared more similarities with cities of the former Confederacy than with other cities along the northeastern corridor. "In the years before the civil rights movement transformed the South, Washington, D.C., was as racially divided as any town in the nation," wrote cultural critic Nelson George in *Elevating the Game: Black Men and Basketball*. "John Thompson, son of a laborer who couldn't read or write, was raised there, absorbing all of the slights inflicted on African-Americans during the years of legal segregation."[8]

Washington recovered slowly from the riots. In particular, neighborhoods like Logan Circle, Brookland, and Shaw—today crammed with well-heeled, mostly white professionals from every state in the union—were once working-class and poor Black havens that took years to bounce back. "It may seem hard to fathom for anyone who moved to DC [since 2000], but in 1980 much of the city remained bombed out, abandoned, neglected," noted the *Economist*. "In the late 1980s and early 1990s the city was America's murder capital."[9] Whereas suburban white flight gutted other urban areas of revenue in the decades after the civil right movement, Washington's Black population share began to shrink in the 1970s.

The city's crime and murder rates have since plunged, so much so that urban entrepreneurs invoke with the city's grittier history with ironic flair. The hipster bar Dodge City near the intersection of U Street and Vermont Street NW, for example, is a tongue-in-cheek ode to a time when gunfire was an ever-present danger in the Shaw neighborhood. Today that same area—a few blocks north and east of two concentrated riot areas in 1968—features a popular Mexican restaurant, a three-story nightclub, a scooter rental agency, mixed-use buildings packed with pricey condos and upscale retail shops, and the city's famed gay-friendly sports bar, Nellies. Vestiges of a once-decaying city that lost nearly a sixth of its population from 1960 to 1980 are still recognizable, but only to longtime residents and sharp-eyed newbies.

Washington is hardly the only American city to struggle with racial tensions or the effects of gentrification. But as the federal city, it is a unique case. Washington operated under national supervision for nearly two centuries until the federal government granted the city home rule status in 1973. In the span of just six weeks in 1967, President Johnson appointed Walter Washington as the city's first Black mayor and Thurgood Marshall as the Supreme Court's first Black justice. Yet aside from Marshall, the dozen-plus members of the Congressional Black Caucus, and Reagan's secretary of housing and urban development, Samuel Pierce, the faces of the national government during the 1980s were more or less as white as they had been during every administration since the founding of the republic. Washington residents were still predominantly chocolate, but the Reagan Administration officials who arrived from California and other far-flung places in January 1981 were decidedly vanilla.

One figure dominated city politics during the 1980s like nobody else: Marion Barry. Barry was a bona fide civil rights leader who served as the SNCC's first chairman. He fought shoulder to shoulder with other major activists, including King. Barry advocated for home rule and, at age thirty-five, won a seat on the city school board and was immediately elected board chair. He then won election to the first class of city councilmembers. Surviving the 1977 "Hanafi Siege" assassination attempt by a Nation of Islam splinter group only further raised Barry's profile.[10] In 1978, Barry narrowly won a three-way Democratic primary race in which beleaguered incumbent Walter Washington finished third. In the heavily Democratic city, Barry coasted to victory in the general election with 71 percent of the vote.

Marion Barry was hugely popular and politically skilled. He deftly navigated among federal officials, white developers, Black entrepreneurs, local labor unions, and the city's poorest residents, who formed his loyal base. He broke ground on major projects, including the Washington Convention Center and the revitalized the Georgetown waterfront. His summer jobs program improved the city while putting many of its impoverished citizens to work. Barry's drug use, infidelity and other poor decisions led to an FBI sting and his 1990 arrest. Despite his tainted legacy, Barry's impact is undeniable and unmatched. Although technically the city's second mayor, for many living Washingtonians Barry is effectively the city's first and forever mayor.

At the start of a conservative retrenchment that continues to this day, former California governor Ronald Reagan's arrival at the White House reshaped 1980s Washington. A dozen years after the 1968 riots set the city ablaze, Reagan rose to power pledging to incinerate as much as possible of Lyndon Johnson's Great Society. Republicans and conservatives who continue to revere him tout the Gipper's anticommunism and consequent military buildup to hasten the end of the Cold War. Or they champion his economic policy of income-tax cuts and business deregulation. Key components of Reagan's agenda, however, carried starkly racial implications: a law-and-order platform that emphasized tougher sentencing; the steady rollback of civil rights victories won during the previous two decades; more strictures on and heightened public enmity toward safety-net programs and those who benefitted from them; and an unapologetic assault on affirmative-action programs. Compared to Reagan's revanchist agenda, Republican president Richard Nixon's 1970s "New Federalism" seemed like a quaint, soft-on-crime, nanny-state project.

Washington during the 1980s began to shed its turbulent and racially divisive past to become the modern metropolitan magnet it is today. Streets and businesses that had been looted and burned in 1968 were slowly rebuilt. Gentrification, however, steadily crowded poorer Black natives out of neighborhoods remade for throngs of newer, more affluent arrivals seeking power and profit. Operating

Unlikely Incubators

in parallel universes at City Hall and the White House just three blocks apart, Washington the city was run by its most famous and beloved mayor at the same time Washington the power center of American politics was run by the conservative movement's most famous and beloved president.

Despite Reagan's antigovernment rhetoric, the federal footprint—whether measured in budgets, agencies, employees, or growing legions of lobbyists—expanded significantly during the 1980s. So did Washington's cosmopolitan ambitions. America's former murder capital now forms the core of one of the best educated, richest, and most influential metropolitan areas in the world. Neighboring suburbs in Maryland and Virginia are home to six of the wealthiest counties in the United States.[11] Beyond the monuments and museums that draw tourists from around the world to Washington, the city offers Michelin-rated restaurants and hosts professional teams in the four major North American men's sports, as well as teams in Major League Soccer, the Women's National Basketball Association, World Team Tennis, and the Arena Football League. Modern Washington and its suburbs form a metropolis with a technology corridor second only to Silicon Valley and America's longest average traffic commute. Today, Chocolate City is a boom city, especially the city's affluent Northwest quadrant. Many of Washington's longtime Black residents scattered across the other quadrants, however, have yet to share in the city's rising fortunes.

Mall Murders, the McDuffie Riots, and Marielitos

A thousand miles to the south, Miami during the 1980s was a cultural melting pot experiencing its own complicated transition. Like Washington, Miami and Miami-Dade County (called Dade County until 1997) are still highly segregated. Greater Miami's segregation, however, is notably triracial. Demographic fault lines separate the middle class and more affluent white residents from predominantly Black neighborhoods like Liberty City, Brownsville, and Overtown, as well as from newer Caribbean and Latino hubs, including Allapattah, Hialeah, and the aptly-named Little

Haiti and Little Havana. From 1950 to 1980, Dade County's Black population grew steadily from 13 percent to 17 percent. During the same period, the county's Latino population exploded from 4 percent to 36 percent.[12]

Waves of Caribbean immigrants contributed to both increases. Born in Cuba, the Dominican Republic, Haiti, Jamaica, Puerto Rico and other islands, these immigrants and their progeny self-identify in Census reports as Black or Latino, and in some cases both. The Cold War struggle between the United States and the Soviet Union to control Cuba created a refugee crisis that lured hundreds of thousands of Cubans to Miami and South Florida. In search of a better future, economically desperate Haitians relocated their families to Miami as well. Puerto Ricans also found South Florida to be a proximate and comfortable home on the U.S. mainland. In 1973 Puerto Rico–born Maurice Ferré became the mayor of Miami and the nation's first major-city Latino mayor. In the five decades since, Miami has produced a string of mostly Cuban-American mayors and members of Congress. Millions of Miami-Dade County Latino votes helped elect Mel Martínez and Marco Rubio to the U.S. Senate.

By 1980 the Caribbean influx had combined with Latino arrivals from Central and South America to make Miami the first major bilingual American city, replete with Spanish and English daily newspapers, local signage, and ATMs.[13] Today, the influence of America's Latinos—particularly two full generations of Mexican Americans driving the population growth of states including California, Texas, Arizona, and Nevada—is greater in scale and much more geographically diffuse. But in 1980, a full six years before Ronald Reagan signed the 1986 Immigration Reform and Control Act, Dade County was a rare beacon within the hemisphere for Latinos seeking asylum or simply a new life in the United States.

Unfortunately, the early 1980s were a tumultuous turning point in Miami's evolving racial dynamics. In a span of ten months during late 1979 and early 1980, Miami was rocked by three dramatic events that exacerbated the city's rising racial tensions: the Dadeland murders, the McDuffie riots, and the Mariel boatlift. Each epi-

Unlikely Incubators

sode drew the nation's attention to—and permanently changed—Miami, Dade County, and South Florida.

Miamians unaware of the toll that drug-war violence would soon exact upon their city were shocked into reality by the 1979 Dadeland Mall murders. With local and national media a few miles away covering the trial of notorious serial killer Ted Bundy, on the afternoon of July 11 a white van spray-painted with black letters reading "Happy Time Complete Party Supply" parked outside the Dadeland Mall's Crown Liquors store. The van was a cleverly disguised armored vehicle packed with weapons and bullet-proof vests. Three men wielding MAC-10 submachine guns exited the van, entered the liquor store, and shot drug lord German Panesso, his bodyguard, and two store clerks. As innocent shoppers fled in panic, the gunmen sprayed the parking lot with bullets during their escape.

Police later attributed the Dadeland murders to Miguel Velez, also known as Carlos Arango. Nicknamed "Cumbamba," Velez was a notorious hit man for Colombian drug kingpin Griselda Blanco. In May 1981 Velez and his associates allegedly orchestrated similar assassinations of Blanco rivals Octavio Mejia and Hernan Granados. Mejia was brazenly gunned down in broad daylight outside Midway Mall. Granados's fate was even more grisly. He was kidnapped from a Ramada Inn, and his chopped up body was later found stuffed into a cardboard box. In a strange twist of fate, Velez was eventually captured in Louisiana for his role as part of a four-man team that killed Barry Seal, the CIA agent turned drug runner turned FBI informant played by Tom Cruise in the 2017 film *American Made*. The Medellin Cartel ordered Seal's murder to prevent him from testifying against drug lord Jorge Ochoa.[14]

The drug cartels' choice of Miami as their landing base for marijuana and cocaine smuggling made turf wars and gangland-style violence inevitable. The horrific Dadeland episode merely signaled the start of the drug-related crime wave to follow. In 1980 Miami suffered a record 573 murders, a standard eclipsed the following year with 621 homicides.[15] Drug-syndicate murders and related crimes dominated local media coverage. Although not every murder was drug related, there was little doubt that the bloody era of the so-called "Cocaine Cowboys" had arrived and would not soon abate. By 1981 the FBI's ranking of the ten most crime-ridden U.S. areas included three South Florida cities: Miami, West Palm Beach, and Fort Lauderdale. An estimated 70 percent of all cocaine and marijuana smuggled into the United States came via South Florida, and one-third of the region's murders were attributed directly or indirectly to the drug trade. So much illicit money flowed through the city that Miami's Federal Reserve branch maintained a greater cash supply than the other twelve branches combined.[16]

Popular culture painted a pastel-brushed image of Miami as a fast-paced city mixing sun-drenched glamour with gory, sensationalized drug violence. Al Pacino's portrayal of a fictional Miami drug kingpin in Brian DePalma's 1983 film *Scarface* shocked audiences with its notorious chainsaw scene. The movie included so much violence, sex, and profanity that thirty-two minutes of the original film were edited out for its release on broadcast TV.[17] Premiering a year later and running for five seasons, NBC's *Miami Vice* presented a safer, distilled version of Miami's drug culture. With actors Don Johnson and Philip Michael Thomas playing the undercover narcotics duo Crockett and Tubbs, *Miami Vice* was a staple of Friday night television in the mid-1980s. The show's flashy juxtaposition of crazed villains and sexy beachgoers paled against the real gangster lifestyle of mid-1980s Miami. Indeed, Miami's intersecting criminal and celebrity cultures were more sensational than their fictional portrayals in films and television. In his book *Hotel Scarface*, Roben Farzad described Miami's legendary Mutiny Hotel, the storied late-night destination where drug lords, movie stars, politicians, star athletes, and models mixed and mingled. Drug kingpin Nelson Aguilar held court there, and celebrities including Dallas Cowboys running back Tony Dorsett, actor Paul Newman, and Senator Ted Kennedy partied with abandon.[18]

Five months after the Dadeland murders, on December 17, Miami police beat to death thirty-three-year-old African American insurance salesman Arthur McDuffie. The dozen police officers who either participated in or witnessed the beating—all of them white—initially claimed that they pursued McDuffie on his motorcycle because he popped a wheelie and gave police the finger while running a red light. In their report police said that McDuffie's massive head trauma resulted from his own reckless driving while he attempted to elude police, which caused him to fall, lose his helmet, and split open his head. In fact, after beating McDuffie so brutally he slipped into a coma, officers ran over McDuffie's motorcycle to bolster their cover story. Four days later, McDuffie died in a nearby hospital.

Miami's state attorney, Janet Reno, led the investigation into McDuffie's death. Aided by the confession of one guilt-ridden police officer who witnessed the episode, Reno's team concluded that police officers harassed McDuffie, broke his glasses and watch, and then assaulted him—most likely with a nightstick or galvanized pipe—for no reason other than that he was a Black man enjoying a late-night motorcycle ride through the city they ruled. The future first female U.S. attorney general charged four officers with manslaughter and a fifth for tampering with evidence as part of the failed cover-up. During the winter and spring of 1980, Miamians closely followed developments in the trial, which was relocated to Tampa to ensure both an impartial jury and the hopes of maintaining public safety back in Miami.

On May 18, 1980, those hopes were dashed when the Tampa jurors acquitted all five officers. Word quickly reached South Florida, infuriating Black Miamians. Within hours of the verdict, Black neighborhoods including Brownsville, the Black Grove, Liberty City, and Overtown descended into violent lawlessness. Rioters assaulted random white pedestrians and motorists with rocks and bottles, pulled them from their cars, and beat some of them to death. City authorities were unprepared for the chaos. Police quickly instituted a curfew for a fifty-two-square-mile section of the city, but the McDuffie riots—alternatively known as the Liberty City riots—continued unabated for three days. When it was over, eighteen were dead, another four hundred injured, and more than three hundred businesses were damaged or destroyed. Loot-ers set ablaze the Norton Tire Company warehouse. It burned for six days, its smoke visible for miles.[19]

White Miamians under siege fled the streets or abandoned their vehicles on foot. Many were aided by courageous Samaritans, including Black Miamians horrified by the violence. Edward Sofen, chair of the University of Miami's Department of Political Science and Public Policy, was among the lucky survivors. Sheltered by a Black Episcopal minster after escaping his besieged vehicle, the professor suffered an orbital skull fracture but avoided the fate of victims whose lives were permanently altered by brain damage or disfigurement.[20] During an appearance on the nightly news broadcast of local station WTVJ, McDuffie's mother, Eula, exhorted people to stop rioting. On the same broadcast, Larry Little—who grew up in Overtown, starred for the two-time Super Bowl champion Miami Dolphins, and was a friend and neighbor of Arthur McDuffie—issued a similar plea for calm.[21] Rioting continued anyway.

During the riots of the late 1960s and early 1970s, deadly violence was uncommon and most of the fatalities were Black victims killed by white police officers or national guardsmen. In stark contrast, the 1980 Miami riot featured Black protestors attacking random, unsuspecting white victims. "The bare statistics of the riot—18 dead, $80 million in property damage, 1,100 arrested—do not in themselves set Miami apart from similar disturbances in Watts, Newark and Detroit a decade earlier," historians Bruce Porter and Marvin Dunn wrote. "What was shocking about Miami was the intensity of the rage directed by blacks against white people: men, women and children dragged from their cars and beaten to death, stoned to death, stabbed with screwdrivers, run over with automobiles; hundreds more attacked in the street and seriously injured."[22]

The explosion in violence was the byproduct of long-simmering racial tensions in Miami. As in other American cities, a series of previous slights and injustices fueled suspicion and anger among Black residents toward municipal police and authorities. Indeed, Arthur McDuffie's death followed three widely reported police transgressions in 1979, including a police officer's molestation of an eleven-year-old Black girl and the shooting of a twenty-two-year-old Black man by an off-duty white officer.[23] More than a decade before a California jury acquitted the Los Angeles police officers who assaulted Rodney King, the McDuffie jury's acquittal of the police officers who murdered an innocent Black professional provided the same spark. "You had very, very angry people on the streets during those years," Robert Simms, director of the city's Community Relations Board in 1980, told the *Miami Herald* on the twenty-five-year anniversary of the riots. "By the time McDuffie happened, the precedent was set: 'When politicians start messing with us, let's get it on.' The verdict was seen as an injustice. And so the riots in 1980 were on." The riots decimated neighborhoods like Brownsville. Many of the looted and burned local businesses never returned. Rebuilding took years, and some neighborhoods never fully recovered. Decades later, the poverty rates in these African American communities are the same as if not higher than they were in 1980.[24]

Because the violence and looting concentrated in Liberty City (although it also occurred in other neighborhoods), many locals and the media still refer to episode as the "Liberty City riots." The neighborhood certainly suffered the most personal violence and property damage. But even before the McDuffie murder, Liberty City was a socioeconomic powder keg ready to explode. For most of the previous half century, it was a planned neighborhood that served as the backbone for Miami's Black middle class. It then suffered the triple heartbreak of drug addiction, violence, and economic deterioration. As journalist Roshan Nebhrajani explained, "In the 1960s integration began allowing blacks to move into neighborhoods previously off limits (although redlining kept some parts of the city de-facto segregated). Many of those with money left Liberty City to buy homes in, for example, Miami Shores. That began the drain of economic and intellectual resources, which accelerated the second part of the downfall: the spread of crack and the crime that followed. The cheap, highly addictive drug swept through the community."[25] The Kerner Commission report's findings, now a dozen years old, remained as relevant as ever.

Miami native and noted documentarian Billy Corben vividly remembered how tense the racial situation was in the city during his youth. Known for the documentary *Cocaine Cowboys* and his two-part ESPN 30 for 30 chronicle of the Miami Hurricanes football program entitled *The U*, Corben noted that the McDuffie riots were only the first of three major race riots during the 1980s; similar outbreaks occurred in 1984 and 1989. "People think of Miami as an international and cosmopolitan city, but we were still the Jim Crow south," well into the decade, said Corben. "That is how we got hoods like Overtown and Liberty City because, for example, African Americans were not allowed to stay overnight in Miami Beach. All African Americans who worked hotels and other businesses in Miami Beach had to be tagged and finger-printed to identify them. And if it's after dark and you're black you better be heading out of town. McDuffie was a culmination of all of this."[26]

More recently, Liberty City is enjoying a cultural renaissance. The area served as the backdrop for the Oscar-winning 2016 feature film *Moonlight* and was the focal point of a 2018 HBO documentary (*Warriors of Liberty City*) about the neighborhood's youth football tradition. In the documentary longtime Hurricanes football booster Luther "Luke Skyywalker" Campbell—credited by Peabody Award–winning rap documentarian Shad Kabango as the godfather of the Miami rap scene[27]—is hailed as the key patron of the neighborhood's youth football program. Liberty City takes pride in having sent dozens of future stars to the Miami Hurricanes football program and in delivering more players to the NFL than any community in America. "Some of the scars from the 1980 riots have faded, but some will never heal completely," said notable Miami sports observer Dan Le Batard. "I'd also say that that time in Miami—that period—had a lot of Scarface in it. Miami was a dangerous, violent, sunny place with a lot of temptation and fun and excess. The (Hurricane) program reflected all of that."[28]

The six-month Mariel boat lift began a month before the McDuffie verdict and subsequent riots. Few events had a more dramatic impact on modern Miami than the mass immigration of political refugees from Mariel port in Havana. The boat lift that eventually brought 125,000 Cubans and Haitians to South Florida was triggered when thousands of Cuban artists and political dissidents announced that they wanted asylum abroad. Thousands showed up and were welcomed into Havana's foreign embassies, especially the Peruvian embassy.

Frustrated Cuban president Fidel Castro surprised the world by declaring that any Cubans seeking asylum could depart from Mariel port so long as somebody came to pick them up. Peru is a long way from Havana, but the Florida Keys are just a ninety-mile boat ride away. Almost immediately, boats of every size and shape departed South Florida for Mariel to embark Cuban defectors. The U.S. government quickly set up a reception center in Key West for the new arrivals. During the peak month of May 1980, more than eighty-five thousand Cubans arrived in Florida.[29]

Castro poisoned Cuban-U.S. relations by making false claims about the Marielitos, as the émigrés came to be known. "In order to save face, Castro put forward the narrative that the Cubans who sought to leave the island were the dregs of society and counter-revolutionaries who needed to be purged because they could never prove productive to the nation," wrote historian Julio Capó Jr. "This sentiment, along with reports that he had opened his jails and mental institutes as part of this boatlift, fueled a mythology that the Marielitos were a criminal, violent, sexually deviant and altogether 'undesirable' demographic." When asked in 2017 to cite an example where immigrant labor negatively affected the work prospects of native-born or naturalized Americans, noted anti-immigrant Trump Administration adviser Stephen Miller pointed to the 1980 Marielitos.[30]

The Marielitos were not the first Cubans to arrive in South Florida. Like earlier Cuban immigrants, they brought with them to America a fierce anticommunism and a reflexive devotion to the Republican Party. But as María Cristina García explained in *Havana USA*, her book about the influence of Cuban-American immigrants to Miami during the twentieth century, the Marielitos differed from the earlier wave of Cuban immigrants:

The first-generation exiles were forced to leave their homeland and adapt their customs and traditions to the realities of life in the United States, but in the process they forged a hybrid society, a uniquely Cuban-American culture. *Marielitos* found the emigrés to be too Americanized, but Cuban Miami was still familiar enough to accommodate them, along with the thousands of other emigrés who chose to resettle there in the middle and late 1980s. Miami had become Havana USA: the border town between Cuba and the United States.[31]

The Cuban influence in Miami has since dominated the city's culture and politics. The rapid transformation of a major American city in such a short period by a single ethnic group of immigrants is virtually without precedent.

Fairly or not, Miami in the 1980s became synonymous with America's illicit drug culture and the new challenges posed by Latino immigration. As early as November 1981, *Time* magazine's "Paradise Lost" cover story by James Kelly identified Miami and South Florida as a metropolitan area in distress. The idyllic scenes long associated with Miami culture—sun bathers, mangroves, and palm trees—were "being crowded out by some altogether different scenes, a collection of photos not found in any Chamber of Commerce travel brochure," wrote Kelly. "Here is a picture of a policeman leaning over the body of a Miamian whose throat has been slit and wallet emptied. There is a sleek V-planed speedboat, stripped of galleys and bunks and loaded with a half-ton of marijuana, skimming across the waters of Biscayne Bay. Here are a handful of ragged Cuban refugees, living in a tent pitched beneath a highway overpass."[32]

Miami remains an arrival point for illicit drugs, but the racial tumult and drug-related violence in the city today pale in comparison to the Cocaine Cowboys era. The state's 2016 Uniform Crime Report found that Miami's overall crime rate has dropped by a third since its mid-1980s peak. But the declines are not uniform across the city. As the *Miami Herald* explained, "For all the improvement, many of the homicides in Miami and Miami-Dade happen in the same places, in the central core of the county in neighborhoods including Liberty City, Brownsville, Allapattah and Little Haiti. That means though shooting deaths are down overall, the violence seems intense to the people who live in those neighborhoods."[33] As has so often been the case for Black and Latino Miamians, progress is real but incremental.

Confronting Racial History on Campus

Georgetown is a religious college as old as the nation. The University of Miami is a secular university founded less than a century ago. Their ages and histories notwithstanding, both universities had to grapple with a problematic evolution from exclusively white student bodies to the more diverse and inclusive institutions they are today. Those transitions did not occur overnight or without incident. The identities of both universities are indelibly wedded to their complex, long-ignored past racial sins. Recently, each campus was forced to confront its complicated racial history.

Something remarkable happened on Georgetown's campus during a four-year span from 2014 to 2017. A set of activists forced university leaders to account for Georgetown's historical connections to slavery, and specifically for the 1838 sale by the university's Jesuit priesthood of 272 Maryland plantation Black slaves to two Maringouin, Louisiana, planters, Henry Johnson and Jesse Batey. Prompted in part by a provocative op-ed published in the *Hoya* student newspaper by undergraduate history major Matthew Quallen, Georgetown alumnus Richard Cellini formed a working group to investigate what happened to those original 272 slaves and their descendants. (During the next five years, Georgetown sold another 32 slaves.)[34]

Cellini and his GU272 Georgetown Memory Project quickly learned three startling facts. First, that the income generated from the slave sales helped rescue the financially strapped university from almost certain bankruptcy in the late 1830s. Second, the whispered tale—passed down through generations of Georgetown students and administrators—that the slaves died soon after their arrival in Louisiana from a mysterious swamp fever was a convenient, self-deluding fiction. And third, according to a team of genealogists hired by Cellini and GU272, many descendants of those slaves could be identified and were still alive.[35] In fact, a significant number of the more than four thousand GU272 descendants still live in or near the small town of Maringouin, where their enslaved ancestors were shipped in 1838. Today, the GU272 project maintains a database of all known living descendants, grouped into forty-nine family clusters.[36]

Coincidentally, Georgetown history professor Adam Rothman and some of his students had also been tracking the history of the slaves and their descendants. Cellini and Rothman quickly decided to combine resources. Along with growing pressure from students and alumni, their joint efforts compelled Georgetown president John J. DeGioia to form the Working Group on Slavery, Memory, and Reconciliation in September 2015. DeGioia tasked the group to study the issue and determine what actions Georgetown should take. "The university itself owes its existence to this history," Rothman, an appointed member of the working group, told *New York Times* reporter Rachel Swarns.[37]

The working group issued its findings in April 2016. A few months later, DeGioia announced the university's response to the working group's recommendation. Georgetown removed from campus buildings the names of former Georgetown presidents Thomas F. Mulledy and William McSherry, the two Jesuit priests directly involved in the slave sale. The university also established a preferential admissions policy for any GU272 descendant who applies to Georgetown.[38] In fall 2017 Mélisande Short-Colomb and Shepherd Thomas became the first GU272 descendants to matriculate at Georgetown. Two years later Georgetown students voted to pay a $27.20 fee per student per semester into a fund that supports descendants of the GU272 slaves.[39]

Reconciliation and reparations are thorny matters that raise uncomfortable questions and compel difficult, often controversial choices. But a movement initiated by a handful of vigilant students, faculty members, and alumni—and eventually adopted by administrators and the university's board of trustees—forced

Georgetown to acknowledge its historical connections to slavery and take remedial action to address its legacy.

The University of Miami was established long after slavery ended, but well before most of the nation's governmental, business, cultural, and educational institutions were integrated by law or in practice. As mentioned in the previous chapter, in the first half of the twentieth century Miami complied with the so-called "gentleman's agreement" by refusing to permit its varsity teams to compete against integrated programs from other colleges. In his 1975 history of the university, Charlton Tebeau cited the cancelled 1946 football game between Miami and Penn State's integrated squad as a pivotal moment in the university's racial awareness. According to Tebeau, Bowman Foster Ashe, at the time Miami's first and only president, remarked that the letters he received approving of his decision to abide this segregationist practice "bothered him more than those that disapproved."[40] The university clearly needed to rethink its segregationist practices, both on the ballfields and in the classrooms of Coral Gables.

After Ashe died in 1952, the process of integrating Miami fell to his two immediate successors, Jay F. W. Pearson and Henry King Stanton. By 1958 Miami began offering its first wave of integrated courses, but only if faculty and students met in off-campus buildings, typically at public high schools or middle schools at night. Off campus, a five-member graduate course in education for aspiring public school teachers that included three white students and two Black students finally broke Miami's color barrier in 1958.[41]

Miami students and administrators alike initially disagreed about whether and when to fully integrate the main campus. By a 14–11 margin the student government council in 1958 passed a resolution calling for full desegregation. But as Tebeau described, university officials continued to hedge:

President Pearson's position remained conservative all along. On January 14, 1959, he stated the opinion of the Board of Trustees and the administration that integration of the University of Miami was inevitable. The only question was when and how. He refused, he said, to take the leadership to change Florida's educational policies "just to prove we are leaders." Nor, said he, would he seek the enrollment of an unqualified student "just because we should prove that we will take one."[42]

Finally, in 1961, a year before Pearson stepped down, the university's Board of Trustees voted unanimously to integrate the entire campus.

The early ranks of Black and other minority students to matriculate were thin, and the daring students in those first two decades faced the kinds of pressures familiar to any group that breaks down social barriers. In 1968 Black students seeking greater resources for themselves and for the recruitment of Black faculty conducted a sit-in at President Stanton's office. Miami's integration, like that of many other universities of the era, was slow and limited in scope, met significant resistance, and was accepted only grudgingly by many white students, administrators, and alumni.

In February 2017 a group of African American alumni returned to the University of Miami for a "U Trailblazers" event organized to honor the minority student pioneers from the 1960s and 1970s. The event was the culmination of efforts by the Black Alumni Society's First Black Graduates Project Committee, which tasked itself with chronicling and celebrating the lives of the university's first generation of Black students. After four years of extensive research of library archives and *Ibis* yearbook entries, committee co-chairs Denise Mincey-Mills, Antonio Junior, and Phyllis Tyle proudly unveiled the Black Alumni Society's *We Were Pioneers* exhibit at the university's Otto G. Richter Library. At a ceremony attended by a number of notable Black alumni and administrators, university president Julio Frenk commended the pioneers.[43]

Cuckoo's Nest and the Two Dunbars

Before Georgetown hired John Thompson in 1972 as head coach, Hoyas men's basketball was an unremarkable program that received little attention from the national sports media or even its own city's top basketball prospects. The Hoyas had only qualified for a national postseason tournament—the NCAA tournament or the second-tier National Invitational Tournament (NIT)—three times during the previous sixty-three years. Of the teams that qualified, the 1942–43 "Kiddie Korps" squad coached by Elmer Ripley was easily the most accomplished. Depleted by graduation and military-service deployments, Georgetown finished 22-5 and made it all the way to the championship game, but lost to Wyoming. Led by captains Dan Knaus and Billy Hassett, the Hoyas were outgunned by Wyoming's Kenny Sailors, the player credited with inventing the jump shot. The Hoyas lineup included Henry Hyde, a backup forward who would later serve for more than three decades as a Republican congressman from Illinois and become known for his staunch opposition to abortion and his role in Bill Clinton's 1998 impeachment.

For decades prior to integration, Georgetown's basketball rosters were full of white prep stars from Catholic high schools in New York and New Jersey. Either because they were not recruited to play for all-white Georgetown or because they could play for better teams in more prominent conferences, local Black superstars including Elgin Baylor, Dave Bing, Austin Carr, and John Thompson himself all left town to play elsewhere.[44] Thompson's predecessor, John Magee, was a personable and competent coach, but he demonstrated little appetite for the type of aggressive recruiting needed to build a competitive, top-flight national program. The season before Thompson was hired, Magee's 1971–72 team finished a dismal 3-23. A self-effacing Magee later claimed unusual credit for saving the university by forcing it to dump him and hire Thompson. "You don't change things when you are 10-16. Sure, maybe you change the coach, but you don't change anything else," said Magee. "But we lost so much they were shocked. So, they changed. I shocked them into it."[45] Even after Thompson took over, nobody thought the small Jesuit school with a mostly white, Catholic student body would someday be identified by its almost all-Black rosters and the first Black coach to win a Division I team-sport national championship.

Born in 1941, Thompson was raised in a highly segregated Washington where the economic disparities and cultural chasm between the mostly white, transplanted political class and its majority-Black residents were as pronounced as anywhere in America. Thompson's Catholic family resided in an Anacostia neighborhood where too few young Black men escaped poverty and others ended up imprisoned or dead. But Thompson's determined mother parlayed young John's smarts and athleticism into a scholarship to Archbishop Carroll High School, the Catholic prep academy named for the same man who founded Georgetown University.

Thompson excelled at Archbishop Carroll, helping lead the school's team to a fifty-five-game win streak that remains a city record. In his senior year, Thompson accepted a basketball scholarship to play for Providence, a Jesuit college that, like many of its fellow Catholic universities, was on the progressive front line of athletic integration. "Most of the Catholic colleges had been among the leaders in integration and had also used their basketball programs to gain national attention, not to mention the extra money that poured in from grateful alumni when the teams did well," Thompson biographer Leonard Shapiro explained. "Georgetown, with a healthy endowment and graduates at the tops of the chosen fields who often contributed generously had never felt the need to upgrade its basketball team."[46] At a time when many young Black men in urban Washington had little hope of escaping poverty, John Thompson found a way out. He would return soon enough.

After a successful collegiate career with the Providence Friars, Thompson was selected by the Boston Celtics in the third round of the 1964 NBA draft. Thompson was a serviceable backup center to Celtics legend Bill Russell, but not a star during his short-lived pro career. In two years with Boston, Thompson appeared in just seventy-four games, averaging about ten minutes of playing time and 3.5 points per game during the 1964–65 and 1965–66 seasons. Drafted away from the Celtics by the Chicago Bulls in the NBA's 1966 expansion, Thompson never played for the Bulls and instead came home to Washington.[47] An economics major in

Unlikely Incubators

college, Thompson found work in the city's urban nonprofit sector. A little more than a year after his return, his hometown was set ablaze during the April 1968 race riots.

Thompson caught his first break when he was hired as the varsity boys basketball coach at St. Anthony's, a Catholic prep school located less than a mile from Archbishop Carroll, in Washington's Brookland neighborhood. In six seasons at St. Anthony's, Thompson racked up an impressive record of 122-28. He stole headlines away from the region's powerhouse high school, DeMatha, coached by the legendary Morgan Wooten. With Thompson's star rising, Georgetown president Rev. Robert Henle soon came calling. "I hadn't given much thought to college coaching and, truthfully, I wasn't sure I was ready for Georgetown, but I let them consider my name," said Thompson, recalling his recruitment at age thirty by Georgetown. "I have a big ego, and I was curious to see what other people thought of me."[48]

Wooten and Thompson disliked each other. Thompson's revival of St. Anthony's led local sportswriters to compare his program to Wooten's long-dominant DeMatha, which has sent more players to the NBA than all but one other American high school. The Wooten-Thompson rivalry escalated into a cat-and-mouse feud in which both coaches avoided tournaments where their two teams might meet on the court. Their mutual enmity grew to new levels when Wooten, who reportedly turned down the head coaching job at Georgetown in 1966, lost out to Thompson in 1972 for the same position.[49]

Admissions director Charles Deacon led Georgetown's seven-person search committee that interviewed Thompson along with Wooten, Jack Ramsay, then the head coach at fellow Jesuit university St. Joseph's, and George Raveling, an African American assistant to head coach Lefty Driesell at nearby University of Maryland. The committee sought to duplicate what the Maryland Terrapins had achieved in College Park. "We were aware of what a basketball team can do for a university in terms of positive publicity," Deacon recalled. "And, we were influenced by what Lefty Driesell was accomplishing at Maryland."[50]

Interestingly, Thompson's 1972 hiring was motivated by more than the promise of reviving the school's dormant basketball program. The violence that tore Washington apart during the 1968 riots, and which again overtook the Georgetown campus three years later during the 1971 May Day riot, rattled university leaders. In the previous decade, Georgetown had also faced rising demands to admit women to the "Yard," the university's primary, all-male college known in shorthand by its central geographic location. As a senior poised to graduate in 1968 from the university's School of Foreign Service, Bill Clinton showed up uninvited to a Yard debate over whether to unify the student governments of Georgetown's various schools: the School of Foreign Service, East Campus, the Nursing School, and the Yard. Dressed in a black leather jacket, Clinton lashed out at Yarders clad in their requisite coats and ties who told students from the other schools, like Clinton, they were unwelcome to participate in Yard meetings. "I come from the land of prejudice but I have never seen prejudice such as I've seen tonight," Clinton said.[51] The campus phased out its coat-and-tie dress code for men and began admitting women to its main campus starting with the fall 1968 semester.

Three years later, on May 3, 1971, roughly three thousand of the thirty-five thousand anti–Vietnam War protestors who had been driven from the National Mall by city police retreated to Georgetown's campus to find safety. But police stormed the campus without the university's permission, released tear gas on the protestors and then arrested several of them. The ensuing chaos of the May Day Riot caused the university's faculty to formally vote to cancel all final exams that semester.[52] The days of Georgetown sitting atop its hilly perch, safely removed from the tumult of national politics and social movements, were over.

The era's social unrest compelled university leaders to rethink Georgetown's relationship with local citizens and the federal city it called home. The Reverend Timothy S. Healy, who succeeded Henle as Georgetown's president, wanted the university to do more. Healy later described DC as a cuckoo's nest in which "local people make the nest" but the cuckoos "fly in and out [but] don't really care a lot about what they do in, or to, the nest." He admitted Georgetown's culpability in this disconnect:

> I think Georgetown has been, to an extent, one of the cuckoos. After the 1968 riots it became obvious that the university's position wasn't very smart or defensible—socially, intellectually, morally or empirically. We began making some changes, some statements to the local community that we were going to try to be at least more responsible and useful. I think it's fair to say that hiring John Thompson was one of those statements.[53]

Charles Deacon, chair of the search committee that hired Thompson, described Georgetown's detachment from its urban surroundings to the *Washington Post's* John Feinstein in similar terms. "Back then, we were living on the fringes of the community, not as part of it. We were living in an ivory tower. We had to change that, we had to actively recruit students from inner-city schools in Washington," Deacon recalled. At the time of 1972 Thompson's hiring, only about fifty Black students a year applied to Georgetown, and only two percent of Hoyas undergraduates were Black.[54]

So it came to pass that Thompson was hired not only to coach the Hoyas but also, in part, to heal the fractious, disconnected relationship between Washington's mostly African American native population and its white-dominated institutions. As if the job of reviving a dormant basketball program with a 3-23 record the previous season were not burden enough, Thompson was expected to help Georgetown take greater social responsibility in Washington at a moment of unnerving political and social unrest less than four years after race riots tore the city apart. With all that pressure, is it any wonder Thompson at first hesitated to accept Henle's offer and took some convincing to accept it? "When I made him the job offer, he said before accepting he would like to say a few things," Henle recalled. "He said he would not play kids and let them flunk out. He said they've got to get a Georgetown degree. He said he'd like to have another position to ride herd on the kids academically. And he wanted a white assistant who he thought could recruit white students better. We gave him what he wanted."[55] That added position—something rare for college programs at that time—would be filled by Mary Fenlon, a nun Thompson brought along with him from St. Anthony's to serve as the team's academic supervisor. Thompson took the job. The university announced his hire on March 13, 1972.

Thompson built Georgetown into a contender by recruiting top talent. When he was first hired, however, neither he nor the Hoyas program had yet to achieve the national reputation that eventually lured top prospects to Georgetown. So Thompson recruited in the one place where his reputation allowed him to immediately attract young talent: his own backyard. Thompson's first recruiting class consisted of five African American players from Washington, including four St. Anthony's seniors he had coached the year before—Greg Brooks, Aaron Long, Jon Smith, and Merlin Wilson—plus Springarn High's Billy Lynn. Smith set the school's new career scoring record and Wilson set the career rebounding record.[56] By mid-season, and nearly two decades before Michigan more famously did so, John Thompson started five Black freshmen.

The transformation of the Hoyas roster was immediate. Georgetown's first Black player, Bernard White, arrived in 1966, but he played sparingly during three seasons.[57] Coach Jack Magee's rosters featured at most two Black players.[58] So an all-Black, five-member freshman class was a stunning change, to say the least. "Although blacks played for the Hoyas before . . . the arrival of five African Americans was unprecedented and immediately demonstrated Thompson's intention to bring minority student-athletes from Washington to the university," observed Georgetown alum Zack Tupper.[59] As described in chapter 1, some white alumni and boosters were incensed by the program's sudden transformation.

As his reputation grew and the Hoyas improved, Thompson expanded his recruiting reach. Two schools in particular—one in Washington, the other in Baltimore—served as important pipelines for Thompson and his Hoyas. Amazingly enough, both schools were named for the same noted Black poet: Paul Laurence Dunbar. Baltimore's Dunbar High School is remembered as the more famous feeder program of the two because it produced David

Wingate and Reggie Williams, both of whom starred on Georgetown's 1984 championship team. During his early years at Georgetown, however, Thompson turned to Washington's Dunbar High
School in search of talent that would help him resuscitate the
Hoyas' basketball program. There, he found two of Georgetown's
biggest stars of the late 1970s: guard John Duren and power forward Craig Shelton. During their senior year, Duren and Shelton
led Dunbar to an undefeated record and a No. 1 national ranking.
The duo were prized regional, if not national, recruits.

Thompson claimed that he landed both local prep stars with a
simple pitch. He told them that if they came to Georgetown "they
could play together, their families and friends would be able to
watch them, and they'd get a good education," Thompson recalled.
"They bought it. It wasn't a big recruiting battle." Thompson biographer Leonard Shapiro instead attributed Thompson's success in
landing Duren and Shelton to his relationship with Dunbar head
coach Joe Dean Davidson: "Thompson and Davidson met when
Davidson was coaching junior high school basketball in Washington and Thompson was recruiting one of his players for St.
Anthony's. 'We got to be friends,' Davidson said a few months
before his death in May 1990 of a heart attack. 'And John sometimes cultivated friendships to suit his purposes.'"[60]

Along with superstar point guard Eric "Sleepy" Floyd, John
Duren and Craig Shelton formed a potent trio in the late 1970s
on Thompson's first nationally recognized teams. Although Shelton missed most of his freshman year nursing a knee injury and
a broken wrist, the power forward excelled during his remaining
three seasons at Georgetown, amassing more than 1,400 points
and nearly 700 rebounds.[61] Known as "Big Sky" for his rebounding prowess, Shelton left his mark on the Big East Conference in
1979–80, the conference's first season and Shelton's senior year.
Before graduating, Shelton scored 10 or more points in every conference game, including Georgetown's upset of second-ranked Syracuse that broke the Orangemen's fifty-eight-game home winning
streak. Thompson described Shelton as the most intense player
he'd ever coached.[62] An elusive guard, John "BaBa" Duren scored

1,587 points and dished out 583 assists during his four years at Georgetown. In his senior campaign, Duren set the single-season Hoyas assist record with 220, an average of 7.1 assists per game. He was named to the All-Big East team and honorable mention All-American that year.[63] In the 1980 NCAA tournament, Duren and Shelton led the Hoyas to their first NCAA tournament victory in the Thompson era.

What Thompson built by culling talent from one Dunbar he perfected by recruiting top players from the other. The Purple Poets of Baltimore's Dunbar High School were coached by Bob Wade, the man later tapped to replace Lefty Dreisell at the University of Maryland when the Terrapins fired Dreisell following the tragic drug-related death of Maryland superstar Len Bias. In the early 1980s, the Poets were arguably the best high school team in America. Dunbar boasted back-to-back undefeated seasons in 1981–82 and 1982–83. Thompson was not the only coach with an eye on the Poets, of course. Coaches from top Division I programs, including Dreisell and North Carolina's Dean Smith, kept close tabs on Wade's prep stars.

Forward David Wingate was one of several notable players Thompson recruited from Baltimore Dunbar. Wingate starred on the 1981–82 Poets team that finished a perfect 29-0. In addition to Wingate, the team considered one of the best high school squads ever assembled featured three other future NBA players: Muggsy Bogues, Reggie Lewis, and another future Georgetown star, Reggie Williams. Late in his senior year, Wingate had apparently narrowed his college choice down to Maryland and Georgetown. He said he had never noticed Georgetown until Patrick Ewing arrived in 1981 and the Hoyas "really started making some major noise" during Wingate's senior year at Dunbar. "And when Big John Thompson, the head coach, comes walking into your house for a recruit visit, he makes a very extraordinary impression," Wingate recalled. According to sports-culture historian Alejandro Danois in *The Boys of Dunbar: A Story of Love, Hope, and Basketball*, Wingate's mother helped close the deal for Georgetown. She wouldn't discuss any other school with her son, but "her face would light up when she mentioned John Thompson, whom she felt was the exact type of role model, similar to Coach Wade at Dunbar, that David needed."[64]

Georgetown's rise required that the program also expand beyond the limits of the small but quaint McDonough Memorial Gymnasium. Opened in 1951 and named for a former athletic director, McDonough is a small, windowless venue that seats just four thousand spectators for basketball games. Although Thompson revived the basketball program within a few years, almost a decade passed before the Hoyas graduated from playing home games at McDonough to playing them at the Capital Centre at the start of the 1981–82 season. In their first game at the new and bigger venue, the Hoyas beat San Diego State, 71–53. Georgetown still hosted five home games that year at McDonough, but played only twice more in their old arena during the remainder of the 1980s, and just four more times during the Thompson era.[65] A young, local beat sportswriter named John Feinstein described the significance of Georgetown's big step up to an area suitable for a nationally competitive program:

> The move from homey, on-campus McDonough to the 19,035-seat Capital Centre represents much more than a geographic shift from Northwest Washington to Landover, Md. It is a final step for Georgetown in a 10 year climb from a 3–23 team in 1972 to this year's team, picked by some to win the national championship. . . .
>
> The move means Georgetown is reaching for the big dollars that increasingly have become a part of college basketball with each passing year. It means the school must sell itself in the media day after day, because it has 12 dates in the big building.
>
> It even means the Jesuits who run the school, from the Rev. Timothy S. Healy, university president, down, are willing to wince slightly, then smile when their marketing people cite *Playboy* magazine in their advertising.[66]

Not everyone on campus was thrilled by the decision to move the games off campus and across the city to the giant arena in Prince George's County, Maryland. Charles Deacon—the same admissions director who chaired the search committee that tapped Thompson to coach the Hoyas—expressed his worries to Thompson and athletic director Frank Rienzo: "When I heard about the move I was against it. I called John and Frank right away and told them so. I think ideally kids should be able to have a drink at The Pub [a campus hangout] and then walk down the hill to the games. But we also have a responsibility to the Washington community as a whole, and with 4,500 seats we can't fill the responsibility in McDonough. That's why we had to do it, community responsibility, that's part of our job here, too."[67]

John Thompson's hiring in 1972 to revive Georgetown basketball was consequential to Washington for all the reasons described above. The city was only four years removed from crippling race riots, and the university needed to become more invested in the city's fortunes. The Hoyas needed a modern program that recruited players nationwide and hosted games in a large, off-campus arena worthy of a national contender in one of the nation's newly dominant conferences. And there was a final reason why Georgetown's revival mattered. In 1972 Washington had no hometown professional basketball team. The NBA's Baltimore Bullets played thirty miles away, and even when the team changed its name—first to the Capital Bullets, later to the Washington Bullets—and moved to the Washington area, the franchise played its home games at the Capital Centre in Landover, Maryland. Sure, the Hoyas' basketball success under Thompson and the rise of the Big East Conference eventually compelled Georgetown to move their home games across the Maryland border to the Capital Centre, too. But when Thompson arrived in 1972, neither of the two biggest basketball draws in the Washington metro area—the Bullets and the Maryland Terrapins in nearby College Park—called DC home. Thompson and his Hoyas gave district residents a true hometown basketball team worth following.

One Vote from Oblivion and the "State of Miami"

It came down to a single vote. By a 6–5 margin, the University of Miami trustees in 1976 voted to keep the school's varsity football program, which had been in disarray in recent years. But within a decade, the Hurricanes would win the first of five national championships en route to becoming the most successful, most imitated and, yes, most hated college program in America.

Prior to the 1980s, Hurricanes football had a spotty history. Perhaps influenced by its surrounding mixed-race community, Miami in 1950 became the first Deep South Division I football team to host a visiting program with Black players. In offering Ray Bellamy a scholarship in 1966, Miami also distinguished itself as the first Deep South school to integrate its football program. These firsts were a significant departure from the university's decision to cancel a 1940 football game against the UCLA Bruins because the Bruins featured four Black players, including Jackie Robinson, and another game six years later against Penn State for the same reason.

The Hurricanes enjoyed a football heyday during the 1950s and early 1960s under the stewardship of Andy Gustafson, whose sixteen seasons as head coach remain a school record. Miami had eleven winning seasons during Gustafson's tenure, but only won one of its four bowl games. (The team suffered a two-year NCAA bowl ban after being found guilty of providing prohibited benefits to players and recruits.) Quarterbacks Frank Curci and George Mira were among Gustafson's biggest stars, and both players remained part of the Hurricanes family. Curci served as head coach for two years in the early 1970s, and Mira's son later played for the 'Canes.

Miami's schedule in those days consisted mostly of other conference independents, including Pittsburgh, Villanova, the service academies, and in-state foe Florida State, with whom Miami began its now storied rivalry in 1951. The 'Canes also played their other in-state rival, Florida, every year. Because South Florida was an alluring destination for visiting teams, the 'Canes played a remarkable three-fourths of their games during this era at home at Burdine Stadium, renamed the Orange Bowl in 1959. Fourteen of the first seventeen Miami-FSU games were played on Miami's home turf, in fact. "For years, Miami had the dubious distinction of being a place where good teams went for a vacation," noted Craig T. Smith in a book recounting Miami's most fabled wins. "Sort of a scheduled trip to Hawaii, without the Pacific Ocean flight, mai tais, and the leis. The nickname 'Suntan U' emerged."[68]

Gustafson left after a dismal 3-7 season in 1963. Aside from the remarkable career of future Pro Football Hall of Famers defensive end Ted "The Stork" Hendricks and running back George Foreman, the Charlie Tate–coached teams of the late 1960s and early 1970s garnered little attention, and they qualified for only two bowl bids. By the late 1970s, the football program was in tatters. During the six-year stretch before Miami turned the program over to Howard Schnellenger in 1979, the Hurricanes had five different coaches. Attendance had plummeted and the team's facilities were a mess. "Morale was terrible," remembered John Green, the administrator hired away from the University of Georgia to revive Miami football. "There was a lot of dissension with the players and with the coaches. The athletes made fun of the program. It was a joke."[69] Lou Saban, the last of the five coaches in that dismal six-year span, had a decent record as an itinerant NFL coach with the Boston Patriots, Buffalo Bills, and Denver Broncos. Saban arrived less than a year after the university's trustees came within one vote of disbanding its football program. In the opening weeks of Saban's first season he underwent triple-bypass surgery and his wife committed suicide. Miami football seemed cursed.

Enter Howard Schnellenberger. Before taking the University of Miami job in 1979 at age forty-five, Schnellenberger had acquired extensive experience as an assistant at the collegiate level and as an NFL assistant coach and head coach. The Miami job represented not so much a demotion for Schnellenberger as an experimental return to the collegiate ranks—a rehab project embraced by a proven coach with both college and professional championships on his resumé. Even in 1979 Schnellenberger couldn't possibly have foreseen that reviving dormant college programs—and, in the late-career case of Florida Atlantic University, creating one from scratch—would become his specialty. After Schnellenberger retired *New York Times* sportswriter Marc Tracy observed that his reputation for reviving programs would probably prevent his election to the College Football Hall of Fame, which requires a career minimum winning record (.600) higher than his. "Schnellenberger's perennial rebuilding of what had been second-tier programs can get lost amid the gaudy won-lost records of opportunistic, savvy coaches who hop, skip and jump up the ladder to the best jobs," wrote Tracy.[70]

Born in Indiana in 1934 but raised in Kentucky, Schnellenberger had been groomed to be a coach from the moment he first stepped on a playing field. He was a three-sport star at Louisville's Flaget High School. Under the tutelage of football coach Paulie Miller, Schnellenberger played at the Catholic prep school alongside fellow Kentuckian and future Heisman Trophy winner Paul Hornung. Schnellenberger almost chose Indiana University for college, but was lured away at the last moment by Paul "Bear" Bryant to play for the University of Kentucky, where Schnellenberger made the 1955 All-American team. After graduation Schnellenberger's coaching career began with a two-year stint as an assistant to Blanton Collier, the man hired to replace Bryant at Kentucky after Bryant departed for the University of Alabama. In Lexington Schnellenberger became fast friends with Don Shula, another young, newly married assistant on Collier's staff.

In 1961 Schnellenberger left Kentucky to join Bryant at 'Bama. After he won three national championships in five years with Bryant's all-white teams, Schnellenberger was hired by George Allen in 1966 for his first NFL stint as the Los Angeles Rams' receivers coach. Three years later, Shula, now the head coach of the Miami Dolphins, tapped his old friend to be the Dolphins' offensive coordinator and receivers coach. At Shula's side Schnellenberger won two Super Bowls and helped guide the 1972 Dolphins team (featuring quarterback Bob Griese, running backs Mercury Morris and Larry Csonka, and wide receiver Paul Warfield) to what remains the only undefeated season in NFL history. "I had a unique preparation in serving as an apprentice to all of them [Miller, Collier, Bryant, Allen, and Shula]," Schnellenberger wrote in his autobiography. "No one else in the world can make that claim. No one else studied or was mentored by these five Hall of Fame coaches."[71]

Schnellenberger's success with the Dolphins won him the head coaching job with Shula's old team, the Baltimore Colts, in 1974. It was a disaster. Winning just four of seventeen games, Schnellenberger was fired three games into his second season. For the first time in his adult life, he found himself not working on a football sideline. In 1975 Schnellenberger retreated to Miami to serve again as Shula's offensive coordinator. Four years later, he arrived in Coral Gables to take over the Hurricanes' floundering program. Although he briefly considered leaving the University of Miami after just two seasons to take the head coaching position at his alma mater, Kentucky, Schnellenberger stayed five years—just enough time to lead Miami to its first national championship.[72]

Schnellenberger's career with the Dolphins contributed directly and indirectly to his eventual hiring at the University of Miami. He had a local reputation as a highly successful coach during his two stints as Shula's assistant with the two-time Super Bowl champions. The Dolphins' success also caused the University of Miami to consider abandoning its football program and then, once it decided to keep football by that fateful single vote, take the necessary steps to revive the program. "My junior year, we voted 6–5 to keep football. We were going to drop football and [Schnellenberger] took it from there to a national title," remembers Art Kehoe, who was playing for the Hurricanes when Schnellenberger arrived and who stayed on after graduation to become his assistant, thus beginning his own, long coaching career at his alma mater. "The guy's an unbelievable coach. . . . Heck, we couldn't pay the phone bill. And now we've got five national titles and played for 11 of them and he's the main fabric of all that. He started it all."[73]

As with Thompson's revival of Georgetown basketball, keeping local talent at home was an important element in Miami's rise to national prominence. In Florida, where Florida and Florida State typically competed for the best prep football players, Miami was the last dog at the recruiting bowl. As the saying went, the Gators got the state's blue chips, while Miami had to settle for cow chips.[74]

Schnellenberger quickly changed the recruiting equation in the Sunshine State. He declared that the Hurricanes would dominate recruiting in what he called the "State of Miami"—the southern Florida triangle formed by Tampa, Daytona Beach and Miami's metropolitan Broward and Dade counties.

Schnellenberger and his staff recruited in some of the toughest urban neighborhoods, places where Saban and his predecessors dared not go. "Before 1979, very few Afro-Americans would consider coming to the University of Miami," Schnellenberger, in the parlance of the time, said. "They looked at it as a great big ivory tower."[75] In the pre-Schnellenberger era, a few hometown white recruits like future Chicago Bears player and coach Jim Dooley stayed home to play for the Hurricanes. But the University of Miami's allure to South Florida's rich pool of talented high school gridiron stars skyrocketed after Schnellenberger resuscitated the Hurricanes and won the 1983–84 national championship. In the three decades since, dozens of Black Hurricanes superstars have emerged from Miami's public high schools, including Carol City (Santana Moss); Central (Najeh Davenport and Willis McGahee); Killian (Randall Hill and Sean Taylor); Norland (Duke Johnson); Northwestern (Melvin Bratton and Brett Perriman); and Senior (Eddie Brown and Andre Johnson). The 'Canes first Black coach, Randy Shannon, is another Norland alumni, and Miami-Dade County's private Catholic all-boys Christopher Columbus High School sent Alonzo Highsmith, plus Latino players Mario Cristobal, Joaquin Gonzales and Carlos Huerta to Coral Gables to play for "The U." High schools from neighboring Broward and Palm Beach counties also produced platoons of Hurricanes stars and future NFL players.

Sportswriters debate whether Schnellenberger or his successor Jimmy Johnson was the most influential Hurricanes head coach in the program's history. Johnson strung together the dominant teams and record winning streaks during the mid-1980s, and also helped burnish the team's demonstrative, bad-boy image and reputation for intimidating play. But as chapter 6 discusses, he and successor Dennis Erickson are also rightly associated with the many off-the-field problems that also came to define Miami football. Regardless, it's clear that without the Howard Schnellenberger–led revival, the Hurricanes head coaching job would never have been coveted by the likes of Johnson, Erickson, and the coaches who followed them. Schnellenberger turned a narrow, program-saving vote into a national championship that his successors then transformed into a college football dynasty.

Urban Revitalization

In the 1980s Washington and Miami braced for two different but equally dramatic transformations. Washington adapted to the rise of the conservative movement in national politics and the simultaneous, Marion Barry–led revitalization of city life under recently acquired home rule. While recovering from the turbulence of horrific race riots and adapting to having become the nation's entry point for cocaine and other illicit drugs, Miami absorbed an influx of Latin American immigrants whose arrival immediately reshaped life in in the city, Dade County, and South Florida. The long-term impacts of these political and demographic changes are still evident in the cultural identities of both cities. "Both minority communities in the Washington, DC and Miami areas were in the midst of a vicious drug plague at the time in the 1980's," wrote Alejandro Danois.[76] "The drug-related violence and negative associated ancillary effects were endemic in both cities. The drug trade was escalating, claiming lives in terms of both death toll and the scourge of addiction. Marginalized folks found themselves in the crossfire, both in a literal and figurative sense with both cities, at some point, earning the distinction as being both the country's Drug and Murder Capital."

The racialized aspects of both cities' transitions served as fitting cultural backdrops to the simultaneous revivals in the Georgetown basketball and Miami football programs, both of which were undergoing their own racial transformations. Young Black or Latino kids from Washington and Miami grew up amid the tumult of their neighborhoods. A few of the most talented athletes made the short trip from where they grew up to the nearby campuses of Georgetown and Miami, seeking an education, perhaps wealth and fame, and at the very least new opportunities. Early in their programs' revivals, they could hardly imagine that they were about to become part of the two most memorable, if unlikely, collegiate sporting dynasties.

For both programs and schools, the path to dynasty began at the top. Desperate to reverse their respective programs' fortunes at the same time they were adapting to emergent sociopolitical and racial changes, Miami and Georgetown gambled by hiring new coaches—one white, one Black. The paths that Schnellenberger and Thompson blazed toward their first Division I head coaching jobs were marked by curious parallels. Both men were raised in working-class Catholic families. Both were collegiate stars in their respective sports before opting for coaching as a profession. Both men valued discipline and were strong recruiters who found and developed talented student athletes. Most importantly, both spearheaded reclamation projects that soon proved more successful than anyone could have foreseen.

Hoyas alumni are keenly aware that the pop-cultural appeal of Georgetown's all-Black team and imposing Black coach quickly changed the university's national image. "I've had a lot of people come to me and ask me about what school I go to, and I say Georgetown University and these people go, 'Is that an [historically Black college],' and I'm like, 'No, what ever gave you that idea?'" said Georgetown graduate Nazareth Haysbert, recalling his undergraduate days. "For nine out of 10 of those people, their reason for thinking Georgetown is an HBC is because of the basketball team."[77] Few people outside the metropolitan Washington area or the Jesuit college circuit had ever heard of Georgetown before its basketball program became a national powerhouse. Almost overnight, it attained misrecognition as a historically Black college.

Billy Corben—the University of Miami alum who directed the critically acclaimed two-part ESPN 30 for 30 documentary about the Hurricanes football program—cautions against labeling his alma mater a football school. "The University of Miami is not and has never been a football school—capital F, capital

S. Football was never prioritized," he said. "What you had happen at Miami was not by design. It was by happenstance thanks to a series of athletic directors hiring a series of coaches recruiting magnificent players. It was a self-motivated engine." Corben criticized administrators who tried to cast Miami as the "Harvard of the South," gladly fundraising off the successes of a football program they view as little more than an "ATM machine." As evidence of the university leadership's disregard for the Hurricanes' football legacy, Corben cited the lack of program recognition on the physical campus: "Find me the monuments, the statues, the plaques. [University President] Donna Shalala knocked down the one football monument: The Orange Bowl."[78]

Georgetown University and the University of Miami were unlikely campuses to give rise to the transformation of major-college televised sports in the 1980s. Two private schools, neither of which had longstanding traditions of sporting glory in, respectively, college basketball and college football, blossomed into iconic programs. Their players, coaches, logos, colors, reputations, and records became nationally recognized symbols for a new era of mass-marketed, immensely profitable and minority athlete–led televised collegiate sports.

Title Town

At times I've been obsessed by the national championship. . . .
Now I have one. I don't want 10 like John Wooden.
I just wanted to get one.

—JOHN THOMPSON, Georgetown University head basketball coach

Honestly, for maybe the next week or so, it was like waking up in
the morning and trying to make sure it wasn't a dream.

—ALBERT BENTLEY, University of Miami running back, on winning
the 1984 Orange Bowl and national championship

At least outwardly, Miami head coach Howard Schnellen- berger remained calm. His assistant coaches had no such luxury. They ran onto the field, yanking the jerseys of Miami's players and herding them back to the sidelines. Everyone in attendance or watching live on television understood why excited Hurricanes players had charged the field prematurely. Thanks to Hurricanes defensive back Kenny Calhoun's deflection of Nebraska quarterback Turner Gill's two-point conversion pass, Miami led the top-ranked and undefeated 'Huskers, 31–30. With just forty-eight seconds remaining, the Hurricanes were mere moments away from one of the biggest upsets in college football history.

But the 1984 Orange Bowl wasn't over yet. The Hurricanes still needed to field the inevitable onside kick from Nebraska and run out the clock. After doing just that, the ecstatic Hurricanes rushed the field again, this time with impunity. Miami players lifted Schnellenberger onto their shoulders and carried him toward midfield, where he dismounted to shake Nebraska head coach Tom Osborne's hand. The next day, the Associated Press crowned the team, which had been unraked in the preseason, the 1983 Division I football national champions. The Hurricanes dynasty had begun.

Three months later at the opposite corner of the continental United States, the final seconds of the 1984 NCAA men's basketball title game in Seattle's Kingdome provided far less end-game drama. The game was no blowout, but the Georgetown Hoyas led the Houston Cougars most of the game and by no fewer than five points during the second half. In the closing minutes, a desperate Houston head coach, Guy Lewis, abandoned the Cougars' 1-3-1 defensive trap. His players repeatedly fouled the Hoyas in the hopes that Georgetown might miss free throws and allow the Cougars to claw their way back. The gambit failed. With sixteen seconds left to play, Lewis and Hoyas coach John Thompson pulled most of their starters. On Houston's defeated bench, white towels served both real and metaphorical purposes. Stunned guard Reid Gettys stared blankly ahead with a towel stretched atop his head. Superstar center Hakeem Olajuwon bowed his head and wept into his. Final score: Georgetown 84, Houston 75. The Hoyas were national champions.

The most anticipated moment for the victors came when Thompson bear-hugged senior Hoyas guard Fred Brown. In the waning seconds of the 1982 championship game two years earlier in New Orleans, Brown had thrown the ball right to UNC's James Worthy, a tragic turnover that sealed the Tar Heels' victory. Two years later in Seattle, Brown, his coach, and his teammates experienced relief and redemption. "You know what's interesting with that picture?" CBS color commentator Billy Packer asked, as Thompson's hug lifted Brown off his feet. "He was hugging him when he made the big mistake, too."

Miami and Georgetown were champions, but their national debuts were strikingly different. Nobody predicted during the 1983 preseason that the Hurricanes would win the title by defeating powerhouse Nebraska in the 1984 Orange Bowl. Miami's resurrection in just a few years surprised and overjoyed even the program's biggest devotees. Art Kehoe, a former offensive guard for Miami who has spent his career on the Hurricanes coaching staff, was a graduate assistant on the 1983–84 title team. He remembered coming onto the field that night with the kicking squad a full ninety minutes before kickoff. Hurricanes fans already in the stands gave the players a standing ovation. "The Orange Bowl, from start to finish, it was just the craziest I've ever seen it in my life," Kehoe recalled. "It was the greatest win for me. I still think it's the biggest win in the history of our program."[1]

Georgetown, on the other hand, had been ranked second in the preseason and was expected to make a deep run in the 1984 NCAA tournament. That's not to say that the Hoyas' victory was anticlimactic. The victory was the first national title for Georgetown, the first for the newly formed Big East conference, and the first for any Division I team with a Black head coach. After the game head coach John Thompson expressed relief: "At times I've been obsessed by the national championship. I've awakened in the middle of the night in the summer saying 'national championship.' Now I have one. I don't want 10 like [UCLA's] John Wooden. I just wanted to get one."[2]

The 1983–84 season changed both teams, both universities, and major-college sports. Neither of these once-struggling programs was supposed to rise so high, so fast. Nor were the Hoyas or Hurricanes expected to leave lasting imprints on college sports, especially for African American athletes and fans. Yet by the mid-1980s Georgetown and Miami were dominant teams in their respective sports, and had also emerged as cultural touchstones for a new generation of Black athletes and fans. The 1983–84 season was the crowning moment in the rise of Hoyas basketball and Hurricanes football.

Unheralded, Unranked, and Unrelenting

At the outset of the 1983 football season, sportswriters were not bullish about the Miami Hurricanes' prospects. Miami did not make the Associated Press Top 25 preseason rankings. In fact, the writers had held the previous year's team in higher regard, ranking it No. 15 in the preseason. That 1982 team turned out to be a near miss, 7-4 squad that won all seven games against unranked opponents but lost all four against ranked teams. Although three of those four losses were narrow defeats on the road—17–14 at Florida, 16–14 at Notre Dame, and 18–17 at Maryland—the 1982 team's lack of a substantial win cost it a bowl bid. In today's era of bowl-game proliferation, Miami's 7-4 record would surely have been good enough for a third-tier bowl bid. Instead, on Thanksgiving weekend the Hurricanes ended their 1982 football campaign unceremoniously and unranked.

Early hints of the 1983 title team's stifling defense, however, were evident in the 1982 squad that only twice surrendered 20 or more points. But the 1982 Hurricanes could not seem to figure out whom to play at quarterback. With the benefit of hindsight, some observers now regard Miami's 1982 quarterbacking corps—seniors Jim Kelly and Mark Richt, junior Kyle Vanderwende, and freshmen Vinny Testaverde and Bernie Kosar—as the best signal-calling group ever assembled on a college roster. The problem for Schnellenberger, offensive coordinator Kim Helton, and quarterbacks coach Earl Morrall was what to do when they lost Kelly, the senior starter and a possible Heisman Trophy contender, to a season-ending injury against Virginia Tech in the third game of the year. Richt stepped in and took the most snaps that season, but completed only 48 percent of his passes and threw just 4 touchdowns against 9 interceptions. Vanderwende completed more than 60 percent of his attempts, but played sparingly.[3] Testaverde took only a few snaps and was ultimately redshirted along with Kosar. In hindsight the irony is that Kosar was the only one of the five quarterbacks who never played a down in 1982. The next year, the side-arm slinging Kosar beat out Vanderwende and Testaverde for the starting job and led the 1983 'Canes to the national title.

The Hurricanes' performance in their 1983 season opener seemed to validate the Associated Press football writers' decision to exclude Miami from their preseason Top 25. Against in-state rival Florida, the Hurricanes turned over the ball seven times in a disastrous 28–3 loss. ESPN's Andrea Adelson pointed to the Florida defeat as a key moment for Schnellenberger and his players, who expected their coach to rip into them after they returned to Coral Gables from Gainesville. "Had Schnellenberger delivered the firestorm players expected, he may have lost the team," Adelson reported. "Schnellenberger had dished out plenty of punishment after ugly losses in the past, making his players scrimmage on Sunday until they figured out how to cut out all the mistakes." Schnellenberger and his assistants noticed from game film just how talented the team was, despite the turnovers that effectively gave the Gators the game. Oddly enough, in his first college game, Kosar tied a school record for completions despite Miami never reaching the end zone. Schnellenberger chose to encourage, rather than scold, his team. "If I had taken the other approach, then they would have not only been embarrassed and down and divided, they would have been pointing fingers," he told Adelson.[4]

As if a switch had flipped, the unheralded Hurricanes reeled off 10 straight regular season victories. The key win early that season was a primetime, nationally televised Saturday night 20–0 shutout of thirteenth-ranked Notre Dame. Although the Fighting Irish proved to be a middling team that finished the year with a 7-5 record, the 'Canes victory over one of college football's most storied programs boosted Miami's profile and catapulted the 'Canes into the national rankings. Thanks to their stingy defense and Kosar's accuracy, the Hurricanes steadily rose in the polls the rest of the year. They climbed to No. 6 by the time the team arrived in Tallahassee to face Florida State, their other in-state rival, in the final regular-season contest for both teams.

Against the Seminoles, Miami nearly blew its chance to play for the national championship. Both teams scored two touchdowns, but thanks to a first-quarter safety that FSU scored on a blocked punt, the Seminoles led 16–14 lead entering the fourth quarter. That score held until the final two minutes, when Kosar marched Miami deep into Florida State territory on just four plays. After missing two earlier field goal attempts, Jeff Davis sealed Miami's 17–16 win with a 19-yard chip shot. Unheralded at the start of the year, the 'Canes finished the regular-season schedule ranked fifth nationally.

The victory over Florida State earned Miami a bid to play juggernaut Nebraska on January 2, 1984, in what was effectively a home game at the Orange Bowl. Despite that advantage, bookies made Miami an 11-point underdog against the top-ranked and undefeated Cornhuskers. Even if the Hurricanes pulled an upset, they would need some if not all of the other three teams ahead of them in the rankings—the University of Texas, Auburn University, and the University of Illinois—to lose their bowl games.

Nebraska was more than formidable; it was frightening. The Cornhuskers averaged an eye-popping 52 points per game during their twelve regular-season wins. (The 1983–84 Nebraska men's basketball team only averaged 69 points per game.) Five times, Nebraska scored more than 60 points, including 84 points against the overmatched Minnesota Golden Gophers. Nebraska's vaunted offense featured two of 1983's five Heisman Trophy finalists. Running back Mike Rozier won the award and quarterback Turner Gill finished fourth in the balloting. The 'Huskers opened the season by demolishing defending champion Penn State, 44–6, and ended the year as the lone remaining undefeated team in Division I. "Nebraska is so much better than any other team in the country, it's a joke," sportscaster Bryant Gumbel bellowed on the *Today Show*.

Few sportswriters noticed that across the line of scrimmage, Miami boasted the nation's second-ranked scoring defense. That year, Miami held seven of its eleven regular-season opponents to seven points or fewer, including back-to-back home shutouts of Purdue and Notre Dame. The defensive corps was led by the team's lone All-American, linebacker Jay Brophy, who registered 135 tackles along with 3 interceptions. Senior linebacker Ken Sisk paced the 'Canes veteran defensive corps team with 139 tackles, and cornerback Kenny Calhoun chipped in with 97 tackles and 3 interceptions.[5] Still, nobody gave the Hurricanes much chance of winning. Most prognosticators expected Nebraska to cruise to a comfortable victory despite having to play on the Hurricanes' home turf. The familiar confines of the Orange Bowl seemed to be Miami's lone advantage.

Had the bookmakers known in advance the score would be 17–0 at the end of the first quarter, they no doubt would have presumed Nebraska was pummeling Miami. Instead, the Hurricanes sprinted to that lead on the strength of two Bernie Kosar touchdown passes to the 'Canes top receiver, Glenn Dennison, plus a Jeff Davis field goal. A few days earlier, Miami linebacker Jay Brophy had said that his team needed to stop the Cornhuskers on their first two offensive possessions.[6] The Hurricanes went one better, stopping Nebraska's supposedly unstoppable offense on its first *three* possessions. Schnellenberger—architect of the famed No-Name Defense during his Super Bowl days with the NFL's Miami Dolphins—had devised a brilliant scheme to slow the 'Husker offense.

By halftime, and thanks in part to a "fumblerooski" trick-play touchdown scored by 'Husker offensive lineman Dean Steinkuhler, the Nebraska offense had awakened to shrink the deficit to 17–14. The fact that legendary Nebraska head coach Tom Osborne had to dip into his bag of trick plays so early in the game, however, was an admission that the 'Huskers knew they were in trouble. Sure enough, in the second half momentum shifted back to the Hurricanes when they restored their 17-point lead with two third-quarter rushing touchdowns. Fatefully for the Hurricanes, after freshman running back Alonzo Highsmith scored the first of those two touchdowns, kicker Jeff Davis clanged an ugly extra point kick off the left upright and in. Had Davis missed, the unforgettable final minute of the game and the result might have been very different.

With Miami ahead 31–17, Nebraska's star-studded offense again rallied with an early fourth quarter touchdown. Miami's offense stalled all quarter, and when Nebraska running back Jeff Smith scored an 8-yard touchdown run with forty-eight seconds to go in the game, the 'Huskers closed the gap to 31–30. Smith scored after taking a gutsy option-play pitch from Turner Gill that faked out Hurricanes cornerback Kenny Calhoun to create just enough space for Smith to find the corner of end zone. Nebraska had turned to Smith in the second half because Heisman-winner Mike Rozier, after racking up 149 rushing yards, left the game with an injured ankle. Smith, a talented replacement, amassed 109 yards and had rushed for an earlier touchdown. The stage was set for Nebraska coach Tom Osborne's fateful decision.

Trailing by a point, Osborne could either kick an almost certain extra point to settle for the tie, or attempt a two-point conversion to either win the game or lose it. (The overtime format now in place did not exist in 1984.) After the game Osborne told the media that he never hesitated or considered settling for the tie. Two of the other three top five teams, Texas and Illinois, had lost their bowl games earlier that day, and third-ranked Auburn had squeaked out a narrow win. A tie and a 12-0-1 record might have been sufficient for Nebraska to finish atop either the United Press International coaches' poll or the Associated Press writers' poll, or perhaps both. (The two polls determined the champion during the pre-playoff era.) But Osborne preferred to leave no doubt. He opted to go for the 2-point conversion, betting the game and the national title on a single play.

The 'Huskers already used their final time-out to design Smith's nail-biting fourth-down touchdown run on the previous play. Forced to make a quick decision, Osborne called for quarterback Gill to roll out right and either pass to Smith in the end zone or, if the Miami defense blanketed Smith, tuck the ball under his arm and run to the end zone himself. As the players lined up, the tension on both teams' sidelines and among the capacity Orange Bowl crowd of 72,549 spectators was palpable. "This is for the national championship for Nebraska," NBC play-by-play announcer Don Criqui intoned expectantly. Gill rolled out and had plenty of time and space to spot Smith, who gained some separation from Miami cornerback Kenny Calhoun, the same player Smith beat to the end zone on the previous play for the touchdown. But Gill's pass was short and slightly behind Smith, allowing Calhoun to dive and deflect the ball off Smith's face mask and into the ground incomplete. The hometown crowd erupted. Miami players flooded the field. After the Hurricanes recovered Nebraska's onside kickoff, Kosar ran out the clock to give Miami the win.

Although some fans and writers questioned Osborne's decision, during his postgame remarks he defended himself, saying that the 'Huskers were "playing to win." Schnellenberger applauded the decision, too. "Tom Osborne is a champion and he went for it like a champion," said the Miami coach. "There was never any doubt in my mind he was going for two points."[7] On the strength of the Hurricanes' victory, the coaches and writers voted them consensus national champions. "It's unlikely that any team in the history of college football ever got higher for a game than Miami did for Nebraska, and if you missed Monday night's Orange Bowl, you missed an emergence," Sports Illustrated's John Underwood wrote presciently.[8] This was, indeed, the Hurricanes' coming out party—the start of a dynasty.

In years to come, Miami would enjoy many more wins, four more titles, several undefeated and arguably more dominant teams—and, yes, a lot of controversy. But that night in Miami, the program basked in the glow of its first championship. Thirty years later, Miami running back Albert Bentley, who scored what turned out to be the winning touchdown for the Hurricanes, recalled those heady days immediately following the 1984 Orange Bowl victory. "Honestly, for maybe the next week or so, it was like waking up in the morning and trying to make sure it wasn't a dream," remembered Bentley, adding that even with his eight-year NFL career to follow, the 1984 Orange Bowl game remained the most exciting win of his life.[9]

Second Time's the Charm

In a matter of seconds, John Thompson had to morph from the first Black head coach in the NCAA championship game into something more important: a calming, avuncular figure. The final moments of the 1982 title game in the New Orleans Superdome—the first Final Four held in a domed stadium designed for football—were televised agony for Thompson and his players. Georgetown sophomore guard Fred Brown had just committed one of the most colossal blunders in the history of televised sports. With the clock ticking down and the Hoyas trailing UNC by a point after Tar Heels freshman Michael Jordan sank a clutch jumper, Brown was dribbling just inside half court with the national championship on the line. For reasons he later admitted he could not explain, UNC's James Worthy was caught way out of defensive position, standing aimlessly out near the half-court line and guarding nobody. Like some weird contagion, Worthy's momentary confusion infected Brown. The Hoyas guard turned to his right and, before he realized who was standing next to him, threw the ball directly to an unsuspecting Worthy. The turnover cost Brown, the Hoyas, and their coach a chance to win the championship.

A crestfallen Brown walked toward the bench, where Thompson greeted him with a hug. "You won more games for me than you ever lost, so hold your head up," Thompson consoled him.[10] Here was the perverse cruelty of big-time amateur sports on full display. Etched forever into the minds of millions of viewers that day and every Georgetown fan are the twin images of Brown's turnover and his subsequent emotional collapse into Thompson's waiting arms. Both Brown and the Hoyas would focus on recovering from that moment during ensuing seasons.

The next year was star center Patrick Ewing's sophomore campaign, but the 1982–83 Hoyas were rebuilding following the graduation of five seniors. Adding physical injury to the emotional scars from the previous year, the 1982–83 squad played half its games without Fred Brown's leadership while he recovered from off-season knee surgery. The team also lacked a true power forward to complement Ewing. The season was hardly a disaster, but it was a disappointment. The Hoyas started out with six straight wins against nonconference, unranked teams. They then dropped four of their next seven games, including an embarrassing loss to unranked crosstown opponent American University. The first of those four Georgetown losses came against the Virginia Cavaliers in a highly anticipated, nationally televised match in Maryland's

Capital Centre that pitted Ewing against the Cavaliers' 7-foot All-American center Ralph Sampson.

The Hoyas' Big East season was also disappointing. After a solid 6-1 start in conference play, Ewing and his young supporting cast stumbled down the stretch, finishing fourth in the conference standings with a respectable but uninspiring 9-5 record. For the only time in Ewing's four-year career, the Hoyas were bounced from the Big East tournament in the first round. Georgetown entered the NCAA tourney having slipped all the way to No. 20 in the Associated Press's end-of-season rankings.

After a too-close-for-comfort 68–63 victory over Alcorn State in the opening round of the NCAA tournament, the Memphis State Tigers ended Georgetown's underwhelming season in the second round, 66–57. Despite Thompson making forty personnel substitutions in a desperate effort to keep the score close against the bigger, Keith Lee–led Tigers, the Hoyas were outrebounded 37–22. "Because of their size we needed more help on the boards," Thompson lamented. "That size factor—after Patrick, we taper off."[11] At the end of the season, the Hoyas had won neither the regular-season conference title, nor the Big East tournament title, nor an NCAA championship game appearance. They achieved all of those during each of Ewing's other three years.

Georgetown again began its 1983–84 season with the highest of expectations. The Hoyas were ranked second nationally, as they had been at the start of the previous year's frustrating season. But 1983–84 ended with the team crowned the national champs. With a record of 34-3, the Hoyas dominated the Big East Conference and also captured the conference tournament trophy. The Hoyas became the first of four original Big East teams to win an NCAA title. (Among the Big East founding programs, Villanova—too soon for the Hoyas' liking, as it turned out—plus Syracuse and Connecticut would eventually win championships, too.) Patrick Ewing was voted most valuable player of both the Big East Conference and NCAA tournament. The U.S. Basketball Writers Association and *The Sporting News* named John Thompson national coach of the year. Although some Hoyas teams may have been better, especially the following year's squad, no Georgetown team before or since accomplished as much as that storied championship team.

Going into the 1983–84 season, Thompson recruited for Ewing a useful sidekick: Michael Graham, a six-foot-nine-inch, 270-pound intimidating bald freshman from the gritty streets of the nation's capital. Graham's role was akin to the enforcer's role in hockey. Sure, Graham was expected to contribute on the score sheet with points, rebounds, and blocked shots. Box scores could not account for Graham's primary duty, however, which was to absorb much of the physical and psychological abuse normally directed at Ewing so the Hoyas' All-American center had more room to dominate.

Graham attracted ample attention during the course of the regular season, but in the 1984 Big East conference tournament his role as menacing enforcer was in full effect. In the final against Syracuse, the Hoyas' primary conference rival, Graham took a swing at Orangemen forward Andre Hawkins. At first referees appeared to eject Graham from the game. After briefly conferring, however, officials instead charged Graham only with a regular foul. At that point the Hoyas trailed. Georgetown rallied to tie the game and won in overtime, 82–71, snatching the Big East crown from Syracuse. Infuriated by his team's loss, Orangemen head coach Jim Boeheim disparaged Georgetown's rough play and the officials who—perhaps sensitive to Thompson's repeated complaints about unfair double standards—had let Graham off easy. "Michael Graham, in front of 19,000 people, punched my player, and the ref had the nerve to call it a two-shot foul," Boeheim fumed. He then threw a chair against a wall as he stormed out of the press room. Sportswriters rank the 1984 final among the greatest games in Big East history.[12]

Boeheim's protests aside, the Hoyas dominated the 1984 Big East tourney at Madison Square Garden and deserved to win the title. They beat the Otis Thorpe–led Providence Friars by 20 points in the quarterfinals. In the semis Georgetown dispatched a talented St. John's squad featuring future NBAers Chris Mullin, Bill Wennington, and Mark Jackson, 79–68. The Hoyas outrebounded their three Big East foes by a whopping 120–70 margin. Tourney most valuable player (MVP) Ewing made 25 of 32 field goal attempts in Georgetown's three games, including a 27-point, 16-rebound performance in the overtime win against Syracuse. Georgetown point guard Michael Jackson joined Ewing on the all-tournament team.

In the press conference after the title game, the media focused on the Hoyas' physical play. Asked about the tourney's on-court tensions, Jackson said: "We prefer to call it playing hard. Sure, it makes you feel proud if somebody says they're scared of you. But we only take that so far. The rest is press talk." Ewing marveled at the way he was depicted as a perpetrator rather than a victim. "I'm over-aggressive? I'm usually the one that had the concussion or got hit in the eye," Ewing quipped.[13] There it was again: equal measures of Hoyas intimidation and "Hoya paranoia," the dynamic cocktail that made Georgetown a national target but also a national sensation.

Georgetown entered the 1984 NCAA tournament with the same rank it held when the season began: second behind only UNC, led by consensus All-Americans Michael Jordan and Sam Perkins. The 1984 tourney was the last before the NCAA expanded to a sixteen-team format. In that era the top sixteen seeds overall—four per region, which obviously included the West Region's top seed, Georgetown—needed to win only five games to capture the crown. The Hoyas' tournament path to its eventual showdown against Houston in the championship game began in Pullman, Washington, a city named for the man who invented the eponymous sleeper train car. Pullman is roughly three hundred miles east of Seattle, where Thompson's team intended to return two weekends later for the tournament's showcase Final Four.

Georgetown's opening-round opponent, Southern Methodist University, had other ideas. Perhaps the Hoyas underestimated the Mustangs. Maybe the thinner air inside Friel Arena at Pullman's 2,300-foot elevation winded the Hoyas. Whatever the case, coached by Dave Bliss and led by 7-foot center and future NBA first-round pick Jon Koncak, the Mustangs put a scare into Georgetown by building an 8-point lead, 24–16, in the first half. In the next two seasons the NCAA would institute the 3-point basket and a

45-second shot clock. But in 1984, many NCAA games remained low-scoring affairs, particularly when teams chose to hold the ball for long stretches on offense. The Mustangs' lead was not insurmountable, but it was substantial by that era's standards.

The Hoyas' second-round defeat by higher-ranked Memphis State a year earlier in the 1983 tourney was a mild disappointment. But losing as the West Region's top seed in the first round to SMU would have been an inexplicable failure and a shock to the college basketball world. Facing that prospect, Georgetown's stifling defense took charge. After playing zone for most of the first half, Thompson switched the Hoyas into a man-to-man, full-court press for the final twenty minutes. SMU only mustered 12 points the rest of the game, including a remarkable nine-minute stretch in the second half during which the Hoyas held the Mustangs scoreless. The game also took on the increasingly familiar, combative dynamic of so many Georgetown games. At one point Michael Graham got into a scrap with SMU's Carl Wright. Georgetown simply imposed on the game its style and will: a suffocating defense paired with the Hoyas' trademark intimidation.

SMU did not die quietly. A baby hook shot by Mustangs forward Larry Davis tied the game at 34 with just under three minutes to play. Inside the Hoyas huddle, Ewing exhorted his teammates: "We're not going home, and that's it." Georgetown seemed content to hold the ball for the final shot, but SMU fouled Hoyas senior guard Gene Smith with fifty seconds remaining. A 64 percent free-throw shooter, Smith went to the line but missed the first free throw of a one-and-one. Ewing, who until then had scored a mere eight points, snatched Smith's miss, spun around, and scored to give the Hoyas a 36–34 lead. "He leaned inside, then 360'd left, a great, great move," SMU's Davis marveled after the game. Ewing's coach was similarly impressed. "I don't think Patrick could describe what he did," Thompson said. "Sometimes [Bill] Russell"—the Hall of Fame Celtic center Thompson had once backed up—"could not, either."[14] The Hoyas escaped with a 37–36 win. "I hope that's the bad ball game we have to get out of our systems," Thompson said afterward.[15]

Thompson's wish turned prophetic. Following the SMU scare, Georgetown returned to form at UCLA's storied Edwin W. Pauley Pavilion with two solid victories to clinch the West Region's slot in the Final Four. Despite narrowly beating UNLV earlier in the season, the Hoyas coasted to a relatively comfortable, 62–48 rematch win over the Runnin' Rebels in the regional semifinal. Ewing and point guard Michael Jackson each tallied 16 points, and the Hoyas held all but one UNLV player to single digits. In the regional final, Georgetown faced the Dayton Flyers, the darling of the tournament. The Flyers, coached by Don Donoher, had already upset higher-ranked Louisiana State, Oklahoma, and Washington to reach the regional final. But Georgetown beat Dayton, 61–49, ending the remarkable career of the Flyers' all-time scoring leader, Roosevelt Chapman, who led the entire NCAA tourney in scoring that year. Chapman scorched the Flyers' first three opponents for an average of 31 points per game, but against the smothering Hoyas defense he managed just 13 points on 10 shots. After the game Donoher complimented the Hoyas: "I'm greatly impressed with their defense. They're relentless—they're all over you."[16] Georgetown headed to Seattle's Kingdome for its second Final Four appearance in three seasons.

Georgetown's opponent in the national semifinal was third-ranked Kentucky, one of college basketball's blue-blood programs. The Wildcats were coached by the legendary Joe B. Hall, an assistant under Adolph Rupp on the all-white Wildcats team that lost the 1966 national championship game to the Texas Western team with five Black starters. Kentucky was the SEC champion and boasted "twin towers" Sam Bowie and Melvin Turpin to match against Ewing and Graham. The Hoyas had their hands full.

Against the Wildcats, Ewing got into early foul trouble, and Thompson had to bench him. Kentucky took advantage of Ewing's absence to build a 27–12 lead. With about three minutes left in the first half, the Hoyas found themselves in a position eerily similar to the SMU game two weeks earlier, but this time trailing by nearly twice the margin against a more talented and experienced Kentucky team that won the Mideast bracket as the region's top seed. Again, Georgetown's tenacious defense went into lock-down mode. Over the game's remaining twenty-three minutes, the Hoyas suffocated the Wildcats, outscoring Kentucky 41–13 to advance to the championship game.

Hoyas upperclassmen, including Ewing and Fred Brown, both of whom endured the painful loss to UNC two years earlier, had earned the chance to redeem themselves and play for the title. The UNC loss remained in the back of Hoyas veterans' minds, although they may have claimed otherwise. On the eve of the 1984 tournament, a reporter asked senior Brown if memories of 1982 weighed on him and the team. "I don't recollect two years ago. I don't recollect last year," Brown bristled. "I've got more important responsibilities. I don't have time to recollect last night."[17] Georgetown never had to face the tournament's top-seeded Tar Heels, however, because Bobby Knight's Indiana Hoosiers eliminated them in the East Regional final.

Georgetown instead met the Guy Lewis–coached Houston Cougars in the title game. The Cougars brought their own memories of a painful championship nightmare. The year before, Houston suffered a heartbreaking loss on a buzzer-beating catch-and-dunk by North Carolina State Wolfpack freshman Lorenzo Charles in the 1983 title game. (The Wolfpack remain the most unlikely and lowest-seeded team ever to win the NCAA tourney.) Whether Georgetown or Houston would erase its sorrows in Seattle, college basketball fans and the media expected to be treated to an epic battle between college basketball's two most dominant centers: Ewing and the Cougars' Akeem (later Hakeem) Olajuwon. With a lineup that also featured Alvin Franklin, Michael Young, and future NBA Hall of Famer Clyde Drexler, Houston was just as deep and talented as Georgetown. The Cougars lost just once all season.

Georgetown controlled the game from start to finish. The Hoyas surged to a 10-point lead by halftime, then held off the Cougars in the second half to win 84–75. Unfortunately, the Ewing-Olajuwon matchup was a dud. With only 10 points, a foul-plagued Ewing again spent a lot of time on the bench, a problem for the Hoyas mitigated by the fact that Olajuwon was also hamstrung by foul trouble. Former Dunbar High teammates Reggie Williams (19 points, 9 rebounds) and David Wingate (16 points) picked up the scoring slack for the Hoyas. The most poignant contributions, however, came from Fred Brown. The only Georgetown senior in the lineup—senior captain Gene Smith was sidelined with a bruised ankle—Brown played only fifteen minutes. In that limited time, however, he tallied 4 points, grabbed 4 rebounds, and dished out 4 assists. Although he is still remembered for his turnover in the heartbreaking 1982 loss to UNC, in Seattle two years later Brown got redemption and a memory to cherish forever.

The Hoyas' victory completed a run of 11 straight wins to conclude their season with a 34-3 record. The only blemishes on that record were losses to conference opponents St. John's and Providence, plus a mid-season loss to DePaul. In front of the Kingdome's capacity crowd of 38,471 spectators, Thompson and his elated players cut down the nets. After the game a sportswriter asked Thompson if his team—which would lose only Brown and Smith to graduation and expected to return stars Ewing, Graham, Williams, Wingate and Michael Jackson—could repeat in 1984–85 (Graham did not return, but the others did). In a moment of unwitting prophecy, a tongue-in-cheek Thompson downplayed his team's prospects: "I think our chances are terrible. The hardest thing in the world is to come back. These kids will be too cocky. Our chances are going to be very hard. Very, very hard."[18]

The university community and fans across Washington celebrated the team. Five days after Georgetown won the title, Mayor Marion Barry and the city government declared April 7 "Georgetown Hoyas Championship Day." The team gave President Ronald Reagan a Hoyas T-shirt during a celebratory event held on the White House lawn, then rode through the city in the annual Cherry Blossom Festival parade. The Georgetown entourage ended the day by congregating on the front steps of the District Building to be honored by the mayor and city council. "We have a double reason to celebrate," Barry beamed. "Some of the players grew up here in the District, and the rest are our adopted, honorary citizens."[19]

In November, coach John Thompson and center Patrick Ewing returned to the White House for a *Sports Illustrated* cover photoshoot, a visit memorialized by a series of pictures of the smiling president bracketed by Thompson on one side and Ewing on the other, each of them brandishing a basketball and a wide smile. Above the shot selected to grace the cover of the magazine's 1984–85 college basketball preview issue is a title cleverly paraphrasing Reagan's famed quip about Jimmy Carter during the 1980 presidential debates: "They're They Go Again." The Hoyas were expected to win a second back-to-back championship during Ewing's senior year.

Race and Rosters

The face of major-college football and basketball has changed dramatically during the past four decades. Nothing makes the changes in the racial composition of the rosters and coaching staffs more apparent than rewatching broadcasts from earlier eras. Black players in Division I basketball and football were plentiful in the 1980s, but not to the degree they are today. Minority coaches, administrators, and broadcasters were rarely, if ever, seen on the sidelines, in press conferences, or in telecast booths.

Indeed, watching Miami's 1984 Orange Bowl victory over Nebraska today feels like a climb into a sports media time machine. The production quality of the images, graphics, and replays hearkens back to an era when joystick Atari sets littered American living rooms. Given subsequent advancements in athletic training and on-campus workout facilities—not to mention the 1990s explosion in the use of performance-enhancing drugs—the players on both squads were smaller than the bulked-up players now. Athletes' celebrations following touchdowns or key defensive plays were nothing like those seen in televised games in the decades since. Players jumped up and down, or patted each other on the tops of helmets or buttocks, but otherwise demonstrations were restrained. Only when Miami's Ed Smith initially thought he had scored on a sparking, catch-and-run touchdown pass from Bernie Kosar did Smith point toward the stands with both index fingers as if he were shooting celebratory pistols. (The touchdown was erased by a clipping penalty.) On the field and onscreen, the production was understated and visually subdued.

But the most striking visual contrast from that memorable 1984 Orange Bowl is the racial composition of both teams. Of Nebraska head coach Tom Osborne's ten assistant coaches, only wide receivers coach Gene Huey was Black.[20] In fact, each of the twenty-five teams the Associated Press ranked in its end-of-season poll that year had white head coaches, plus white offensive and defensive coordinators. Not a single African American held any of the top seventy-five Division I coaching jobs.[21] The Cornhuskers' three offensive superstars—quarterback Turner Gill, running back Mike Rozier, and wide receiver Irving Fryar—were Black. But ten of the Cornhuskers' eleven defensive starters were white (Black cornerback Neil Harris was the exception). By comparison, Nebraska's 2017 starting defensive unit featured nine Black players and only two white players. "What I remember about that time is the way we looked at teams, and it was easy to label teams as a black or white team," said USC sports historian Todd Boyd. "Nebraska was a white team."[22]

Nebraska was and remains a predominantly white state, and its flagship university had a predominantly white student body in 1983. To the program's credit, starting an African American quarterback (Turner Gill) was a rarity at that time. With a few notable exceptions like future Republican congressman J. C. Watts, who started at quarterback for the University of Oklahoma in the late 1970s, almost every Division I college quarterback from that era was white. In the twenty years from 1963 to 1983, seven quarterbacks had won the Heisman Trophy, all of them white, whereas twelve of the thirteen running backs who won the Heisman were Black. "This juxtaposition of white quarterback and black running back becomes even more significant given that most coaches believed blacks lacked both the intelligence and the leadership ability to lead offenses," sports historian Joel Dinerstein wrote.[23]

Miami's 1983–84 coaching staff and player roster were more diverse than many of their counterparts but included far more white players than they would in the coming years. Quarterback Bernie Kosar, tight end Glenn Dennison, and most of Miami's offensive line were white. Even the Hurricanes' starting defense in the 1984 Orange Bowl featured just five Black players and one Latino, defensive end Julio Cortes.[24] Yet, compared to other powerhouse programs like Nebraska, Notre Dame, and Penn State, the 1983–84 Hurricanes were a veritable rainbow coalition. Latino players were rare, yet Cortes and offensive lineman Juan Comendeiro were among a small cohort of Latinos who had a major impact on that year's Hurricanes team. Backup linebacker Jacinto "Jack" Fernandez, who played brilliantly in place of Miami's leading tackler Ken Sisk after Sisk left the game with an injury, was a surprise hero in the Hurricanes' 1984 Orange Bowl victory.

The team's racial and ethnic diversity, which would hardly merit mention today, caught the attention of *New York Times* sportswriter George Vecsey at the time. "There were enough Hispanic names in that [Miami roster] to truly represent the increasingly Hispanic city," Vecsey observed in his column the day after the Orange Bowl. "With a hometown player like Jacinto Fernandez coming off the bench to play a terrific game at linebacker, and with black hometown heroes like Fred Robinson, Miami's victory should create some healthy vibrations for the school and the city."[25] Vecsey correctly identified the racial reformation that began in Coral Gables with Howard Schnellenberger and accelerated under his successor Jimmy Johnson.

In retrospect, it is remarkable how white the rosters of many major Division I programs remained well into the 1980s. Not until the rise of Miami and Florida State as national powers did the traditionally white programs in the Big 10 Conference and now-defunct Southwestern Conference begin recruiting heavily in major cities and the football-rich states of the former Confederacy. ESPN's Adam Rittenberg explained how Jimmy Johnson and FSU's Bobby Bowden triggered this transformation:

> If etymologists [*sic*] tackled the origins of modern college football, their research would lead to two coaches, one talent-rich

state and the annual games that changed everything. . . . Miami and Florida State were college football's hubs from the mid-1980s through the mid-1990s, spreading new ways of recruiting, evaluating and utilizing personnel to all corners of the country.

Johnson and Bobby Bowden were at the controls. The results were historic. Miami and FSU each had a national title and seven top-five finishes between 1986, Johnson's third year at the U, and 1993, when Bowden won his first national title with the Seminoles. No other program had more than four top-five finishes during that span.[26]

The emphasis both coaches placed on recruiting speed at nearly every position in the lineup—not just receivers, running backs, and cornerbacks, but linemen and linebackers too—forced other Division I coaches to start recruiting outside their traditional home states and regions, particularly in the South. That meant recruiting more Black players.

Once Miami and in-state rivals Florida and Florida State changed their recruiting objectives, their rosters became more integrated, and soon thereafter so did those of out-of-state teams hoping to contend for national honors. "The quick rise in success for both Miami and FSU, both of whom developed modern offenses of their day—pro-style for college was considered an innovation then—coupled with defenses that emphasized speed over power, suddenly forced other schools to both alter their own styles and invest more heavily in recruiting South Florida," said Chuck Todd, *Meet the Press* host, Miami native, and avid Hurricanes fan. "Supply and demand have since helped South Florida become the heaviest recruited three counties in the country."[27] In his autobiography, former Hurricanes head coach Jimmy Johnson described his love for the "ethnic swirl" of South Florida as a true "cross section" of the local community that attended games. Yet Johnson also realized that, in retrospect, his early teams failed to fully reflect that diversity: "I looked around and realized that, in the middle of all that talent in South Florida, we'd had a predominantly white team, and that a lot of talent had been bypassed. I wasn't going to bypass anybody, as long as he was a good player and could handle the academics. By 1986 the number of black players at Miami had significantly increased."[28]

Georgetown's championship season also delivered a powerful message about the new racial dynamics in major-college sports. The 1966 Texas Western team featuring five Black starters had won the national championship two decades earlier. But head coach Don Haskins and several of the contributing players on that squad were white. Georgetown's 1983–84 roster was an all-Black team led by the first Black coach to win a Division I team sport championship in NCAA history. Only assistant coach Craig Esherick, academic adviser Mary Fenlon, and one of the Hoyas' three managers were white. Simply put, no previous NCAA Division I team champion in any sport, men's or women's, looked like the 1983–84 Georgetown Hoyas.

In subsequent conversations, John Thompson made clear how he felt about breaking through the coaching glass ceiling. He repeatedly stressed the fact that he was only a novelty because others before or alongside him were deprived the opportunities he had, and that to suggest that he was unusually talented or smart was wrong. "I was very proud of winning the national championship and I was very proud of the fact that I was a black American, but I didn't like it if the statement implied that I was the first black person who had intelligence enough to win the national championship," Thompson told ESPN *Up Close* host Gary Miller during a televised 2001 interview. "I might have been the first Black person who was provided with an opportunity to compete for this prize, that you have discriminated against thousands of my ancestors to deny them this opportunity."[29]

Thompson's hire at Georgetown ramified across Big East coaching staffs, which steadily began to add Black assistant coaches. St. John's Lou Carnesecca hired Ron Rutledge for the 1978–79 season. Syracuse head coach Jim Boeheim in 1983–84 added Wayne Morgan to his staff.[30] Today, the Big East is the only one of the so-called "Big 5 power conferences" in which half of the head coaches are African American.[31] For example, in the 2018–19 season the

Big 10—now a fourteen-member conference clinging to its out-dated name—had not a single African American head coach.[32] The contingent of minority coaches at top-tier programs steadily grew after 1984, but those increases have been neither uniform nor permanent.

The 1984 NCAA tournament field included several Black coaches from non-HBCUs, most notably Temple's John Chaney and Tulsa's Nolan Richardson. Thompson's Georgetown team winning the tournament meant so much more for Black sports fans, however. Thompson was quite aware of the message his ascension sent to observers, especially African Americans: "We had a hell of a lot of people in those stands cheering for us that weren't black. But did it have a special connotation for black people? Sure, based on discrimination and segregation and based on lack of oppor-tunity that people had. When I was the first African-American to win a Division I national championship, it had a special connota-tion because it meant opportunities for other people."[33] Thomp-son's comments about his barrier-breaking role in college sports often reflected the duality of being recognized for achievement, yet saddled with the repeated obligation to contextualize that achievement within the longer, racist history of college athletics.

A program once consisting mostly of white Catholic prep stars from New York and New Jersey was now a home-grown team beloved by Washington natives and by the city's African Ameri-can residents in particular. Speaking to the *Washington City Paper* three decades later for a commemorative piece about the 1980s Hoyas teams, longtime local talk-radio personality Kojo Nnamdi explained how Georgetown's rise led locals to finally adopt the Hoyas as their own:

> Washington was always a good basketball city, but we never had a good basketball college in the city. There was Maryland, but it was outside of the city. We never had a good basketball college in the city that African Americans could really relate to.
>
> Because in large measure they were being so heavily criticized by other coaches and the media, the feeling developed in the city

in general, the African-American community in particular, that, "They're ours. We have to circle the wagons. We have to defend them. We have to protect them. And therefore, we have to adopt them."[34]

The Ewing-era teams had a dramatic effect on Georgetown University, of course. Fans and students took great pride in the Hoyas' successes. High school students did, too; undergraduate applications to Georgetown rose 45 percent from 1983 to 1986.[35] Georgetown was no longer a sleepy Jesuit school tucked into a tony corner of Washington along the Potomac River. It was a destination college with a national brand built primarily by its Black basketball head coach and his team's intimidating but winning reputation.

Miami football and Georgetown basketball were racial pioneers. At a bridge moment in major-college men's sports between the era of overt racism and the multiracial competitive environment of today, both programs helped blaze a new path for college athletes, coaches, administrators, and fans. Many Black and other minority athletes and a few coaches paved the way before them, and thousands more followed. Those two championship seasons—coming just three months apart, and delivered by two very different coaches at two very different universities—heralded the changing racial dynamics of major-college televised sports.

Championship Hangovers and Near Misses

To the shock of many across South Florida, the 1984 Orange Bowl marked the end of head coach Howard Schnellenberger's days at Miami. When he was hired, the coach known for his trademark bushy white mustache and tobacco pipe promised that Miami would win a national championship within five years. He delivered exactly on time. Perhaps that sense of timely accomplishment made it easier for him to leave the University of Miami for a chance to coach in the fledging United States Football League (USFL). Schnellenberger inked a deal with owner Sherwood Weiser to coach and become part owner of the Washington Federals, which Weiser pledged to relocate to Miami.

But the USFL suddenly abandoned its original springtime schedule in favor of playing in the fall, putting USFL games in direct competition with Division I college football and the NFL for ticket sales and television audiences. Schnellenberger balked. The deal that would have paid him $5 million over the first three years collapsed. Meanwhile, after a ten-day search Miami had already tapped Jimmy Johnson to replace him. Schnellenberger went on to rebuild the University of Louisville's dormant program and create Florida Atlantic University's team, but his Hurricanes days were over. "Who knows how many national titles Coach Schnellenberger would have won if he'd stayed?" Larry Coker, who later coached the Hurricanes, wondered. "His success would have been off the charts."[36]

The sudden coaching change was less disruptive than expected—or so administrators, assistant coaches, and players claimed at the time. Bernie Kosar, the team's star quarterback, said that after Schnellenberger sat him down to explain the reasons behind his departure, Kosar felt even more respect toward his departing coach. Returning players and incoming recruits also stuck with the program despite the change in leadership. On the job less than a year, Miami athletic director Sam Jankovich expressed confidence in Johnson's ability to effect a smooth transition. To that end, Johnson shrewdly retained six of Schnellenberger's nine assistant coaches, including Gary Stevens, Bill Trout, Joe Brodsky, and Hubbard Alexander.

Johnson promoted Trout to defensive coordinator. Defense was a particular area of concern to Johnson because the 'Canes lost to graduation seven of their eleven defensive starters from the championship squad. "Both have been successful," said Trout, when asked to compare Miami's departing and incoming head coaches. Trout then offered a telling distinction between Schnellenberger's and Johnson's interpersonal styles: "But they have very different approaches to the game. Howard coached the coaches more than the kids . . . Jimmy hasn't been in the pros, so he gets more emotionally involved with the kids."[37] Ultimately, Johnson left a larger and more lasting imprint on Miami football. But Schnellenberger is rightly regarded as the man who revived a program on life support when he took over in 1979.

The more emotive Johnson's first season with the 'Canes was a rollercoaster. Starting the season ranked tenth nationally, Miami dispatched top-ranked Auburn in its opening game and seventeenth-ranked in-state rival Florida the following week. The two wins catapulted the Hurricanes to No. 1 in the polls just two weeks into Johnson's reign. But Miami lost two of its next three games and immediately became a longshot to defend its national title. The season ended in dismal, even bizarre fashion. The 'Canes lost their final three games, including the Fiesta Bowl to UCLA, by two points each.[38] The way Miami lost its last two regular-season games, both at home in the Orange Bowl, stung Johnson and his players.

By the time unranked Maryland arrived in Miami on November 10, the Hurricanes had climbed to sixth in the national rankings and were playing with renewed confidence after five straight wins. Quarterback Bernie Kosar and running back Alonzo Highsmith were certified superstars. Kosar eventually finished the season with 3,642 yards passing and 25 touchdown passes, and Highsmith amassed a combined 1,163 rushing and receiving yards.[39] Miami pummeled the visiting Terrapins in the first half, 31–0, quieting the home crowd as both teams headed into the locker room for intermission. The game was over—until it wasn't.

Maryland coach Bobby Ross inserted backup Frank Reich at quarterback for the second half. Reich promptly led the Terrapins to six second-half touchdowns and a 42–40 victory sealed when Miami missed a potentially tying 2-point conversion. At the time it was the greatest comeback in NCAA Division I football history. Johnson repeatedly cited that blown lead whenever opponents or the media later criticized his squads for running up the score against overmatched foes. The Maryland loss also contributed to the 'Canes emerging reputation. "The comeback never would've happened if it had not been for the attitude of the Miami Hurricanes," former Maryland placekicker Jess Atkinson told the *Washington Post* three years later. "Those guys were the biggest cheap-shot, trash-talking, classless outfit of football players I've ever seen in my life ... and it gave us a little extra incentive."[40]

Thirteen days later, in a nationally televised game on Friday night of Thanksgiving weekend, Miami hosted the Boston College (BC) Eagles. Led by quarterback Doug Flutie, who won the Heisman Trophy that season, the tenth-ranked Eagles were more talented than the Terrapins. In a high-scoring, back-and-forth game, Kosar and Flutie combined for more than 900 passing yards. With Miami leading 45–41 after running back Melvin Bratton's third touchdown of the game with 28 seconds to play, Flutie and the Eagles took possession after the ensuing kickoff at their own 20-yard line. Needing a touchdown to win, Flutie quickly drove BC near midfield. Then on the final, unforgettable play, he raced around as time expired and then launched what's since been described as the "Hail Mary" touchdown pass to wideout Gerard Phelan. Although technically throwing a 48-yard touchdown, Flutie scrambled so far back in the pocket to evade Miami's rush that he actually threw the ball more than 60 yards—into heavy storm winds.

Final score: Boston College 47, Miami 45.

"It's a great thrill to have participated in a game like this," Jimmy Johnson mused. "But it could have been even greater—with six less seconds."[41] In two consecutive games that rank among the most storied contests in college football history, Johnson watched his team lose leads—one large, one late. Each 2-point defeat was decided on the final play of the game. The only benefit of those two gut-wrenching losses is that for years to come Johnson and his players tapped into the pain and embarrassment they experienced at the end of the 1984 season for extra motivation.

Miami's dynasty lasted well beyond the Johnson-Erickson era of the 1980s. Starting with the 1983–84 team, the Hurricanes won four titles in nine seasons under the supervision of three different head coaches. In an eight-year stretch combining the final four years of Jimmy Johnson's reign and the first four under Dennis Erickson, Miami won eighty-eight games and lost just seven. By any measure Miami was a dynasty and was without question the most dominant college football program of the 1980s. The program again surged during the mid-1990s under Erickson's successor Butch Davis. Yet 'Canes players and fans still felt that Miami never quite received the credit it deserved. "If you put all those same accolades on a Notre Dame or a Penn State, man, that's all you'd see and hear," Michael Irvin said on the eve of Miami's 1993 Sugar Bowl loss to Alabama, which cost Miami a fifth title in ten years. "But people look at Miami, and because of what they think we stand for, they get tired of seeing us win. We just don't get the respect we should."[42]

In 2015, a few days after Clemson dealt Miami a 58–0 whupping, the worst loss in Hurricanes football history, sportswriter Brian Goff examined the history of Miami's recruiting classes. For nearly three decades starting in the 1980s, the Hurricanes attracted and developed an incredible talent pool of players. But the number and quality of top recruits has since waned. "A deeper look into the best of the best players going to Miami—first and second round drafts picks—is revealing. From 1985–93, during the golden era of Miami football, 24 players were selected in the first or second rounds of the NFL draft. That number holds also for the years (1996–2004) of the scandal-laded resurgence of the 'Canes." As Goff pointed out, Miami's pro-level talent fell by half thereafter as in-state teams including Florida and Florida State, and even upstarts like Central Florida and South Florida, became more competitive. The Southeast Conference, led by Alabama but including powerhouses like Georgia and LSU, also emerged as the premier conference and choice of many prep superstars. Goff concluded: "[Because those programs] can draw off some of the players that would have supplied greater quality depth at Miami, it would seem as though the golden era will not likely return."[43] How shallow has the talent pool in Coral Gables become? In the 2020 NFL draft, the same Miami program that once boasted three of the top nine draft picks in 1987 watched as both Florida International University and Florida Atlantic University—once laughingstocks within Sunshine State football circles—each had a player drafted before Hurricanes linebacker Shaquille Quarterman was selected by the Jacksonville Jaguars with the 140th pick.

Only once during the past forty seasons was Miami's first pick drafted at a lower position.[44]

The program's struggles after Larry Coker left in 2006 are painfully evident. In the subsequent thirteen seasons, Miami cycled through four different coaches—Randy Shannon, Al Golden, Mark Richt, and current head coach Manny Diaz—plus a fifth, interim coach for the remainder of the 2015 campaign after Golden's mid-season firing following the 58–0 humiliation by Clemson. The 'Canes won 96 games against 70 losses, a middling 57.8 percent share, during those thirteen seasons. By comparison, the Hurricanes suffered only 53 total defeats across twenty-four seasons starting with Howard Schnellenberger's 1983–84 title team. In that stretch the 'Canes posted 238 victories, for a stunning 81.7 percent win rate.

Miami's declining reputation and fortunes during the past thirteen seasons are also evident from its recent bowl history. Thanks to the proliferation of postseason bowl games—and despite a two-year, self-imposed bowl ban while the program was under NCAA investigation in 2011 and 2012—Miami nevertheless earned bowl bids in ten of its remaining eleven eligible seasons. However, the Hurricanes played in mostly second- and third-tier contests, including the Russell Athletic Bowl, the Emerald Bowl, the New Era Pinstripe Bowl, and two Independence Bowls. Worse, the 'Canes won just one of those ten postseason games. During a twenty-year span from 1983–84 to 2002–3, Miami played for a chance to win the national championship nine times and won five titles. The dynasty days are over.

Georgetown's valedictory lap the year after winning the 1983–84 championship was setting up to be a perfect encore and possible back-to-back title. The Hoyas were ranked No. 1 heading into the 1984–85 campaign. Ewing returned for his senior season and would fulfill twin expectations by being voted the nation's top player and later picked first by the New York Knicks in the 1985 NBA draft. With the exception of Michael Graham, who never returned after his impactful freshman year, Ewing's supporting cast (Reggie Williams, David Wingate, Michael Jackson, and Horace

Broadnax) was back. The Hoyas had the best starting lineup in college basketball. They were loaded with an even more talented and experienced roster than they'd had the year before.

Georgetown also finished the season with a better record, 35-3, and a more dominant run through its schedule. In twenty-six of those thirty-five victories, the Hoyas won by double digits, and their only two defeats during the regular season were back-to-back losses by a combined 3 points to nationally ranked Big East rivals Syracuse and St. John's. Georgetown twice avenged the Syracuse loss—by a whopping 27 points in both teams' Big East regular-season finale and by 9 points in the Big East tournament semifinal at Madison Square Garden. At that point the Georgetown-Syracuse rivalry was bigger and more heated than ever.

With a national television audience watching that Big East semifinal, tempers flared again. This time, Ewing and Syracuse star point guard Dwayne "Pearl" Washington exchanged elbows during separate incidents. An angry Ewing retaliated, swinging wildly and barely missing Washington with a punch that emptied both benches. "He gave me a forearm shiver," Ewing recalled during an interview a few months after Washington died in April 2016 from brain cancer at age fifty-two. "It knocked the wind out of me. I got mad and tried to throw a punch. Thank god, it missed. If I'd have hit him, I probably would've broken my hand and I don't know what would've happened to him."[45] The Hoyas rarely initiated fights, but they did not back down from attacks. Georgetown won the 1985 conference tournament, their second title in a row and fourth in the Big East's six-year history. For good measure, the Hoyas avenged their earlier loss that season to St. John's three times—later during the regular season, in the final of the Big East tourney Georgetown won, and in the NCAA seminal game.

Lost amid the focus on the titanic rivalry games with the Orangemen and Redmen that year was the Hoyas' narrow survival in two very close games against another Big East foe, Villanova, their surprise opponent in the NCAA title game on April 1, 1985, at Rupp Arena in Lexington, Kentucky. Villanova's dramatic win over defending-champion Georgetown in the 1985 NCAA title game is considered one of the greatest upsets in the history of major-college team sports. Perhaps along with North Carolina State's 1983 defeat of Houston, it is also regarded as the biggest upset in an NCAA title game. The loss prevented the Hoyas from becoming the first team to win back-to-back championships since UCLA. The Wildcats' amazing performance—including a near-perfect second half in which Villanova shot 90 percent from the field—is precisely the Cinderella storyline television executives dream about every year when the March Madness tournament tips off. Images of rapturous Villanova head coach Rollie Massimino emerging from a group bear hug with his assistants to cross the court and shake a defeated John Thompson's hand are perfect fodder for the signature "One Shining Moment" videos that now conclude the tournament broadcast each April. Scads of articles and two books have been written about the epic Villanova-Georgetown 1985 final.[46]

Might having Michael Graham back for his sophomore year have helped Georgetown repeat as champions? Maybe, maybe not. What is certain is that Graham will be remembered as a rare casualty during that glorious 1980s era. Raised in poverty in Washington, he was a volatile young man battling personal and familial demons. Thompson had a soft spot for Graham, who had fathered a child while still in high school. With his bald head and physical aggressiveness, Graham became a symbol of Georgetown's ferocity. "The indomitable, stoic center Patrick Ewing was the face of the Hoyas," sportswriter Alan Siegel recalled. "But for a short, profoundly memorable stretch, nobody embodied Georgetown's establishment-rankling ethos more than Graham." The 1984 title game was Graham's last as a Hoya. He didn't handle the spotlight well and soon dropped out of Georgetown. He tried to revive his college career at nearby University of the District of Columbia, but flamed out there, too. During Graham's short pro career with the Seattle Supersonics, he never played a single NBA game. Even future Chicago Bulls coach Phil Jackson, known for deftly handling the combustible Dennis Rodman, only made it eleven games as Graham's coach for the Albany Patroons in the Continental Basketball Association before he and Graham got into a verbal spat in the middle of a game. The Patroons cut Graham loose. He played sporadically for a few years in Europe before retiring.[47]

Georgetown would remain a national contender during the remainder of the 1980s and well into the 1990s. The Hoyas routinely advanced to the Elite Eight round of the NCAA tournament, even when Georgetown fielded less talented rosters than during the Ewing era. A young 1987 team led by senior Reggie Williams advanced to the Elite Eight by beating Danny Manning's Kansas Jayhawks in the Sweet Sixteen round. That "Reggie and the Miracles" Hoyas squad exceeded expectations by finishing in a three-way tie atop the Big East's regular-season standings. They then won Georgetown's fifth Big East title after soundly beating Providence in the semis and hated rival Syracuse in the final. Williams won the tourney's MVP award.[48]

Had Georgetown not lost in the Elite Eight round to Thompson's alma mater and Big East rival Providence—then coached by Rick Pitino and featuring star guard Billy Donovan—Georgetown would have reached a remarkable fifth Final Four in seven years. The 1987 Final Four in New Orleans included Providence and Syracuse, the two conference rivals that Georgetown had defeated a combined five times that season and had just beaten on consecutive nights to win the Big East crown. An inexperienced team tying for first in the Big East regular season, winning the conference tourney, finishing No. 4 in the national rankings heading into the NCAA tournament, and losing only five games—all to conference opponents, including two who made it to the Final Four—this was considered a *down* year for Georgetown in the 1980s. "To a Hoya, style is synonymous with winning," *New York Times* sportswriter Roy Johnson wrote about that 1987 team. "And going into this season, questions about the young Hoyas made it seem as if Georgetown and its coach, John Thompson, would endure a rare season of humility, much to the glee of their Big East rivals."[49]

Thanks to Reggie and the Miracles, the Hoyas experienced only a slight drop-off following their dominant four-year run with

Patrick Ewing in the lineup. The following season, the 1987–88 team finished just 20-10 but featured emerging stars like Charles Smith and Mark Tillmon. With the arrival the next year of Alonzo Mourning and Dikembe Mutumbo, the Hoyas surged to the top of the polls again during the late 1980s and early 1990s, when John Thompson's controversial signing of point guard Allen Iverson heralded the last great run of the Georgetown dynasty.

The first half of the 1980s was an unparalleled moment for Georgetown and the emergence of the NCAA tournament as a national entertainment extravaganza. Four of the NCAA tournament's most memorable title games came during the span of just six years: the titanic 1979 matchup between Indiana State's Larry Bird and Michigan State's Magic Johnson; the 1982 final featuring Michael Jordan's game-winning jumper and the Fred Brown turnover in the final minute of North Carolina's victory over Georgetown; Lorenzo Charles's buzzer-beating dunk to cap North Carolina State's storybook championship in 1983; and Villanova's near-perfect-game upset of Georgetown two years later. To the eternal chagrin of Hoyas players, students, and fans, Georgetown lost two of those classic games. Without those losses, John Thompson and his Patrick Ewing–led teams could have had (along with the Christian Laettner–era Duke teams of the early 1990s) the most successful four-year stretch in men's college basketball history since the UCLA dynasty ended. Because so few of today's collegiate superstars stay for all four years of their eligibility, as both Ewing and Laettner did, the Georgetown dynasty of the early 1980s endures, relic of a bygone era in Division I basketball.

Convenient Foils

Within a span of three months, Georgetown basketball and Miami football won their first national titles. Those championship runs were remarkable in a number of ways. Only a few years and one coaching hire earlier, the Hoyas and Hurricanes were unheralded programs that attracted little national attention, and what little notice they did attract generally focused on the miseries suffered by both teams. The years mired in mediocrity were quickly forgotten when John Thompson and Howard Schnellen-berger revived the two programs and led each to prominence and national championships.

With success came greater scrutiny, of course, and not all of the increased attention that Georgetown and Miami attracted was favorable. With the spotlight fixed on both schools, the Hoyas and Hurricanes became magnets for thinly veiled racial animos-ity. Opposing fans and some members of the sports media gladly advertised their disdain for the Hoyas and 'Canes. Because they won—and, more specifically, because of the way they won—Georgetown and Miami quickly evolved from no-name teams into champions, but also convenient foils. Neither program was flaw-less, and Hurricanes players in particular had more than their share of run-ins with NCAA rules and the law. Derision and scorn—much of it emanating from an overwhelmingly white chorus of fans, boosters, conference officials, NCAA administrators, and media writers—were the price paid for the two programs' rapid rise to national contenders.

To be fair, there was an undeniable "you asked for it, you got it" aspect to the hostility directed at Georgetown and Miami. Both programs invited, even welcomed, the enmity of opponents, critics, and the media. That hatred fueled the competitive fires of coaches and players in Washington and Coral Gables. All that ire, however, was offset by a potent and disruptive counterforce. Mil-lions of mostly African American fans quickly came to identify themselves with one or both programs. Georgetown and Miami thus became the collegiate sports equivalent of Rorschach tests for racial identity and solidarity. Young Black men in particular adorned themselves with the colors and logos of both programs. Popular culture, including but not limited to rap music, quickly appropriated Hoyas and Hurricanes iconography. The die was cast for Georgetown basketball and Miami football to transcend the normal expectations for major-college sports programs and become cultural phenomena.

[5]

John and Jimmy, Patrick and Michael

If I saw someone coming at me the wrong way, I went back at 'em.

—JOHN THOMPSON, reflecting on his coaching career at Georgetown

----

When you go into a program with great success,

they don't want to change things.

—JIMMY JOHNSON, on being hired as Miami's new head coach

During the 1980s Georgetown had one coach, John Thompson. Miami had three, the middle and most influential of whom was Jimmy Johnson. One Black and the other white, Thompson and Johnson came from very different backgrounds. Thompson was born and raised in Washington DC and vaulted from the high school coaching ranks straight to a Division I head coaching job. Johnson grew up in working-class Port Arthur, Texas, worked his way up through the college coaching ranks, and had already coached at Division I Oklahoma State before his arrival in Coral Gables. Despite their contrasting biographies and coaching philosophies, they bore a striking similarity; they were controversial yet successful coaches who understood how to recruit, groom, and mentor talented young minority athletes.

Patrick Ewing is the greatest player in Georgetown history and was the most dominant college basketball player of the 1980s.

Ewing's family relocated from Jamaica to the United States when he was a teenager so the talented young center could sharpen his skills at a Boston prep school. His recruitment to Georgetown and his four years playing for the Hoyas included some of the most notable games and episodes in the program's history. From the lows of racist taunts to the highs of the Hoyas' 1984 championship run, Ewing was a central figure in many of Georgetown's most glorious and controversial moments. Miami wide receiver Michael Irvin had a similar impact. He was key to the Hurricanes becoming the decade's most dominant college football team. He starred in some of the most memorable Miami games of the 1980s. His spectacular catches and on-field demonstrations helped turn Miami football into a national powerhouse. Hero to some and lightning rod to others, Irvin helped make the Hurricanes a program to either root for or revile.

These four men were essential to the successes of the two programs that transformed Division I men's team sports during the 1980s. Thompson and Johnson built their teams into national powerhouses by revolutionizing how their programs recruited and coached players, and both men are now enshrined in their respective halls of fame. Ewing and Irvin dominated during their college days, enjoyed Hall of Fame professional careers, and remain key figures in their respective sports to this day. Other players, coaches and administrators contributed to the sports dynasties at Georgetown and Miami, of course. But Thompson, Ewing, Johnson and Irvin helped build—and to this day, still embody—the enduring "Hoya paranoia" and "The U" mythologies.

Most Abnormal Coach of All

Georgetown's 1972 decision to hire John Thompson as head basketball coach was a gamble. Because even successful prep coaches have limited recruiting networks, Division I athletic directors and search committees rarely entrust the overhaul of their programs to high school coaches. Most universities instead hire a college head coach with a rising profile from a smaller school or conference, or tap an up-and-coming assistant coach groomed by a proven mentor at a top program.

Thompson's biography, however, was unusually impressive. His local roots in Washington and his NBA experience were rarefied credentials for a high school coach. So, too, was the potential value of his race. For some young Black athletes, playing for a Black college coach is uniquely alluring. Only two years earlier, Illinois State hired Will Robinson as the first Black head coach in Division I. Thompson understood his unusual advantages and exploited them to win the job and then build the Hoyas into a national juggernaut.

Thompson's rebuilding project at Georgetown showed progress almost immediately. Under his stewardship, the Hoyas improved from 12-14 and 13-13 in his first two seasons to an 18-10 winning record by his third year. That season, Georgetown—although still a conference independent—played in the 1975 Eastern College Athletic Conference tournament's South Region. Thanks to a buzzer-beating shot by Hoyas guard Derrick Jackson, Georgetown won the regional bracket and its automatic bid to the NCAA tournament. This was Georgetown's first tournament bid in thirty-two years and only its second NCAA appearance. The Hoyas reached the tournament again in 1976. After missing the next two seasons, Georgetown played in the NCAA tourney eighteen of the next nineteen seasons from 1978–79 to 1996–97. No prior or subsequent Hoyas coach has come close to matching Thompson's remarkable run.

Thompson's third season was marred by a notoriously racist episode that remains a flashpoint moment in his career and the history of Georgetown basketball. The details of the episode remain in dispute. After the Hoyas won seven of their first nine games that year, they lost their next six. Newly spoiled fans and students started to grumble. One night a banner was discovered in the Georgetown gymnasium that read "John Thompson the N—— Must Go!" In some accounts, the banner was found in the gym after hours. Other witnesses claimed that they saw it thrown onto the court during a game. Still other accounts indicate the banner included an added word, reading "John Thomp-son the N—— Flop Must Go!"

Who made the banner and why? A former athlete who refused to identify himself told university officials that two drunk George-town football players created the banner because they were angry about the relocation of the football team's locker room. Years later, a retired Nike representative claimed that Thompson made the banner himself in order to distract attention from his coaching struggles, a dubious accusation given that Thompson led both the 1974–75 and 1975–76 teams to the NCAA tourney.[1] Whoever made the infamous banner, the episode remains an ugly yet enduring component of Thompson lore.

Sportswriters Bruce Lowitt and Ira Rosenfeld contended that the banner incident masked a deeper, overlooked story. During the team's six-game losing streak, Thompson benched Jonathan Smith, the Hoyas' leading scorer. Despite signing the team's required log-book indicating that he had attended all his classes, Smith had in fact skipped several sessions. When Thompson found out, he benched Smith. The team suffered, but neither Thompson nor any of his players discussed the reasons for Smith's benching until the day after the banner incident, when the players held their own press conference. With local media listening, Smith defended Thompson's decision. Teammate Felix Yeomans went even fur-ther. After citing all the good Thompson had done for his play-ers, Yeomans said, "If this is what it is to be a n—— flop, this is what we want to be."[2] The banner episode was the first time the public witnessed the abiding devotion and respect players felt toward Thompson.

By the mid-1970s Thompson's was turning heads regionally, even nationally. He quickly attracted the attention of more established coaches like the University of North Carolina's Dean Smith, the 1976 U.S. Olympic men's basketball coach. Four years after an offi-ciating controversy in Munich cost the 1972 U.S. team a victory over the Soviet Union and the gold medal, Smith's team headed to Montreal determined to reassert America's reputation as the world's premier basketball nation. Smith tapped Thompson to

John and Jimmy, Patrick and Michael

be the first Black assistant coach in U.S. Olympic basketball history. Fittingly enough, the 1976 U.S. men's team was the first to feature a majority-Black roster. (The 1972 team was split evenly between six white and six Black players.) The U.S. squad never got the opportunity to exact revenge on the Soviets, who played in the opposite bracket and did not advance to the gold-medal game. But the Americans got redemption. Propelled by leading scorer Adrian Dantley, the United States won all seven games en route to capturing the 1976 gold medal.[3]

The 1976 Olympic roster included four of Smith's Tar Heels but none of Thompson's Hoyas. Smith's roster choices were no slight against his assistant coach: In the mid-1970s Thompson's rosters did not yet boast Olympic-caliber players. Yet the Olympic team included two Washington DC natives, Notre Dame's Dantley and North Carolina State's Kenny Carr, both of whom left their hometown to sign with more prestigious programs than Georgetown's. The fact that two local prep stars chose to play elsewhere testified to the incomplete, though steady, progress that Thompson had made.

Nevertheless, Thompson's early successes at Georgetown and his role with the 1976 Olympic team bolstered his profile in national basketball circles. His recruiting prowess and win-loss record eclipsed those of his predecessor John Magee, but Georgetown was still a few years away from becoming a national powerhouse. To reach that next level, Thompson needed to attract top prep superstars from the Baltimore-Washington area, the kind of players who—like Carr, Dantley, and Thompson himself—who would previously never have considered staying home to play for the unheralded Hoyas.

In his early years, Thompson recruited as locally as possible. His first year, in fact, he brought three players with him from his St. Anthony's prep team, all of them Black, plus two other Black recruits from teams he coached against in the Washington area. As his inaugural 1972–73 season progressed—and almost two decades before the University of Michigan's "Fab Five" freshmen burst onto the national scene—Thompson began starting five Black freshmen. Given what a small and unremarkable program the Hoyas were at the time, Thompson's bold move garnered none of the national attention that Michigan coach Steve Fisher and his Wolverine freshmen did many years later.

The racial composition of Thompson's Hoyas contrasted sharply with that of teams from previous eras. Georgetown alumni took notice—and a few took exception. Thompson recounted the story of a woman so upset about the Hoyas' complexion change since his arrival that she called his office directly:

> There was one time the first year when a white lady phoned. She obviously didn't know anything about me, but she was very hot. The day before, there had been a photo in the paper of a couple of my big kids standing on each side of a little white kid. They looked like they were going to mash him. The lady said her father, maybe her brothers, had gone to Georgetown, and if I was the coach I ought to stop what was happening there—abnormal n——s bullying white students. I told her things were worse than she thought and that I was going to send her two tickets to our next game so she could come see for herself, that what she would see would make her blood run cold. I was very sorry that lady couldn't use those tickets. They were for seats right behind where I sit on the bench. I wanted her to get a look at the most abnormal n—— of them all.[4]

The lesson was clear. Although Thompson needed to integrate and improve the roster by adding talented Black players, the team's sudden change in profile generated backlash from some hardline boosters.

During the 1970s, Thompson mostly competed with crosstown Catholic University and other nearby schools for local recruits ignored or overlooked by the big-name programs from the Atlantic Coast and Southeastern Conferences. By the mid-1970s Thompson began to win those battles and could redirect his recruiting focus to talented local players who had, historically, left town. By guiding the Hoyas to that 1976 NCAA tourney bid, Thompson earned his program's first mention in *Sports Illustrated*, which

John and Jimmy, Patrick and Michael

praised the young coach's recruiting prowess. "For many years local schools did not want black athletes," Thompson told Larry Keith. "When they finally decided they did, it was too late. The tradition among the players was to get out. Fortunately we've been able to change that a little."[5]

By the late 1970s, the competitive recruiting environment for major-college basketball coaches had changed. What was once a series of regional competitions had expanded into fierce national battles among the most notable programs and coaches. Summer basketball leagues—especially the late Howard Garfinkel's famed Five-Star Basketball camp—attracted the nation's top prep players. Division I coaches were more than happy to volunteer at Five-Star in exchange for an up-close chance to rate and recruit players. Garfinkel started his Scranton-based camp in 1966, but a circuit of imitator camps soon popped up around the country. "I recruit New York City school kids who play summer games in Utah. Washington summer programs send kids to Las Vegas. Kids go overseas in the summer now," Thompson told *Sports Illustrated* in 1980. "When I was in high school in D.C., we were lucky to go to Baltimore. There are no foreign courts anymore. Good players will play wherever the game is."[6]

Baltimore's Dunbar High School thirty miles north of Washington proved to be a rich feeder program that provided Thompson coveted superstars like David Wingate and Reggie Williams, who later helped lead the Hoyas to the program's first Final Four appearances and the 1984 championship. Named for African American poet Paul Laurence Dunbar, the Baltimore school's Purple Poets, coached by Bob Wade, were a national prep powerhouse. As recounted by Alejandro Danois in *The Boys of Dunbar: A Story of Love, Hope, and Basketball*, Wade's greatest team featured not only Wingate and Williams, but eventual Division I stars Reggie Lewis (Northeastern) and Tyrone "Muggsy" Bogues (Wake Forest). All four were later drafted into and played in the NBA. (Wade's prep school successes, like Thompson's, led to his hire to rehabilitate a nearby Division I program, in his case the University of Maryland.)

Thompson had a major advantage in the recruiting wars: his race. For some prep prospects, playing for a Black coach on an almost all-Black roster had a certain allure. But Thompson's appeal was not the byproduct of racial tokenism. He built his reputation with the way he treated his players and the expectations and standards to which he held them. Current players let potential recruits know that Thompson was a tough-love mentor who expected them to attend class and comport themselves at all times with dignity and grace. Thompson and his team sold Georgetown as a program led by a strong, avuncular figure who understood the unique challenges facing young Black athletes.

Thompson's national breakout year was 1979–80. In the Big East's inaugural year, Georgetown finished in a three-way tie with St. John's and Syracuse for the regular-season title, then beat both teams to win the conference championship. Entering the NCAA tourney with a 24-5 record and No. 11 national ranking, the Hoyas dispatched Iona College and local rival the University of Maryland to reach the East Region final against Iowa Hawkeyes. Hoyas guard Sleepy Floyd, who scored 31 points on 11-for-14 shooting, was nearly unstoppable. The Hoyas led the Hawkeyes by 10 points at halftime and expanded their lead at one point in the second half to 14 points. Georgetown was cruising to what appeared to be Thompson's first Final Four. Then everything fell apart. Iowa scored on 15 of its final 16 possessions, including a three-point play by backup center Steve Waite with five seconds left in the game to seal the victory.[7]

Despite the loss, Thompson was a hot commodity. He openly considered taking jobs at the University of Florida, the University of Oklahoma (OU), and the University of Pittsburgh, which was not yet a member of the Big East. Thompson biographer Leonard Shapiro claimed that Thompson's wife Gwen was instrumental in him keeping him at Georgetown: "While Thompson made every effort to keep his private life and his family out of the public eye, their friends knew that Gwen Thompson could be just as strong-willed as her husband. In fact, [she] occasionally sat in on John Thompson's contract talks with the university." Georgetown responded to the growing interest in its star coach by raising his salary after the 1979–80 season. Thompson stayed put.[8]

In 1981 Thompson landed the biggest recruit of his career: Patrick Ewing. Ewing's recruitment and eventual signing with Georgetown created national headlines and a bit of controversy. Mike Jarvis, Ewing's coach at Rindge and Latin High School in Cambridge, Massachusetts, circulated an unusual letter to coaches interested in signing Ewing (i.e., the coach of virtually every major program in the country). *Sports Illustrated*'s Ralph Wiley described the impact of Jarvis' unprecedented move:

> In 1980, Jarvis was determined to keep the Ewing recruiting circus under control. So he sent out to 150 Division I schools the so-called Ewing Letter, which promulgated rules for recruiting Patrick and listed his academic and athletic requirements. The letter explained in detail that because of his culturally poor background Ewing might need daily tutoring, remedial instruction, tapes of lectures and other special educational considerations. The Ewing Letter predictably left people around the country wondering: What, is he that dumb?[9]

The letter went public after Ewing announced on February 2, 1981, his intent to play at Georgetown. Jarvis and Thompson both came under scrutiny. Some insinuated that Jarvis demanded special academic attention for Ewing and that Georgetown made promises to bend its rules to accommodate Jarvis and Ewing.

Thompson was incensed by the insinuations. "I've never seen anything intended to help someone backfire as much as this," Thompson complained. "The guidelines were drawn up to help keep the youngster from being exploited. Jarvis and the family made no stipulations, and there has never been a contractual agreement regarding Patrick Ewing's course of study at Georgetown. What Pat Ewing is getting at Georgetown is no different from what any other student who needs help at Georgetown would get."[10] In trademark fashion, Thompson fired back at his skeptics. "Kids are now starting to choose us for what we are, not to make us something," Thompson told the *Washington Post*'s young beat writer at the time, Michael Wilbon. "Patrick is not coming to a welfare program. We deserved Patrick Ewing." At a time when the Reagan Administration was threatening social safety net and affirmative action programs, Thompson's use of "welfare" was no accident.

Thompson's protective love for his players was noticed from afar. A 6-foot-1-inch guard from Plant City, Florida, Horace Broadnax was a top prep prospect who averaged 23 points a game his senior year of high school. Broadnax remembered watching the Fred Brown turnover and the painful final moments of Georgetown's loss to North Carolina in the 1982 NCAA title game. "The way Coach Thompson treated Brown showed me how much he cared about his players," Broadnax recalled. "It swept me off my feet. But I knew that I couldn't just choose a school because of that. Everything about Georgetown just impressed me." Also watching that night was 6-foot-5-inch Baltimore Dunbar High School forward David Wingate. According to Wilbon, Wingate also cited Thompson's hug as key to his decision to sign with Georgetown. "David told me he just had to be associated with a coach who cares so much about his players," Wingate's Dunbar coach Bob Wade told Wilbon. "I was impressed myself, but I don't know if it's possible to gauge the positive impact that one simple act had on kids."[11]

Some sportswriters criticized Thompson's brusque attitude. Black critics better understood the coach's agenda, motivated to a significant degree by the heightened expectations and scrutiny he faced as a barrier-busting coach. Long before he became a national political commentator on Fox News, Juan Williams profiled Thompson for the *Washington Post* in 1988. Williams saw in Thompson a powerful need for control—over the circumstances of his life, over his program and its players, and especially over his and Georgetown's racial identity and legacy. "He's been after control ever since the fifth grade, when he was mocked for not being able to read and was kicked out of Catholic elementary school by teachers who told his mother he was retarded. Already big, awkward and shy, he was slow to trust anyone from that time on, already anxious to be in charge," wrote Williams. "To gain control in the sports world and keep it, Thompson wins. He knows that if he loses too many basketball games, it won't matter how many of his athletes graduate from Georgetown, it won't matter that he's made Georgetown a source of pride for Washington's blacks. If the team loses, Thompson loses."[12]

In those early years, Thompson's all-Black rosters and his need for control ruffled the feathers of opponents, alumni, and even some of Georgetown's most loyal boosters. But the results were indisputable: Thompson turned Georgetown's dismal program around in less than a decade. He kept local stars from bolting for other programs and recruited top players from across the country. He was an Olympic team assistant coach and raised Georgetown's profile enough for the team to be included in the 1979 expansion Big East Conference. Long a national embarrassment, the Hoyas transformed from an unknown program into a national contender in just eight years following Thompson's hiring in 1972.

Not all of the new attention was positive, however. After he won the 1984 championship, Thompson became a public figure but also a target. "Some media figures . . . said he was arrogant and abrasive and kept his team insulated from the public . . . [and] his team was overly aggressive," sports historian Richard Lapchick recounted. "His personal leadership as the outspoken elder statement of America's black coaches [had] enhanced his status in the black community and alienated many in the white community." Lapchick concluded that Thompson's shattering of longstanding stereotypes created blowback against him and his Hoyas: "He was a big winner with a lot of black recruits [who] were not a freewheeling, footloose team but, rather, one of the most disciplined teams in the country. Even more important, at a time of great negative publicity concerning the academic abuse of college athletes, Thompson's players had one of the highest graduation rates in America."[13] It was easy for some to dislike Thompson, but impossible not to respect him.

Thompson did not apologize for his methods, his combative posture, or his ceiling-breaking role as an African American coach. "If I saw someone coming at me the wrong way, I went back at 'em," Thompson told the *Washington Post* years later. "I was supposed to be grateful because I one was one of the first African Americans coaching. I was supposed to sit there and say, 'Oh, thank you Mr. White Man for giving me a job.' God made me human and equal. Now I'm supposed to be grateful because you're treating me equal and treating me as a human being? No."[14] Thompson's combination of intense defiance and racial pride made him a pioneer and a role model for future Black coaches. Kevin Ollie, a former star forward for conference rival the University of Connecticut (UConn) who played against John Thompson's Georgetown teams in the late 1990s, cited Thompson's example when he was hired in 2012 to succeed his own coach, Hall of Famer Jim Calhoun, as UConn's first African American coach.[15] In his second season, Ollie led UConn to the national championship, putting him in rare company along with Thompson, Nolan Richardson, and Tubby Smith as the only Black coaches to win the NCAA Division I tourney. Such is the reach of Thompson's pioneering career.

John Thompson put the lie to racial inferiority and associated fictions about the tradeoff between physical and intellectual prowess. As a player and coach, Thompson was big, strong, and athletically talented, but also savvy, disciplined, and successful. His players excelled in the athletic arena and graduated at rates similar to if not higher than those of white students or Black players on white-coached teams. Thompson was criticized for many legitimate reasons. He was brusque. He rarely hesitated to chastise the media, conference officials, or the NCAA. He never apologized for his surly demeanor, his quick temper, or his policy stances. But the Hoyas coach was also criticized for the laziest of reasons; he was a Black man succeeding in elite college sports at a time when Black coaches were almost as a rare as minority athletic directors, NCAA officials, and sportswriters. Longtime radio talk show host Kojo Nnamdi, of Washington's public radio station WAMU, summarized the incredible pressures that Thompson faced. "When you become the first black coach with that kind of prominence, people subconsciously expect you to be Martin Luther King,"

John and Jimmy, Patrick and Michael

Nnamdi told Washington's *City Paper*. "They subconsciously feel that if you're prominent, then clearly you're going to be someone who is pleasant, someone who smooths the relationship between you and the media. John Thompson is not that kind of person. He was outspoken, he was brash, he was assertive. And I think a lot of people just didn't expect that."[16]

More Than a Haircut

Born and raised in Port Arthur, Texas, James William "Jimmy" Johnson came from a modest family. At Thomas Jefferson High School, Johnson was a decent student, but his physical talents won him a football scholarship to the University of Arkansas. A defensive end, Johnson was captain of the Arkansas Razorbacks his senior year and won a national championship in 1964. Perhaps most fatefully, Johnson befriended Razorbacks teammate and future millionaire businessman Jerry Jones. Years later, as owner of the Dallas Cowboys, Jones hired his former college teammate and lifelong friend to coach his then struggling NFL franchise.

Not talented enough to turn professional, Johnson began his coaching career immediately after graduating in 1965. Over the next fourteen years Johnson held seven assistant coaching jobs, including stints at Wichita State, the University of Oklahoma, and the University of Pittsburgh. For three years when Johnson was defensive coordinator at Oklahoma, his opposite at offensive coordinator was Barry Switzer, who two decades later replaced Johnson as the Dallas Cowboys' head coach.

In 1979 Johnson finally won his first head coaching position. At Oklahoma State University (OSU) in Stillwater, he turned around a middling program that the NCAA had recently placed on athletic probation. His first year at OSU, Johnson was named Big Eight Conference coach of the year. In a tough conference featuring perennial powerhouses Nebraska and Oklahoma, Johnson kept the OSU Cowboys competitive. But he never led them to a conference championship and through his first four seasons compiled a losing record and just one bowl bid, a loss to Texas A&M in the 1981 Independence Bowl.[17]

Fortunately for Johnson, his fifth and final season at OSU was his best. That Cowboys squad posted an 8-4 record, and their four losses were by a mere 12 points combined. In fact, the team's two best performances of the year were defeats. First OSU lost a 14–10 heartbreaker to a top-ranked Nebraska team that arrived in Stillwater after winning its first five games by an average margin of 58–11. That defeat was followed a week later by the Cowboys' 1-point home loss to fifteenth-ranked Oklahoma. Johnson's 1983 Cowboys finished the season with a victory over Baylor in the Bluebonnet Bowl and a respectable No. 18 national ranking.[18]

Johnson peaked at the perfect moment. After Howard Schnellenberger's surprise announcement that he was leaving Miami for the USFL, Schnellenberger recommended that University of Miami athletic director Sam Jankovich promote defensive coordinator Tom Olivadotti to head coach. A few days after Schnellenberger's announcement, Jankovich and Johnson were both in Dallas attending the annual College Football Association meetings. The two men struck up a conversation. Johnson and his wife enjoyed living in Pittsburgh when he was an assistant coach at Pitt, and he told Jankovich that he hoped to again coach for a big-city university. "To tell you the truth, I wouldn't mind leaving for the beach myself," Johnson hinted. After a ten-day search, the Hurricanes offered Johnson the job.[19]

Jankovich was lucky that Johnson was still available. Johnson had been actively seeking new opportunities in 1984 and interviewed for jobs at both the University of Arkansas and Rice University. According to *Tulsa World* columnist Bill Haisten, the reason Johnson was shopping himself around in early 1984—even to a dismal Rice program that had won just one of its twenty-two games the previous two seasons—was that OSU compensated him so poorly. But Arkansas and Rice hired other coaches. "Considering that Johnson was destined to become such a successful and renowned coach at both the college and NFL levels, it's remarkable that he didn't get the Rice job," Haisten wrote. "Instead, an extraordinary set of circumstances vaulted Johnson to his next chapter."[20]

When he first received Miami's offer, Johnson was still a bit unsure about whether to leave Stillwater for Coral Gables. He had a solid recruiting class that included future Pro Football Hall of Famer Thurman Thomas. Larry Lacewell, a longtime friend who coached with Johnson during their early years together as University of Oklahoma assistants, talked Johnson through the decision. Lacewell asked Johnson if his Oklahoma State Cowboys had ever beaten in-state rival Oklahoma. Nope. How about Big Eight powerhouse Nebraska? Nope. "Well, sooner or later, your fans are going to figure that out," Lacewell recalled telling Johnson. "And by the way, can you win a national championship at Oklahoma State? He just grinned. Well, they *just did* at Miami."[21] Johnson packed his bags and headed for South Florida.

Counting endorsement deals, the new position at Miami immediately doubled Johnson's salary. If the raise did not impose enough pressure, the forty-year-old knew he faced intense scrutiny taking over a program that had just won its first national title. His primary lament was that Miami hired him too late to supervise spring practice. To maintain continuity, Johnson retained six of Schnellenberger's nine coaching assistants. "Any time there are some changes, it's difficult," Johnson said of his new job. "When you go into a program with great success, they don't want to change things. But I'm here to make it as easy a transition as possible. Good things can happen, and good things are going to happen."[22]

Johnson quickly realized the bounty of talent available to him in what Schnellenberger called the "State of Miami" in the southern half of Florida. Schnellenberger's teams were more racially diverse than Hurricanes rosters of previous eras. But to compete nationally or even with powerful in-state rivals Florida and Florida State, Johnson recruited classes full of some of the state's most talent African Americans and Latino prep stars.

Sports historian and cultural critic Todd Boyd attributed Johnson's openness toward recruiting Black athletes to his experience in the 1970s coaching alongside and, later, against Barry Switzer. Like neighboring Nebraska, Oklahoma was the flagship university of a breadbasket state with an almost all-white citizenry.

Unlike the Nebraska teams of that era, Boyd explains, the Sooners were perceived as "more of a black team" because Switzer created an explosive "wishbone" offense at Oklahoma that featured Black players in the key skill positions of quarterback and running back, the most famous of whom was quarterback J. C. Watts.[23] As OU's defensive coordinator from 1970 to 1972, Johnson got a daily, first-hand look at Switzer's wishbone while coaching across the line of scrimmage from offensive coordinator Switzer. Switzer became OU head coach in 1973, the same year Johnson left to take the job as defensive coordinator at Arkansas. After Johnson became OSU's head coach in 1979, he and Switzer competed as Big Eight Conference rivals in what Oklahomans affectionately call the "Bedlam Series" between the state's top two football programs. It wasn't much of a rivalry. Johnson's Cowboys lost all five games to Switzer's offensive juggernaut by a combined score of 176 to 53.[24] The only close game was OSU's 21–20 loss in Johnson's fifth and final season in Stillwater. "I look at Jimmy Johnson and believe he had to be influenced by what he saw Switzer doing at Oklahoma when Jimmy coached against him at Oklahoma State," Boyd said.[25]

Long before they became notable head coaches in their own right, Tommy Tuberville and Ed Orgeron were young graduate assistants on Johnson's staff at Miami. The future head coach at Auburn University and U.S. senator from Alabama, Tuberville recalls Johnson's application of an unusual recruiting criterion. "He was really high on kids who played basketball," remembered Tuberville, saying that Johnson was convinced he could "find out more about a football player from watching him play basketball than anything."[26] Orgeron, who eventually led Louisiana State to the 2019 national championship, remembers learning a different maxim from Johnson; coaches set an example by how they handle the team's leaders and stars. "Coach your best players the hardest and the rest of the team will respect you," Orgeron said.[27]

Like Georgetown's John Thompson, Johnson defended his players, many of whom considered him Miami's first "Black" head coach. Johnson allowed players to express themselves. He rarely chided them for excessive on-field celebrations or intimidation tactics; in fact, he encouraged his players to use sportsmanship tactics to gain an edge over opponents. Johnson's humble beginnings allowed him to empathize with underprivileged Black players who grew up in challenging circumstances. He embraced Schnellenberger's "State of Miami" recruiting territoriality. As for the unusual racial dynamic of being a white coach of urban Black players, Johnson acted like the fun uncle rather than Schnellenberger's stern father figure.

Johnson had a particularly soft spot for one of the best college and pro players he ever coached, Michael Irvin, who starred at wide receiver both on Johnson's Hurricanes teams and later with Johnson's Super Bowl champion Dallas teams. In his autobiography, *Turning the Thing Around*, Johnson stated that to truly understand Irvin's demonstrative style on the field, one had to realize that he was the fifteenth of seventeen children and that his father died right before he started college. Irvin dedicated his career to his father and finished his business degree in four years. "But in 1986, all that America knew was that we had a lot of flamboyant players . . . and that we had a lot of black players out front, many of whom tended to be demonstrative." Johnson further explained what motivated "Mike" Irvin, as he called him during his Hurricanes playing days, to act the way he did:

> If you watched my Miami teams play on television, you may recall how, after catching touchdown passes in home games at the Orange Bowl, Mike would run right up into the lower end zone seats, pointing a finger at fans seated there. Just watching on TV, you might think, "What a hot dog!" But the truth is that that group, which was ethnically diverse, turned out especially to see Mike play. And when he pointed at each of them, he would look them in the eyes individually and they knew that the gesture meant, "This is for you, and you, and you, and you, and you, and you . . ."[28]

Irvin behaved the way he did because of who he was and where he came from, something perhaps not immediately obvious to viewing audiences or white fans from more affluent backgrounds.

After a topsy-turvy and disappointing first year, during John-son's final four seasons at Miami the Hurricanes simply domi-nated. The 'Canes went 44-4, finished each season ranked in the top ten, won the 1987 title, and came within two narrow defeats of sandwiching that championship between two more in 1986 and 1988. Johnson's teams featured star athletes including Bernie Kosar, Steve Walsh, and Vinny Testaverde, the program's first Heisman Trophy winner. During Johnson's five-year tenure, Miami partici-pated in some of college football history's most memorable games. The team's losses include two 2-point stunners against Maryland and Boston College in the 1984 season, the upset defeat by Penn State in the first true national championship game, ending the Hurricanes' 1986 season, and the controversy-filled "Catholics v. Convicts" game against Notre Dame in 1988. Johnson's most mem-orable victories were as glorious as the defeats were debilitating. These included humiliating Notre Dame 58–7; pegging eventual national champion Oklahoma with its sole loss during the 1985 season; coming from behind to beat Florida State 26–25 in 1987; shutting out the top-ranked Seminoles 31–0 shutout in the rivals' season opener the next year; winning consecutive Orange Bowl victories over Nebraska to finish the 1987 and 1988 campaigns; and, of course, defeating Oklahoma 20–14 in the Orange Bowl to cap off the Hurricanes' second—and first undefeated—national championship season.

During his five years at the helm, Johnson was a frequent tar-get for opposing fans and media critics. He took heat for running up the scores in games, particularly the 1985 pummeling of Notre Dame and Miami's pasting of Nebraska in the 1989 Orange Bowl. In the waning minutes of the 58–7 win over Notre Dame, John-son attempted to block an Irish punt and called a reverse play on offense. Rarely do players angrily approach opposing coaches after a game, but Irish quarterback Terry Andrysiak did just that. "Those guys don't have any class," Andrysiak told the media after the game. "I told their coach that."[29] After beating the 'Huskers 23–3 in the Orange Bowl, Johnson again took fire for trying to embarrass the opposition. "I don't understand people and they obviously don't understand me," he replied. "How can anyone criticize me or the team for playing hard for 60 minutes? We were not trying to embarrass anyone. We're just going to run our offense until the end of the game, like it or not."[30] *New York Times* sportswriter Peter Alfano described Johnson's image after five years in Coral Gables: "He has . . . become one of the more controversial coaches in the country, accused of, among other things, lacking tact and running up scores. Johnson, though, appears unaffected by the notoriety. His teams win, and, more important, he is apparently respected and well-liked by his players."[31] Alfano could not know that Johnson's Orange Bowl victory a few days earlier would be his final game on the Hurricanes sidelines. Eight weeks later, Johnson left Miami for Dallas.

Johnson took it as a compliment to be described as a players' coach who identified readily with his charges. But because he allowed his players to express themselves, Johnson was routinely criticized as being a permissive coach who ran a loose program and turned a blind eye to his players' off-the-field transgressions. Johnson mostly ignored these criticisms. He believed the uglier side of Miami's national image was a feature, not a bug. Amid all the controversy surrounding the 1987 Fiesta Bowl against Penn State—his players showing up in camouflage, their staged walkout during the pregame banquet—Johnson touted the benefits of being associated with Miami's rogue image: "I think people see the 'Miami Vice' TV program and the crime it depicts in South Florida and tend to associate it with us. I think it's the finest place in the country to live. We joke about it, saying we're glad we have that image in South Florida, because it keeps people from moving that way."[32] When in Miami, do as the Miamians do.

Although Johnson embraced the program's bad-boy image and turned criticisms into motivation for himself and his players, he eventually harbored a few grudges. After winning the national title in 1987, Johnson expressed relief and a bit of spite that he could finally stick it to his growing legion of detractors. "When people throw stones at our football team, whether it has been at me, or others, we all hurt," Johnson said during the postgame press conference. "And they've been hurt for the last three or four years, like I've been hurt for the last three or four years. This makes the hurt a little better than it was three hours ago."[33]

By the time he bolted Coral Gables for Dallas, Johnson had groomed several notable assistants for their own coaching careers. In addition to Tuberville and Orgeron, two of Johnson's most notable protégés were his defensive coordinator Dave Wannstedt and defensive line coach Butch Davis. Both followed Johnson to the NFL in 1989 to serve as his assistants on the Dallas Cowboys' staff, and both later became NFL head coaches of their own teams. If there is a blemish on Johnson's resume at Miami, it is how few minority assistant coaches he kept on his sidelines. The lone African American on the Hurricanes' bench during the Johnson era, tight ends and wide receivers coach Hubbard Alexander, was a holdover from Schnellenberger's staff. Johnson also brought Alexander along with him to Dallas.[34]

After nearly winning the national championship three years in a row, Johnson decided to make the leap to the NFL to coach for his former college pal, Dallas Cowboys owner Jerry Jones. Johnson arrived in Dallas to find the team on life support. His first year, the team went 1-15. The next year, the Cowboys improved to 7-9 and Johnson was named NFL coach of the year. In his third season, Johnson led the Cowboys to the playoffs. Dallas won the Super Bowl during his fourth and fifth years, making him the first coach in history to win an NCAA title and a Super Bowl.

Johnson's four-year stint coaching the Miami Dolphins was far less successful, but in 2020 Johnson was named to the NFL Hall of Fame's centennial class. He learned of the honor from Hall of Fame president David Baker during the live broadcast of an NFL playoff game. "The only thing I can think of is all of the assistant coaches that worked for me, all the great players that played for me. They're the reason I'm here," Johnson told Baker. "I can't talk. This is so special."[35]

Always a big personality, Johnson has appeared in a few small TV roles, including an episode of *The Shield*, plus two cameos playing himself in the Adam Sandler movies *The Waterboy* and

Funny People.[36] He is a TV fixture as an NFL analyst for *Fox Sports.* His hair is grayer than it was during his glory days coaching in Coral Gables, but Johnson's signature bangs and broad grin are the same as ever.

The Intimidator

The New Orleans Superdome, March 29, 1982. Georgetown and North Carolina faced off in the national championship game played before the largest in-person basketball audience ever assembled to that point. By the time the fans in attendance and the millions watching at home made it to the second TV timeout, anyone previously unfamiliar with the impact freshman center sensation Patrick Ewing could have on a game recognized what an commanding presence he was.

Ewing won the opening tip-off. He scored the first points of the game on a baseline jumper. He collected the game's first rebound. Tar Heels star forward and national player of the year James Worthy took his first shot of the game, a 12-foot jumper from the elbow, but Ewing snagged the ball as it descended toward the basket—goaltending. After a Ewing blocked shot, the Hoyas scored twice more, including a banked-in layup by Ewing. North Carolina broke the Georgetown full-court press and Michael Jordan and Matt Doherty had a two-on-one against Ewing, but rather than head to the hoop and confront Ewing they pulled the ball out and waited to set up the offense. Eventually Worthy took a pass in the lane and tried a one-handed floater from six feet away. Ewing swatted the ball away in front of the rim—goaltending, again.

On UNC's next possession, Jordan collected a rebound underneath the basket and went up to score. But Ewing's long reach forced Jordan to switch to his left hand to shoot, and Jordan missed. A few plays later Jordan took a pass from point guard Jimmy Black and from the same spot on the left block tried to bank in a lay-up that Ewing slapped away after it hit the backboard—another goaltending. Down 12–6, the Tar Heels worked the ball into the paint, this time to center Sam Perkins. Ewing blocked Perkins's first attempt, but Perkins collected the ball and shot again, only to have Ewing goaltend yet again. Seven minutes into the final, the Tar Heels had eight points on four field goals, but remarkably, none of North Carolina's shots actually passed through the net.

Ewing's repeated violations were not a case of freshman nerves overtaking him. Hoyas coach John Thompson instructed Ewing to goaltend in the opening moments of the game as a way to establish his presence inside and intimidate the preseason and consensus No. 1 Tar Heels. Georgetown lost the game in the dramatic final moments forever remembered for Jordan's game-winning jump shot and Fred Brown's turnover. Yet the opening seven minutes, dominated by Ewing, were equally memorable. He blocked, altered, and changed shots. He rebounded, scored, and intimidated.

The 1981–82 season was just the tenth since the NCAA first permitted Division I freshmen football and basketball players to participate. In years to come—especially as players began to leave early for the NBA, often after just one season—outstanding freshman performances in the Final Four became more common. Louisville's Pervis Ellison in 1986, Syracuse's Carmelo Anthony in 2003, Kentucky's Anthony Davis in 2012, and Duke's Tyus Jones in 2015 all won tournament Most Outstanding Player (MOP) honors as freshmen. Ewing did not win MOP in 1982, though he might have if Georgetown had beaten North Carolina. But Ewing accomplished something greater; he set the standard for freshman dominance in the Final Four. Those opening few minutes against UNC were his breakout moment on the national stage.

Patrick Ewing is the greatest player in the history of Georgetown basketball. He scored 2,184 points and shot an eye-popping 62 percent from the field during his Hoyas career. Ewing set school records with 1,316 rebounds and 480 blocked shots—records he still holds. Along with Merlin Wilson, he is the only Hoyas player to lead the team in rebounding all four years wearing the gray and blue, and only Eric "Sleepy" Floyd scored more points than Ewing in Georgetown history.[37] Ewing was named Big East player of the year twice and is the only player in conference history to win defensive player of the year each of his four seasons. He led the Hoyas to the national championship game in three of those four seasons, and in his junior season Georgetown won the national championship. In his senior year, Ewing won two national player of the year awards and was later drafted first overall by the New York Knicks in the 1985 NBA draft.

Ewing never played basketball until he arrived in the United States from Jamaica, but a teaching mentor named Steve Jenkins introduced the sport to the 6-foot sixth grader. Ewing developed quickly and within six years emerged as the nation's top high school player. He starred at Cambridge's Rindge and Latin High School, which he led to a 77-1 record and three straight Massachusetts Division 1 boys' state titles in 1979, 1980, and 1981. His senior year, Ewing was voted Mr. Basketball USA and was universally regarded by scouts and college coaches as the nation's most coveted prep prospect.[38] He was so good that he was invited as a prep player to try out for the 1980 U.S. Olympic basketball team. Ewing failed to make the roster, but was among the last players cut from the team that never participated in the Moscow games the United States boycotted.[39]

Ewing's coach Mike Jarvis was a key figure in Boston basketball circles for almost two decades. A Cambridge native and Rindge and Latin alum, Jarvis stayed near home to play college ball for Northeastern University, then served as an assistant coach at Northeastern and later at nearby Harvard University. Jarvis left the college ranks to return to his prep alma mater to coach Ewing. In what he later explained was an attempt to reduce the frenzy surrounding Ewing's college recruitment, Jarvis formed a group that included Ewing, his parents, and Steve Jenkins to help steer his star center through the process.[40] Although Ewing visited 6 schools, including UCLA, Villanova, and North Carolina, he soon narrowed his decision to 3 finalists: nearby Boston College and Boston University, plus Georgetown. Jarvis created a stir with the so-called "Ewing letter" sent to the 150 schools recruiting Ewing during his senior year.

At a press conference held at Satch's restaurant in Boston, the shy Ewing announced his decision to attend Georgetown with four simple words: "I have chosen Georgetown." *Washington Post* sportswriter John Feinstein noted: "Those words represented a quantum leap for Georgetown and Thompson. They moved the Jesuit private school, the oldest Catholic institution of higher learning in the nation, from the pack to the upper strata of college basketball."[41]

Thompson prohibited media from talking to freshmen players until January of their first year. Frustrated reporters had to write stories without access to Ewing. Finally, on New Year's Day, 1982, the *Washington Post's* Michael Wilbon published a story that included excerpts from a one-on-one interview with Ewing on the flight back from a holiday tournament in Rochester, New York, that the Hoyas just won. The long-silent Ewing made clear how he felt about the recruiting controversy the previous spring and the whispered insults about his intelligence: "I don't understand why people who have never met me, or don't know anything about me, say I am dumb. I am not dumb. If I was, I would have gone to one of the other schools that offered me all kinds of things. If I was dumb, I would have gone to a school only because of basketball." Ewing also told Wilbon that he remained focused on his studies and improving as a basketball player, but often felt a tinge of homesickness and just wanted to "be treated like any other student."[42]

The on-court realities of Ewing's new life as a freshman superstar, however, precluded him from being treated like most other basketball players, much less "any other" student. Thompson was protective of all his players. But Ewing's stardom and the unique ways in which opponents and fans taunted him during his freshman year required his coach to pay special attention to his 7-foot-tall prodigy. Thompson mostly kept the media away from him, and even when Ewing spoke to reporters he kept his answers and interviews short. During his freshman year the team routinely taped Ewing's interactions with reporters—a practice that the Hoyas claimed was utilized to improve the Ewing's media interactions, but was likely also done to ensure that reporters did not misquote him.

A week after the *Washington Post* article appeared, *New York Times* sportswriter Malcom Moran interviewed Ewing alongside

Thompson in the coach's McDonough Hall office. Thompson assured the reporter that team media policies had not changed since he had arrived at Georgetown a decade earlier. Moran pushed back a bit in the story he wrote, noting that Hoyas players just a few years earlier were allowed to conduct solo interviews with the media. Moran also realized some topics were clearly off the table. "When Ewing was asked how his classes were going—not his grades, just how he had adjusted to college courses and if he enjoyed them—he politely shook his head and apologized for not being able to discuss the subject," Moran wrote. "He turned to look at [Thompson,] who explained that asking Ewing about his classes was an invasion of privacy, similar to asking someone how much money he made."[43] At the end of his freshman year, Ewing was voted Big East rookie of the year and defensive player of the year. He averaged 12.7 points, 7.5 rebounds, and 3.2 blocked shots per game and led the Hoyas to within one point of winning the national championship.[44]

On the court, Ewing manifested a tough yet taciturn personality. He rarely smiled. He nursed grudges about how he was treated and covered. To the media and outside observers, Ewing was a distant, enigmatic, and unapproachable figure. Thompson once mocked reporters for being too intimidated to ask Ewing questions during postgame press conferences. To those who knew him off the court, however, Ewing was very different. He was somewhat shy but also expressive. Ewing liked art, especially drawing. By his senior year, Ewing began painting, "landscapes mainly, because it's a challenge to try and capture how real they are."[45]

After a freshman year full of insults and taunting, Ewing became a different sort of target his sophomore season. In an effort to limit Ewing's impact, teams collapsed their defenses around him. They double- and sometimes even tripled-team him in the paint and routinely bumped, shouldered, and elbowed the tall but willowy center to disrupt him. These tactics worked. Ewing's sophomore year was the only season during which he shot less than 60 percent from the field.[46] After a notably physical conference game against Big East rival St. John's, Thompson finally blew his top, threatening to advise Ewing to declare himself eligible for the NBA draft after just two seasons and creating a media stir. *New York Times* columnist George Vecsey wrote that Thompson's words "left a bad impression," given that Georgetown had so regularly touted the importance of its players finishing their college degrees and had specifically promised Ewing's mother that her son would complete his education. Vecsey admitted, however, that Ewing was a special case because of the rough treatment he endured, and that as his "trusted mentor" Thompson had "earned the right to advise" Ewing to do what was best for him.[47]

A bulkier and more mature Ewing dominated his final two seasons at Georgetown. In addition to winning the 1984 national title and reaching the title game again in 1985, Ewing racked up almost every award and honor available. By the time he graduated, Ewing was the most decorated player in Big East Conference history. In all four years, he won the Big East defensive player of the year award. He was twice named Big East player of the year, selected for the all-conference team three times, and was a two-time Big East tournament most outstanding player. When the Big East dissolved in 2012, a *Bleacher Report* ranking of the top twenty players in conference history rated Ewing first.[48] Nationally, Ewing won the Naismith and Rupp Trophies, was selected a consensus All-American three times, thrice earned NCAA tournament all-tourney team honors, and won the tournament's most outstanding player award the year Georgetown captured its national championship.[49] With the possible exception of Duke's Christian Laettner, Patrick Ewing boasts the most storied four-year college career since the advent of freshman eligibility.

Ewing spent most of his seventeen-year NBA career starring for the Knicks, a franchise that drafted him with the hope of restoring the club's early-1970s glory days. Ewing led the Knicks once to the NBA finals. Nine years after losing to Ewing in the 1985 NCAA title game, 1994 NBA finals MVP Hakeem Olajuwon got revenge when his Houston Rockets beat the Knicks in seven games. Ewing averaged a double-double for the series, with 18.9 points and 12.4 rebounds (plus 4.3 blocks) per game. But he shot just 36 percent from the field.[50] An eleven-time All-Star, member of the 1992 "Dream Team" that won an Olympic gold medal in Barcelona, and selection to the NBA's all-time fifty greatest players team, Patrick Ewing was elected to the Naismith Memorial Basketball Hall of Fame in 2008. He thanked the coaches who taught him from grade school through the NBA. "Thanks for letting me come to Georgetown a boy and leaving a man," he said to John Thompson, who was in the audience. "It was the best four years of my life."[51]

Patrick Ewing's astounding college career rates among those of the great centers who came before him, including Wilt Chamberlain, Lew Alcindor, and Bill Walton. Unfortunately for him, Ewing's college career ended on a sour note. He and the Hoyas suffered the shocking upset loss to Big East foe Villanova in the 1985 title game. The Wildcats played an almost perfect game, making 90 percent of their field goal attempts in the second half. Had the heavily favored Hoyas beaten Villanova, a team they had defeated twice previously that year, Georgetown would have been the first repeat champion since UCLA. The day before that memorable championship upset, Villanova head coach Rollie Massimino was asked about Ewing's impact on the court. "He is an intimidator," Massimino said. "And not in a negative way. It's just that when it comes down to deciding who's going to win and lose in the last four minutes, he's involved in every single play."[52]

The Playmaker

In retrospect, Michael Irvin was a longshot to become a star collegiate and professional athlete. Born into extraordinarily difficult circumstances—the fifteenth of seventeen kids—Irvin was still in high school when his father died, just three days before the start of his senior year. Irvin did not play football his junior year; he only practiced with the team. When his father died, Irvin considered quitting football, but his mother and head football coach George Smith at Fort Lauderdale's St. Aquinas High School encouraged Irvin to persevere. Before he passed away, Irvin's father asked Smith to take care of his son. He agreed. "When I lost my dad, Coach Smith really did become my father," recalled Irvin decades later when he returned to watch his son, Michael Irvin II, play football for St. Aquinas. "There's no way I would be here if it wasn't for that man."[53] Irvin won a scholarship to play for the nearby University of Miami, where won a national championship before embarking on a successful professional career during which he won three Super Bowls with the Dallas Cowboys, was a five-time Pro Bowl selection, and capped his career by being elected to the Pro Football Hall of Fame in 2007.

Perhaps having sixteen brothers and sisters instilled in Irvin his assertiveness and bombast. Whatever their origins, Irvin drew attention almost from the moment he set foot on campus in Coral Gables. During this very first day of his freshman season at Miami, Irvin got into a scrap with an upperclassman who played on Miami's offensive line. Team protocols mandated that freshmen wait until veteran players got first crack at the team's training buffet. When Irvin tried to jump ahead of one lineman, the upperclassman told him he had to wait. Irvin initially complied. But the upperclassman continued to hold up the line while a hungry Irvin waited. Irvin, who admitted years later that the "had never seen food like" the team's buffet, decided he would wait no longer. "All the ghetto came out of me," he remembered. "I took the tray, smashed it across [the lineman's] head. He fell. I hit him and started punching him. They took me to Coach Johnson's office. I'm a freshman and I got in a fight the first day."[54]

Johnson and his coaching staff soon realized that Irvin fought just as hard on the field. He caught 46 passes his freshman year, 9 of them for touchdowns, earning him freshman All-American honors.[55] His 840 receiving yards also set Miami's freshman record, a mark he held until 2016.[56] In his sophomore year, Irvin caught a career-best 11 touchdowns. "People may not have understood what a terrific worker Michael was," Butch Davis, a Miami assistant during Irvin's career, recalled in a video tribute commemorating Irvin's 2007 induction into the Miami Sports Hall of Fame. "He was just a tireless practice player . . . I've seen Michael streaming wet in the middle of those hot summer afternoons in South Florida in his preparation for those big games he was going to play in the fall."[57]

Documentarian Billy Corben interviewed Irvin at length for *The U*, his two-part ESPN 30 for 30 series film about the Hurricanes. The way Irvin spoke about his relationship with coach Jimmy Johnson continued to resonate with Corben. "Michael Irvin talking about how vulnerable he was when he came to Miami—how he had lost his father, how they misunderstood his touchdown celebrations," Corben recalled, citing how Irvin routinely shot his pointer fingers toward the sky after big plays not to boast that he was number one, but instead to pay tribute to his deceased father. Johnson filled a vacuum. "Jimmy became the male role model for Michael. The bond between them was something I always thought deserved more explanation."[58]

Irvin made a lot of finger-pointing big plays for the Hurricanes, but two touchdown catches his junior year were vital to Miami's 1987 national title run. Against in-state rival Florida State in an October 3 matchup of two undefeated teams with more than five dozen future NFL players on their combined rosters, Irvin helped save Miami's championship hopes by leading one of the most storied comebacks in Hurricanes history. Like Miami, in the 1980s the Bobby Bowden–coached Seminoles were a program on the rise. The Hurricanes arrived at Tallahassee's Doak Campbell Stadium in October 1987 ranked third; the Seminoles ranked fourth. In effect, the game was one of two unofficial national semifinals for the NCAA title. The other came in November when Big Eight rivals Nebraska and Oklahoma—both undefeated and ranked first and second, respectively—squared off in Lincoln. Unless any of these four top-ranked teams lost to some other opponent, the Miami-FSU winner would face the Nebraska-Oklahoma winner to play for the national championship in January. (Oklahoma beat Nebraska, 17–7.)

The Hurricanes got off to a dismal start. In front of their home fans, FSU opened a 19–3 lead thanks to a swarming defense and an offense led by Seminoles quarterback Danny McManus and running back Sammie Smith. After Miami's dispiriting loss in the title against Penn State in the final game of the 1986 season, Miami was on the verge of blowing its title chances just four weeks into the 1987 season. At one point during the game, Seminoles All-American cornerback Deion "Neon" Sanders, who spent a good part of the day covering Irvin, told Irvin to just give up. "Michael, you might as well quit running so hard and blocking so hard, 'cause it's all over for today," Sanders advised. "Oh, no. We play Hurricane football all day," Irvin replied. "We're going to keep balling all day."[59]

Poor Steve Walsh, Miami's sophomore quarterback, had the herculean task of trying to rally the Hurricanes in the second half. That task was a microcosm of Walsh's entire season, during which he had the unenviable job of replacing Miami's departed Heisman Trophy winner Vinny Testaverde. Walsh later admitted that he threw up before most games that year. He was something of an outsider. A native of St. Paul, Minnesota, he played high school football a long way from the famed "State of Miami" recruiting triangle that delivered so many superstars to The U.

Walsh had a strong second half. On consecutive possessions, he found wide receiver Brian Blades for a late third-quarter touchdown and Irvin for another early in the fourth quarter. With two 2-point conversions, the 'Canes tied the game, 19–19. Then came Irvin's highlight-reel play on third down with 7 yards to go from Miami's 27-yard line, with the score still tied at 19 and 2:32 to play.

Irvin lined up wide right. The play sent to Walsh from the Miami bench called for an "out," a short pass route in which Irvin would run 10 yards, turn toward the near sideline, catch the ball, and most likely be pushed out of bounds after gaining enough yardage for a first down to keep the drive alive. To understand what happened instead, one must first understand what kind of teammate Irvin was. In a show of solidarity designed to bolster the confidence of his inexperienced quarterback, the poor Black kid from South Florida went to Minnesota during the 1986 summer offseason to train with Walsh. "I spent that whole summer, I moved to Minnesota with [him]," recalled Irvin. "I said, 'We will train together all summer long to prepare for this season.'" By fall, Irvin and Walsh had worked out a set of hand signals to use during the games to

John and Jimmy, Patrick and Michael

call audibles at the line of scrimmage based on whatever formation opposing defenses showed.[60]

When Irvin got to the line of scrimmage, he saw two things. First, Martin Mayhew—not FSU's coverage specialist, Deion Sanders—was covering him. Second, Seminoles safety Dedrick Dodge was lined up too shallow in the middle of the field to provide deep cover if Irvin could get past Mayhew. So Irvin gave Walsh a hand signal, and Walsh called an audible for Irvin to run a deep, straight route down the sideline rather than the 10-yard out. Irvin took a quick stutter step, then bolted downfield. Walsh hit Irvin in stride behind Mayhew, and Dodge arrived too late to catch up. The spectacular 73-yard catch-and-run completed 23 unanswered Miami points.

The 26–25 win over Florida State, sealed when FSU missed a 2-point conversion after a late touchdown, preserved the Hurricanes' undefeated record and eventually put Miami rather than FSU in the Orange Bowl to face Oklahoma. In the third quarter of that championship game, Irvin caught a 23-yard touchdown pass from Walsh for what turned out to be the game-winning score in Miami's 20–14 victory over the first-ranked and undefeated Sooners. In the two biggest games of the Hurricanes' championship season, Irvin had the two biggest catches.

Michael Irvin's career ranks among the best in the Hurricanes' program, which has included two Heisman Trophy winners and a battalion of future NFL players. In his three seasons at wide receiver at Miami before skipping his senior year to turn pro, Irvin caught 143 passes, including 26 touchdowns.[61] He won first-team All-American honors his sophomore year and second-team All-American honors his junior year. His penchant for big plays and his 16.9 average yards per catch earned him the nickname "The Playmaker."

Irvin was, of course, a notably demonstrative player on the field who was instrumental in creating the The U's swaggering image. He chirped incessantly on the field and off, often about his own greatness. In an August 2019 interview with Miami sports talk host Joe Rose of WQAM, Irvin was asked which player most personified

Miami's bombastic reputation. Irvin rattled off a few player names, then paused. He told Rose, "I'm going to tell you the ultimate person that comes to mind really—it's Jimmy Johnson. Jimmy Johnson said to us and me, 'Everybody's talking about *how* we play. I don't worry about that. As long as you win, I'll answer all those questions. You have fun and win, I'll take that pressure. As long as you win—as long as you win—I'll worry about that.' That gave you the freedom, the freedom to have that swag."[62]

Irvin's work ethic and commitment to the program continued after he left. During his junior year, Miami was recruiting Lamar Thomas, a talented receiver from Gainesville. As Bruce Feldman recounted in *'Cane Mutiny,* Thomas was leaning toward signing with the University of North Carolina and had lined up his visit to Chapel Hill. But Irvin called Thomas and told him to forget UNC and come visit him in Coral Gables. Irvin promised Thomas he would mentor him. A suitably impressed Thomas signed with the 'Canes instead of UNC. After Irvin turned pro, he kept his promise to Thomas. Irvin called the freshman repeatedly, encouraging him and providing tips on how to disguise his routes from defenders. Thomas said that Irvin talked a lot about himself during those calls—some things never change—but that he still drew inspiration from Irvin's weekly check-ins. "I enjoyed it because I knew he'd call every week and I knew I had to do something spectacular to keep up with the wide-receiver tradition," said Thomas, who proceeded to break Irvin's Hurricanes career receiving-yards record.[63]

Irvin's twelve-year professional career with the Cowboys exceeded his college exploits. A favorite target of Dallas quarterback Troy Aikman, Irvin helped the Cowboys win three Super Bowls in a four-year span. In the first, Super Bowl XXVII against the Buffalo Bills, Irvin caught six passes for 118 yards and 2 touchdowns. Remarkably, his 2 touchdowns came just 18 seconds apart. Irvin caught the first and, after Bills running back Thurman Thomas fumbled the ball away on the first play from scrimmage after the kickoff, Aikman found Irvin again. Irvin retired as the franchise's leader in receptions, reception yards, and touchdowns. He earned Pro Bowl honors five times.

Both during and after his playing career, Michael Irvin became ensnared in plenty of off-the-field problems. At Miami Irvin allegedly ran over the toes of two students with his car. In Dallas he faced serious accusations that included drug abuse, weapons possession, and sexual harassment. In 1999 he, a Cowboys teammate, and two topless dancers were caught in an Irving, Texas, motel room with cocaine and marijuana. The episode led to rumors of the married Irvin's repeated infidelities in hotel rooms or at the so-called "White House" not far from the Cowboys' practice facility where players routinely consorted with women. Irvin allegedly tried to intimidate one such woman, and her husband, a Dallas police officer, found out. The officer was later arrested when the hit man he hired to kill Irvin turned out to be an undercover informant.[64] Irvin found trouble and trouble found him.

Irvin had to sit out five games the following NFL season. While still on legal probation, he was accused of holding a gun to another woman's head while teammate Erik Williams and another man raped her in Williams's home. The woman later recanted her story, but Irvin appeared too often to be in the wrong place at the wrong time, making some bad and sometimes illegal choices. His reputation and his marriage both suffered. He spent the ensuing years cleaning himself up and trying to make amends. Under the stewardship of Pastor T. D. Jakes, Irvin found God and discovered his spiritual side.

Through it all, Irvin has been surprisingly forthright about his personal failings. His public humility makes him difficult to dislike. Crying sporadically during his 2007 Hall of Fame induction speech, Irvin addressed the personal problems he confronted during his career. "You know, the Bible speaks of a healing place. It's called a threshing floor. The threshing floor is where you take your greatest fear and you pray for help from your great God," he said, before asking his two young sons, then ages eight and ten, to stand up in the audience. He pointed to them:

That's my heart right there. That's my heart. When I am on that threshing floor, I pray. I say, "God, I have my struggles and I made some bad decisions, but whatever you do, whatever you do, don't let me mess this up." I say, "Please, help me raise them for some young lady so that they can be a better husband than I. Help me raise them for their kids so that they could be a better father than I." And I tell you guys to always do the right thing so you can be a better role model than dad.[65]

Irvin upheld his pledge to be a role model in 2011 in an unusual way. He appeared without a shirt on the cover of an *Out* magazine issue focused on gay professional athletes. Irvin told *Out* he realized at age twelve that one of his older brothers was gay. Consequently, he later admitted that during his younger years he felt a need to affirm his own heterosexuality by projecting the image of a ladies' man. Irvin now believes that the NFL is overdue for an openly gay player. In the *Out* article, he discussed the long-whispered rumors that former Cowboys teammate Troy Aikman was gay by saying that he did not believe Aikman was, but that Irvin would have supported his teammate if he were. Irvin drew a direct line between the long struggle by African Americans to achieve equality and that of gay Americans. "I don't see how any African-American with any inkling of history can say that you don't have the right to live your life how you want to live your life," he told *Out*'s Cyd Zeigler. "When we start talking about equality and everybody being treated equally, I don't want to know an African-American who will say everybody doesn't deserve equality." Irvin added that "if anyone [came] out" as gay in the four major North American professional team sports, he would "absolutely support him."[66] Perhaps Irvin's redemptive nature and good deeds have paid dividends already. In 2019 he survived a brief throat cancer scare.

Two decades after his Hurricanes and Cowboys playing days ended, Irvin remains the same big personality he was from that first episode at the Miami training table his freshman year in Coral Gables. He is a provocative analyst on the NFL Network's *Gameday*

Morning Sunday pregame show. He has appeared in three movies, including as a player on the prison football team in Adam Sandler's remake of *The Longest Yard*. Partnered with professional Russian dancer Anna Demidova, in 2009 Irvin made it through seven rounds before being eliminated on ABC's hit series *Dancing with the Stars*.[67] He was over the moon when his namesake son, Michael Irvin II, signed in 2015 to play tight end for the Hurricanes.

Irvin's most notable film turn has to be his art-imitates-life role in the 2017 movie *Slamma Jamma*. Irvin plays a former basketball player with a troubled history. "I read the script and I loved it," he told an interviewer. "The movie is about a player who gets arrested, goes to jail and tries to get his life back. I'm telling you, I escaped that fate by the hair of my chin."[68]

Champions, All

None were born to special circumstance, but each was gifted at birth with rare physical talent. None balked at public controversy, but each promoted racial equality for minority college athletes. None wilted under the intense scrutiny that attends fame, and all earned championship rings and Hall of Fame distinction. John Thompson and Jimmy Johnson, Patrick Ewing and Michael Irvin—during the 1980s these four men left indelible marks on Georgetown University and the University of Miami, as well as on major-college men's football and basketball.

Thompson and Johnson aggressively recruited African American prep athletes and groomed them for excellence and superstardom. Their coaching philosophies and methods differed, but their core assumptions about how to mentor young Black student athletes were similar and equally successful. Both men coached in the college ranks for more than two decades, but the arcs of their careers differed dramatically. Thompson jumped directly from prep school coaching to head coach at Georgetown University, where he spent his entire collegiate career before he retired from coaching. Thompson is associated exclusively with the blue and gray, the Hoyas, and Georgetown's bulldog mascot. Johnson, by contrast, was an itinerant coach moving from one opportunity to the next. Each man claimed a first. Thompson became the first African American coach to win a Division I NCAA title in any sport; Johnson became the first head coach to win a Division I NCAA title and a Super Bowl ring.

Ewing and Irvin led their college teams to championships and set university records in the process. Both capped their All-American collegiate performances with Hall of Fame pro careers. Their collegiate stardom burdened them with a heightened scrutiny born of that era's racialized expectations. Ewing was a regular victim of the laziest and most racist dumb-Black-jock tropes. Critics described his physical, intimidating style of play as menacing, even goon-like. Irvin was lambasted for his demonstrative celebratory antics—behaviors that evinced his underprivileged background, yet were routinely mischaracterized as unsportsmanlike boasting.

All four men's actions, opinions, and style—which routinely offended critics at the time—are considered mainstream behaviors by today's standards. In that regard, college sports adapted to and accommodated them, rather than the reverse. It's impossible to measure precisely how much influence these two coaches and two athletes had. With the benefit of three decades' hindsight, however, it's clear that their methods and manners ultimately won the day. During their glory years at Georgetown and Miami, John Thompson, Jimmy Johnson, Patrick Ewing, and Michael Irvin celebrated their share of winning days, too.

John and Jimmy, Patrick and Michael

[6]

Commodifying Color

Fear is what made Georgetown memorable. . . . But the fear,
back then, had as much to do with race as hoops.

—MIKE DEBONIS, sportswriter

It wasn't that I hated Miami so much as they seemed to exist
on a plane beyond my comprehension.

—MICHAEL WEINREB, sports historian

A half-billion-dollar payout. That's how much the NCAA dis-
tributed to participating football programs and conferences
in April 2015, three months after Ohio State won the NCAA's first-
ever Division I men's College Football Playoff (CFP) championship. The disbursement represented a nearly 70 percent increase
over the $300 million that participating schools received the previ-
ous year, when Florida State won the title in the final game played
under the expiring Bowl Championship Series (BCS) format. A
record 33.4 million viewers watched the Ohio State–Oregon title
game, smashing the previous bowl-game TV-ratings record.[1] After
decades of institutional resistance to replacing the traditional bowl
system, the NCAA's inaugural four-team playoff proved to be as
lucrative as long-time playoff proponents predicted. The NCAA
finally had a football playoff to rival the excitement, viewership,

and revenues of its popular and profitable "March Madness" basketball showcase.[2]

The week before the NCAA announced the record-setting revenues from its 2015 CFP playoff, the Duke Blue Devils beat the Wisconsin Badgers to claim the their fifth men's basketball title in twenty-five years. A thirty-second ad during the championship game cost $1.55 million, more than five times the price of spots during the most popular television show at the time, CBS's sitcom *The Big Bang Theory*.[3] The 2015 tourney generated $1.2 billion in advertising revenues, closing out a ten-year run during which the NCAA's ad revenue haul from the tournament totaled $8.2 billion, plus merchandise sales and other receipts. In fact, the three-week NCAA tourney now rakes in more money than the NBA's two-month playoff and ranks second in total season advertising revenues only to the NFL among all North American sports enterprises, college or professional.[4]

The success of these billion-dollar sporting events depends in no small part on the fact that modern viewership is far more racially inclusive thanks to rapid integration of Division I basketball and football programs during the late 1970s and 1980s. Although the racial changes in rosters were partly motivated by legal pressure and norms of inclusion, the primary reason for the rapid integration of major-college sports was money. The bigger the audiences and the more consumers, the easier it became for universities, conferences, and the NCAA to sign TV deals, ink corporate sponsorships, and sell merchandise.

Sportswriter Dave Zirin offered a useful back-of-the-envelope way to understand the racial commodification of profit-driven, televised college sports since the 1980s. He compares Clemson's 1981 championship football team with the 2016 Clemson team that won the title thirty-five years later. On a salary of $50,000 head coach Danny Ford shepherded the 1981 Tigers squad, which was more than 60 percent white, to the national championship.[5] When Dabo Swinney led Clemson's 40 percent white 2016 team to the crown, his incentive-laden compensation package was approximately $10 million.[6] "How does a $50,000-a-year job become a $10 million-a-year job? We can explain it by the growth of cable sports and billion dollar cable deals—that's where the revenue comes in," Zirin argued. "But that's the result, not the cause. The cause is the excellence of the product on the field and the desire of the consumer to consume that product. And that's entirely a question of the black athlete, and what the black athlete brought to college football and college basketball. It's entirely a question of putting out a product that white consumers wanted to buy."[7]

The selling of Division I basketball and football to the largest possible audiences depended on a number of innovations: the growth and reorganization of athletic conferences, the rise of cable sports television, the reshuffling of game-day schedules, and the addition of more postseason contests. But the growth of major-college basketball and football also meant tapping into sports fans' racialized rooting reflexes, a task perfectly suited for the supposedly villainous Georgetown Hoyas and Miami Hurricanes. Because race transcends the geographical boundaries of in-state and conference competition, Georgetown and Miami emerged as highly marketable national antagonists in the 1980s. The racial posture of both programs appealed to or agitated spectators beyond local fan bases and alumni who traditionally follow a college sports team. Nothing helps sell tickets, television ads, and merchandise like the polarizing appeal of good guy versus bad guy matchups—and in America, nothing polarizes more than race. Whether peopled rooted for or against the Hoyas and the 'Canes, they tuned in and shelled out.

Georgetown basketball and Miami football were major influences on the marketing and sale of major-college televised sports to national audiences. The revolution they led in the mid-1980s improved the quality of the on-field product, but also increased that product's value by deploying a proudly racial posture to attract new fans and consumers to stadiums, television sets, and apparel stores. The transition of amateur basketball and football from regional conflicts into national rivalries required useful foils. Wearing their racial identities on their sleeves, the Hoyas and

Hurricanes played the antagonist's role to the hilt. Georgetown and Miami fed—and fed off—the racial reflexes that supporters and detractors brought to arenas and their living-room couches.

Loving the Hate

In sports, every competitive edge matters. Like stock fortunes, games are often won or lost at the margins—a slight advantage wielded here, an opponent's weakness exploited there. Competitive advantages are mostly athletic and decided long before the opening kickoff or tip-off. Recruiting top athletes, working them into peak physical condition, and developing offensive and defensive schemes to maximize their talents are what separate great teams from the merely good.

Psychological advantages may not help underdogs topple more talented or better-coached teams, but they can decide contests between evenly matched opponents. The most powerful psychological weapon is perceived disrespect. Players and coaches love to plaster their locker rooms with derisive comments from opponents or dismissive predictions by the media. In *The Last Dance,* Jason Hehir's ten-part documentary about the Chicago Bulls' dynasty, viewers witnessed the myriad ways Michael Jordan drew motivation from the smallest slights—even if Jordan had to invent them.

In major-college football and basketball, conference and statewide bragging rights provide perennial motivation. Rivalries between the Ohio State Buckeyes and the Michigan Wolverines, or the USC Trojans and UCLA Bruins, are enduring and inherited. For the past four decades, Miami, Florida, and Florida State battled each other for national football honors, but also for the informal, parochial title of "state champions." Their combined eleven national titles are a byproduct of the ferocious fights to claim Sunshine State superiority. Likewise, competition for conference bragging rights among Georgetown, Seton Hall, St. John's, Syracuse, and Villanova propelled each of these five Big East basketball programs into the Final Four at least once during the 1980s.

Who becomes loved or hated, and why? Local or regional

grudges fuel rivalries, but race can trump geography. Solidarity is especially important to African Americans and other minority fans. Many Black Alabamans rooted against the Crimson Tide when the University of Southern California's integrated football team came to segregated Tuscaloosa in 1970. Conversely, the Los Angeles Dodgers maintain a national following that extends well beyond either New York City or Southern California for the simple reason that Jackie Robinson broke major league baseball's color line as a Brooklyn Dodger. Perhaps Duke University is the best example of nationalizing regional rivalries. The Blue Devils will always have their detractors a few miles away in Chapel Hill and Raleigh. But only after the Duke men's basketball team gained a reputation as a white team—deserved or not—did the Blue Devils become national antagonists hated by viewers far from Tobacco Road.

Georgetown and Miami set a precedent by becoming college teams hated not just by conference or regional opponents but by fans across the country. That kind of fury places undue stress on young amateurs playing in front of live national audiences, especially at hostile road arenas. Hate also provides an unintended blessing, of course. With a permanent target on their backs, the Hoyas and Hurricanes were motivated for every game against every opponent in every corner of the country. Being the bad guy is also good for the business of sports.

Racial identity polarizes. But the fault lines of fandom are never strictly Black and white. Consider how differently two white fans of the same generation perceived the Hurricanes when they were kids: "Meet the Press" host and Miami native Chuck Todd and sportswriter Michael Weinreb, who grew up in State College, home of Penn State. Todd readily admitted that he didn't realize how much the rest of the nation despised the 'Canes until he left his South Florida bubble to come to Washington for graduate school and an eventual career in the national media:

> I certainly perceived an anti-Miami bias watching away games and in hindsight recall much of the criticism leveled at Miami to be

behavioral. It's now clear to me with a lot more distance that the real resistance to Miami was cultural. It was black kids showing emotion in a different way than white kids did in the '70s. This was also the first post-civil rights era of black kids who didn't believe it was their job to fit into a foreign culture like black athletes of the '60s and '70s felt forced to, but instead wanted to create their own identities.

I think, in this sense, Miami was like any cultural pioneer: It received over-the-top pushback from those in charge who feared what change was coming. Watching a Miami game from the late '80s through today's cultural eyes is tame, trust me.[8]

What Todd could not readily see in his 'Canes until he left Miami, Weinreb understood intuitively as a kid raised in the shadow of the legendary Joe Paterno and his Nittany Lions. Weinreb felt a weird mix of disdain and confusion about those 1980s Hurricanes teams. He recalls the sweet satisfaction of watching Penn State upset Miami in the 1987 Fiesta Bowl. Only a year earlier, following Miami's 58–7 slaughter of Notre Dame, he was "perplexed" by the "so what?" attitude of the Hurricanes players and the joy they took in humiliating opponents. "It wasn't that I hated Miami so much as they seemed to exist on a plane beyond my comprehension," Weinreb wrote in *Season of Saturdays: A History of College Football in 14 Games*.

Years later, after the NCAA severely penalized Miami and Southern Methodist University for academic and financial misconduct in their football programs, Weinreb reconsidered the confused contempt he felt toward Miami as a youngster: "The best thing Miami and SMU ever did was that they refused to say they were sorry for the way they won football games. And eventually, their lack of shame forced people to reconsider their ideals." The "radical change" in the product on the field, Weinreb believed, first led to the Bowl Championship Series for selecting the national champion and eventually to the four-team College Football Playoff system that replaced the BCS: "All this utter disregard for the existing structure of the sport in the eighties—the culminating shouts of *So What?*—helped us realize that maybe things could be better than they'd always been. In the end, the black hats turned out to be the good guys after all."[9]

At some point after the 1983 Hurricanes team won the program's first championship under Howard Schnellenberger, but before Johnson's 1987 team won the second, the 'Canes became the team college football fans loved to hate. Many sportswriters specifically cited the 1986 season capped by Miami's shocking loss to Penn State as the year that cemented the Hurricanes' role as national antagonist. "If Miami in 1983 announced itself loudly as a new-wave national champion, in 1986 we were witnessing something different and refined," CBS *Sports'* Dennis Dodd wrote on the thirtieth anniversary of that Miami team. "They knew exactly what they were doing. For the first time that season—it can be argued—one team began to define the game with attitude as much as talent. . . . From the way Miami dressed, played and conducted itself that year, a new sports culture emerged. It wasn't limited to college football. It went beyond yapping and preening and running up the score."[10]

To be sure, that 1986 Miami team earned much of the enmity it received. Players had a number of off-the-field problems, including allegations of and a few official police reports documenting fights with girlfriends and other students, petty theft, gun possession, and the illegal use by almost three dozen players of a phone calling card to rack up thousands of dollars in unpaid long-distance charges. After the 'Canes dismantled the No. 1 Sooners in October that year, *Sports Illustrated's* Rick Reilly penned a scathing critique of the disconnect between Miami's enviable play on the field and its scurrilous behavior off it: "Miami may be the only squad in America that has its team picture taken from the front and from the side. You see a drop of remorse anywhere? Notice anybody seeing the errors of his ways and all that? Nah. In all of the Canes raising, exactly one player has been suspended for one game by [head coach Jimmy] Johnson."[11] Running back Alonzo Highsmith bristled remembering the fallout from defensive tackle Jerome Brown's gun incident that led to his suspension. "Yeah,

Jerome Brown had a gun on campus, and that put the program in a bad light. But [the media] didn't mention how many of us graduated, how we weren't allowed to take those easy courses like other programs get away with." Highsmith also made clear that Miami's rough reputation, rather than being a mark of shame, inspired envy in many opposing teams: "We were brash, and we did a lot of talking on the field, but if you asked the majority of college players, they wished their coaches would let them play like us."[12]

At the end of the 1986 regular season, but before Miami's shocking 14–10 loss to Penn State in the Fiesta Bowl, quarterback Vinny Testaverde won Miami's first Maxwell Trophy, recognizing the nation's most outstanding player. (A few days later he also became the first Hurricane to win the Heisman Trophy.) At the awards ceremony, Testaverde was asked about his team's image. "We thought the whole world was against us," he said, expressing exactly the attitude coach Jimmy Johnson wanted to instill in his team. "There was a lot of bad talk, but all of it brought this team closer. We are like a family. We put our minds on winning a national championship. We want that very badly."[13] Perceived disrespect and an embattled, us-versus-them mentality? To coaches, that's motivational gold.

A fixture of sports commentary in Miami and nationally, Dan Le Batard watched the Hurricanes up close for four decades. What he remembered most vividly about those 1980s teams was their powerful effect on the locals, including a rising cohort of young Latinos: "The teams played free, had style, were dangerous, felt like Miami. And then came the success. And people of all kinds gravitate toward fun winners like magnets to metal. Winning can feel like unity in a community. Winning when it is very much you-against-the-world the way those Canes teams inspired love and hate. I also think an entire generation of Latinos, new to this country, new to this area, didn't have very much locally to cheer for in sports beyond the Dolphins, so a whole generation of Latin kids learned how cool sports could feel from those rebellious, crazy teams."[14]

To whatever degree racist attitudes fueled criticism of the Hurricanes, the person routinely blamed for Miami's makeover was white: head coach Jimmy Johnson. Because rosters change and players wear helmets during games, Johnson was literally the most recognizable face of the program. He was condemned for being too permissive with his players because he allowed them to showboat during games and skirt campus rules. "Johnson, who earned the best villainous nickname ever bestowed on a coach—'Porkface Satan'—got death threats, all because he did to holier-than-thou Notre Dame what it had done to many of its opponents," *Miami Herald* columnist Linda Robertson recalled. "He had the audacity to allow his players to express rather than repress their joy and fire. The Canes chose honest celebration over fake humility. Football has been a lot more fun since."[15] Miami was a team even detractors grudgingly came to respect.

During his interviews with former Miami players for his documentary "The U," Billy Corben was impressed by how much pride the older and more mature Hurricanes alumni still drew from their roles in building Miami's image and unifying the city: "As adults they looked back at that time unapologetically. I was impressed with how the swagger was maintained. It wasn't a show, and it wasn't just kids misbehaving. They were very proud of what they did, how they did it, and what it meant to other people [across Miami and beyond]. There's a bravery in that. All of them were introspective. They weren't in denial about all of this. Most of them arrived at the same conclusion—which is sort of lifting a middle finger. They did the right thing at the time, and stand by it, and are not sorry for it."[16]

Like Miami, Georgetown built a hated-yet-feared national reputation in the 1980s. *Slate* sports columnist Mike DeBonis described the potency of John Thompson's Hoyas teams from that era, specifically Georgetown's ability to dominate other teams through intimidation. "No program since John Wooden retired has left as deep an impression on basketball's collective psyche. Not Phi Slama Jamma. Not the Fab Five. Not Rick Pitino's Kentucky teams. Certainly no team involving [Duke's] Christian Laettner. Fear is what made Georgetown memorable. . . . But the fear, back then, had as much to do with race as hoops. Georgetown basketball under John Thompson was always intertwined with racial politics. That was inevitable when an elite Eastern university, then as now overwhelmingly white, started fielding teams made up almost exclusively of black players." How much the Hoyas' Blackness or their talent contributed to their scariness remains in dispute. There is no dispute about whether those Hoyas teams were frightening.

Intentionally or not, Thompson's often caustic relationship with the media magnified Georgetown's mystique. Thompson shielded most of his players, especially freshmen, from inquiring reporters and only opened the team's locker room after games for about fifteen minutes. Although Thompson's rule protecting freshmen was essentially the same policy as that of his close friend, University of North Carolina head coach Dean Smith, Thompson's refusal to accommodate media requests fueled the "Hoya paranoia" image. "To the media, hungry for backstage access to the ascendant Georgetown program, Thompson's policy was a horror. Some sharp-tongued media type termed it Hoya Paranoia, and the phrase was subsequently replayed in hundreds of headlines and broadcasts," pop culture critic Nelson George explained. "The spoiled sports media, used to having college coaches suck up to them, handle rejection as well as a lovesick fifteen-year-old. Moody stars, close-mouthed teams, or coaches that are just plain quiet try the patience of reporters." Tensions between story-hungry media members and tight-lipped coaches trying to protect their players are common. But Thompson's case was different, George asserted: "That natural hostility toward poor sources was certainly exacerbated by the fact that Thompson, as well as Ewing, were towering black men whose disinterested attitude toward interviews clearly irritated an overwhelmingly white male media."[17]

Georgetown's fearsome posture caught the attention of many young players watching the team at home on TV. Just ask the University of Michigan's "Fab Five" Black freshmen, who took

Commodifying Color

basketball courts and the public consciousness by storm during the 1991–92 season. Chris Webber, Jalen Rose, Juwan Howard, Jimmy King, and Ray Jackson—perhaps the greatest recruiting class in college basketball history—led the Wolverines to consecutive national title games in 1992 and 1993. The Fab Five coupled a chest-bumping, trash-talking style with apparel innovations like baggy shorts and black socks, trends quickly adopted by Black and white players on teams and playgrounds nationwide. Their on-court successes matched the cultural imprint they left on college athletics.

Today, point guard Jalen Rose is a national media figure on ESPN and sports talk radio. Interviewed by *Vibe* magazine's Adelle Platon upon the release of Rose's 2015 autobiography, Rose was asked to what degree a sense of racial "brotherhood" influenced the Fab Five's identity. "No team can replicate it," Rose told her. "It will not happen and if it does, I want to watch their documentary 20 years afterwards and see the response. I felt teams before us had it that I wanted to emulate." Rose then listed his cultural role models: "I idolized John Thompson's Georgetown teams and Jerry Tarkanian's UNLV team so really I felt like what we were doing [with the Fab Five] is just a graduation of what I saw them do because I was a huge fans of theirs."[18]

The 2011 release of the ESPN documentary *The Fab Five* created a minor kerfuffle between Rose and former Duke basketball star Grant Hill about racial norms in college sports. In the documentary Rose derided the Duke team that beat the Fab Five in the 1992 title game as "bitches" and called their Black athletes "Uncle Toms." Hill is the affluent son of Calvin Hill, former superstar halfback for Yale University and the NFL's Dallas Cowboys. Duke rosters during head coach Mike Krzyzewski's era have typically included shares of Black players comparable to those of other top Division I teams. However, thanks to a parade of prominent white stars, including Christian Laettner, Bobby Hurley, Chris Collins, Steve Wojciechowski, Jon Scheyer, J. J. Reddick, and Grayson Allen, Duke's reputation was that of an elitist program comprising privileged white *and* Black athletes—

and the snotty, rich "Cameron Crazies" who cheered them from the stands.

Amid the media stir caused by Rose's comments, Hill remained his usual magnanimous self. In a *New York Times* opinion piece, Hill responded to Rose's comments by telling readers that he drew inspiration from many of the same 1980s icons that Rose did, including Georgetown and even Rose's Fab Five teams. "At Michigan, the Fab Five represented a cultural phenomenon that impacted the country in a permanent and positive way," Hill said. "The very idea of the Fab Five elicited pride and promise in much the same way the Georgetown teams did in the mid-1980s when I was in high school and idolized them. Their journey from youthful icons to successful men today is a road map for so many young, black men (and women) who saw their journey through the powerful documentary."[19]

To burnish their national reputation as a love-them-or-hate-them team, Georgetown had to win. They would have remained just another obscure, mostly Black college team had they not won those Big East tournament titles and made deep runs through the NCAA tourney in the 1980s. Yet other long-obscure programs with rosters headlined by Black superstars become nationally competitive around the same time Georgetown did. That list includes Big East rivals St. John's, Syracuse, and Villanova, plus DePaul, Louisville, Memphis State, and Michigan State. Why did none of those programs have the impact Georgetown did? The short answer, again, is hate. "Until the early 1980s, college basketball largely had been a regional sport. As America fell in love with March Madness, Georgetown became a cultural phenomenon," contended Patrick Hruby in a *Washingtonian* magazine essay about the 1980s Hoyas teams. "Sportswriters likened Thompson and the Hoyas to Darth Vader and the Galactic Empire from the *Star Wars* films. Fans loved the Hoyas, or loved to hate them. Some of the animus stemmed from the school's dominance, as Georgetown went 121-23 over Ewing's four years. And some of it was racial."[20]

In June 2011 the staff at *Sports Illustrated* published its list of the "25 Most Hated Teams of All Time." Only seven college teams made the list, but Georgetown and Miami accounted for three of them. *Sports Illustrated* ranked Georgetown's 1983–84 championship team No. 23 and the 1990 Miami team that forced the NCAA to create new unsportsmanlike-conduct rules No. 11. Which team did *Sports Illustrated* rank No. 1? Jimmy Johnson's 1986 Miami squad. The 'Canes are the only program, amateur or professional, with two entries on the list.[21]

Obviously, the Hoyas and Hurricanes were not the first to embrace the role of racial bad boys. A long list of Black athletes from Jack Johnson to Muhammad Ali preceded them. A less charitable view is that Georgetown and Miami simply applied a long-proven method to the burgeoning medium of televised college basketball and football. The more charitable view is that, as students, they were the first Black amateurs who dared to transform televised intercollegiate team sports by creating and embracing the role of racial villains.

Rap Rebels on Campus

Rap music exploded in the 1980s. It did not take long for rap musicians to identify with superstar Black college athletes, particularly the Hoyas and the Hurricanes. The rebellious, anti-establishment spirit expressed by rap artists and Black athletes created a natural alliance. Each side appropriated the language and symbolism of the other.

Rap music today is so omnipresent and accepted by all races the public hardly notices it in movies, TV, and other pop culture formats. When it first emerged in the late 1970s and early 1980s, however, rap was an almost exclusively African American enterprise. Because rap music was associated with urban lifestyles and violent, even insurrectionist themes, many white Americans viewed the new musical form with suspicion. Establishment politicians and religious figures denounced rap as a nefarious influence on young Americans and clamored for censorship. As sociologist Theresa Martinez noted, rap artists of that era like Public Enemy, KRS-One, and N.W.A. built this new "oppositional culture" style of music atop the simmering anti-establishment sentiments of historically oppressed groups: "The voice in political and gangsta rap lyrics narrate a biting distrust, disillusionment with, and critique of major societal institutions and government."[22] Or as N.W.A. succinctly put it in the refrain of their song of the same title, "Fuck Tha Police."

The mutual affinity between Black athletes and Black rappers derives from their shared racialized masculinity. Both music and sports serve as important cultural markers of Black masculinity in America and are especially potent in conjunction. "Sports and music have long had close and mutually reinforcing ties in shaping African American male experiences and image," music scholar Ken McLeod asserted. "Spectacular black male performance in sports and music can thus be viewed as both a unifying salve to black males yet also simultaneously a reminder of their marginalization and isolation from mainstream society."[23] Synthesis was inevitable between Black male college athletes who listened to rap and rappers who cheered on their favorite Black collegiate stars.

Early 1980s rappers elevated Georgetown's cultural status by adorning the university's signature bulldog logo and blue-gray colors.[24] Despite a deep affinity for his native Los Angeles, N.W.A. cofounder Ice Cube (O'Shea Jackson) on various occasions wore a Hoyas jersey, sweatshirt, jacket, and two different baseball caps. In a 2017 essay for the *Georgetown Voice*, Jonny Amon chronicled other rappers who appropriated Georgetown's identity in lyrical or apparel choices: "Rappers, such as Big Boi of OutKast and Nas, referenced the school's tough play in their music. Chuck D, leader of the rap group Public Enemy, once articulated his dream of forming a rap group called 'Georgetown Gangsters,' where each member wore a Georgetown Starter jacket." Biz Markie donned a Georgetown crewneck in his "Just a Friend" music video. Run-DMC's Darryl McDaniels wore a Georgetown Starter jacket because doing so, said Amon, "meant that you had an attitude [and] that you was bad."[25]

A thousand miles south, the mid-1980s rise of Miami football coincided with the emergence of South Florida's rap music scene led by a young Liberty City deejay named Luther Campbell. The Hurricanes' rebellious on-field exploits melded perfectly with the anti-establishment attitudes of Campbell's hypersexualized rap group. Known by his stage name, Luke Skyywalker, Campbell formed Ghetto Style DJs in 1982. For this low-budget operation started with a few friends, Campbell set up turntables and speakers in "The Pit" of African Square Park to entertain Liberty City locals.[26] After saving enough money to open his own club in Miami, Campbell invited West Coast trio 2 Live Crew—Fresh Kid Ice, Mr. Mix, and Brother Marquis—to perform in Miami. Campbell then joined the trio as their producer, frontman, and DJ. He created his own record label, Luke Records, to produce the group's music. In July 1986—as the most hated Hurricanes team was preparing for its season—Campbell's reconfigured rap ensemble released Luke Records' first album, *The 2 Live Crew Is What We Are*. The album cover showed three of 2 Live Crew's four members, including Campbell, clad in Miami Hurricanes jackets or hats.

Skyywalker and 2 Live Crew quickly became a national sensation and a lightning rod for national controversy. 2 Live Crew's lyrics were sexually provocative, including tracks on their 1986 album entitled "We Want Some Pussy" and "Throw the D." During live performances, scantily clad women danced on stage alongside the rappers. "It was edgy and in your face," said Miami hip hop radio host DJ Laz. "It was like audio porn." The 1989 release of the group's third album, *As Nasty As They Wanna Be*, triggered public outrage from the state capital in Tallahassee all the way to Washington. That album's most popular song, "Me So Horny," became a popular crossover hit with young white listeners. The album's cover—the Crew's four members laying prone on the beach beneath four standing, spread-legged, rear-facing Black women in thong bikinis—was sexually provocative.

On cue, the Christian fundamentalist organization the American Family Association joined forces with Florida Republican governor Mel Martinez to pressure local officials to crack down on 2 Live Crew. Broward County sheriff Nick Navarro banned sales of *As Nasty As They Wanna Be* in local record stores. Shop owners who ignored the edict were either arrested, issued citations, or both. Next, Navarro's team staked out a 2 Live Crew Concert. When the group used explicit lyrics the police arrested 2 Live Crew members and cited them for an "obscene performance." The group's sexually explicit and profanity-laced lyrics led to the first obscenity charge in U.S. history issued against a record store owner.[27] Campbell equated his First Amendment case to a defense of hip hop itself. Campbell and his cohorts won in court. "If we had lost that case, because it was a federal case, everything in hip hop with explicit lyrics would have been deemed obscene, and there would have been case law and precedent already set that would have been on the books," Campbell said years later in the Netflix documentary *Hip Hop Evolution*.[28]

Campbell emerged as a key cultural figure in Black Miami and a notable celebrity within Hurricanes football circles. He frequently consorted with football players and routinely hung out on the team's sidelines during home games. The marriage of Campbell's identity with the Hurricanes' image made perfect sense, according to sports cultural critic Alejandro Danois: "Luke, a celebrity and hero to the marginalized, was as synonymous with Miami football in the '80s as Jack Nicholson was with the Los Angeles Lakers at the same time. Luke and the 2 Live Crew were embedded with the Hurricanes brand, they helped mold its bad boy image. And despite a popular outcry around the country, there's always a faction of the disenfranchised that will forever have a devotion to outlaws. After all, over 35,000 people attended the funerals for Bonnie and Clyde."[29]

Campbell became a major problem for the Hurricanes when local media learned he had created a bounty system in which he illegally promised and delivered cash payments to Hurricanes players as rewards for big hits that knocked opposing players out of the game.[30] But by then Campbell and Miami football had already burnished their rebellious reputations. "There was some-

Commodifying Color

thing about 2 Live Crew fighting the government and its stodg-
iness that fit the image of the Hurricanes who were fighting a
stodgy old college football elite and trying to bring some more
life and entertainment to football," said Chuck Todd, recalling
his teen years growing up in Miami. "I think if you want to talk
about the image and cool of those '80s Canes and the counter
cultural fight that appealed to many of us, you have to include the
2 Live Crew battle with the local government over their live performances. The old guard in all of these instances lost or eventually surrendered."[31] Along with Luke Skyywalker and 2 Live Crew,
rappers including Liberty City native Trick Daddy, Sir Jinx, four-
time Grammy Award winner Rick Ross, and even white rapper
Vanilla Ice wore Hurricanes gear in public and identified with
Miami football.

In 2018 STARZ released a six-part documentary directed by
Andrew Cohn and Adam Rosenfeld about Liberty City's local
football tradition.[32] Luther Campbell remains active in his neighborhood's youth football program. Liberty City has produced a
number of star players for the Hurricanes, including Artie Burns,
Duke Johnson, and Sean Spence. The small community of roughly
twenty thousand residents is also home to star NFL wide receivers Antonio Brown, Amari Cooper, T. Y. Hylton, and Chad Johnson. Liberty City native Barry Jenkins wrote the screenplay and
directed *Moonlight*, the 2016 Oscar-winning film set in this gritty
section of Miami. The alchemy between Black Miami's football
and popular culture is potent.

In the 1980s rap was a countercultural roar emanating from
poor, Black, urban neighborhoods. Young Black men found
power in rap's beats and especially its lyrics. Many in white
America either did not understand rap or viewed it as a threat
to social mores. Its crossover appeal for young Black athletes in
the 1980s was immediate, however. To them rap was an intox-
icating outlet and voice for their generation. Mutual admira-
tion between rap musicians and young Black athletes brought
the two groups together at a rebellious and incendiary moment
for Black culture.

Sports Apparel as Tribal Identity

Athletes and sports teams understand the power of colors and iconography. Uniforms convey a shared identity. Wearing the logos of one's favorite team signifies allegiance to the school from which one graduated or to the city one calls home. At a perilous American moment riven by blue-versus-red polarization, sports identities provide one of the few remaining bonds that can transcend race, religion, and even partisanship. As the Colin Kaepernick episode demonstrated, however, even that bond is tenuous.

Watching old broadcasts of college basketball and football games from the 1970s and 1980s reveals how different the crowds of that era looked. One can spot clusters of color in the bleachers, typically in the student sections or areas reserved for players' families and university bands. By contrast, modern stadiums and arenas feature spectators awash in their team's colors. The intensity of fandom may not have changed during the past four decades, but the dress code clearly has. Today's fans express their manic devotion by suiting up.

In 1964 University of Oregon alumnus Phil Knight formed a handshake deal with his former track coach Bill Bowerman to create Nike. The company had a local following at first and faced considerable competition in the sports apparel segment. Rival Adidas became the early leader in sneaker sales in the 1970s, and Converse was a rising concern. Competition among sneaker companies thus forced corporate executives to find new and creative ways to market sneakers and athletic apparel to consumers. In the early 1980s the collegiate sports apparel industry was still in its infancy, but maturing quickly. Knight saw the business potential of selling shoes and other apparel bearing the colors and insignia of major colleges. University officials quickly realized that copyright control over their logos meant that athletic teams could generate substantial revenues from merchandising deals. Nike innovated, becoming the first shoe company to employ college and pro sports licensing as way to increase its market share. An industry was born.

Nike representative Sonny Vaccaro deserves much of the credit for pioneering the idea of paying university teams to sign deals to wear corporate logos. In the 1970s these arrangements were limited to a handful of basketball and football programs. For sums of from $5,000 to $10,000, plus free gear, the tireless Vaccaro persuaded coaches to outfit their teams with Nike's sneakers. According to Dan Wetzel and Don Yaeger, authors of *Sole Influence: Basketball, Corporate Greed, and the Corruption of America's Youth,* by the start of the 1980s Nike had surpassed Adidas as the top sneaker company: "By 1984, 60 percent of Division I teams were wearing the swoosh, compared to roughly 6 percent who were wearing Adidas. Some would even argue that the college basketball dynasty of the 1980s wasn't Georgetown, North Carolina or Michigan, but Nike, which put its sneakers on the feet of five national champions during the decade." From 1980 to 1983, Nike's revenues increased sixteenfold to $4 billion, $800 million of which came from basketball shoe sales alone.[33] Knight announced in 1990 that Nike had become the world's "largest sports and fitness footwear and apparel company," a feat achieved "by marketing a wide range of quality in a variety of sport categories."[34] The fight among Nike, Converse (which Nike later bought), and Adidas to sign coaches and universities quickly got out of hand, according to Wetzel and Yeager, but there was no turning back. Marketing college sports apparel became big business in the 1980s.

Among the most influential people driving the rise of schools' apparel deals was John Thompson. In 1980 Nike made him a paid consultant and in 1991 the company elevated him to its board of directors. Thompson remained on Nike's board until May 2020, when he retired to an emeritus director position after forty years as either a paid consultant or better-paid board member. "I've known John Thompson for almost 50 years and Nike would not be the company it is today without his many contributions," Phil Knight said in a statement announcing Thompson's retirement.[35]

Thompson's relationship with Nike legitimized the company's association with Georgetown. The Georgetown Starter jacket, in particular, became a must-wear item for young Black Americans during the 1980s in large part because Black pop culture icons made it cool. In his 1986 feature film debut, *She's Gotta Have It*, Spike Lee's chirpy Mars Blackmon character wears the Georgetown jacket and matching Nike Hoyas Dynasty sneakers introduced by the company in 1981.[36] "Most people remember the Terminators . . . but the Nike Dynasty was the signature shoe of Patrick Ewing and the Georgetown Hoyas throughout most of his college career," branding expert Brandon Edler wrote in a commemorative review of the Hoyas' classic footwear. "The sneaker dropped in 1981 and was one of the first major basketball releases by Nike. The shoe inspired classics like the AF1, Sky Force, and Dunks in the early to mid '80s and helped lead Ewing to one of the most successful campaigns in college basketball history."[37]

Nike released its Terminator shoe for the 1984–85 season, Patrick Ewing's senior year. At that point the Hoyas were the defending national champs. Created exclusively for Georgetown as a custom version of Nike's Dunk shoe, the most distinctive feature of which was the "NIKE" corporate name emblazoned zoned in capital letters across the heel. Nike was so confident in the power of its brand that on Georgetown's custom black-and-grey Terminators it replaced its own corporate name on the heels with "HOYAS." (Nike also had the coincidental good fortune that Arnold Schwarzenegger's hit movie *Terminator*, about a time-traveling assassin, opened the third week of October 1984 as the basketball season started.)[38] "The shoe represented something totally unique in the sneaker world," explained Zac Dubasik, writer for SoleCollector.com, a website that covers the sneaker industry. "With signature shoes just about to become commonplace in professional basketball, the Terminator carried the clout of an NBA signature model, while being made specifically for a college. Along with Kentucky's Converse Cons Blue, it represents one of the only times in history that a shoe can be considered a true 'team signature' shoe."[39]

Nike also cleverly paired Spike Lee's Mars Blackmon character in television ads opposite the planet's most popular athlete at the time, Michael Jordan. "Mars's character is an obvious demonstration of the extremes of popular Black male youth culture, as his trendy attire and utter disregard for mainstream existence foreground his marginal existence," USC film school professor and popular culture expert Todd Boyd wrote at the time. "Black Georgetown imagery and the more mainstream form of Blackness associated with Jordan and Blackmon/Lee defines the contemporary state of commodity culture as it relates to basketball and African American culture."[40] In 1991 John Singleton's film *Boyz n the Hood* certified Georgetown's cultural power. Tre Styles, the protagonist played by Cuba Gooding Jr., wears a Hoyas T-shirt in his South Central Los Angeles neighborhood. South Central is about a thirty-minute drive from UCLA, home to the most storied basketball program in NCAA history, but more than three thousand miles from the Georgetown campus. Tre Styles's T-shirt attested to Georgetown's cultural reach.

Miami's relationship with Nike in the 1980s also set a new standard for sports apparel marketing. In 1987 Nike signed the Hurricanes to the first exclusive all-sports apparel contract, covering every athlete of every varsity team, men's and women's alike. The idea for the contract began when University of Miami attorney Robert Ades phoned Nike's Sonny Vaccaro. Ades asked Vaccaro if Nike would be interested in signing a deal to outfit every Miami varsity program. Vaccaro loved the idea and immediately called Nike chairman Phil Knight. "This is it," Vaccaro told his boss. "We hit the motherload. Now we own the school."[41] Or at least they did until 2015, when Miami severed ties with Nike and signed a twelve-year deal with Adidas. "The University of Miami was the first college program to excel as a national brand with championship play on the field, changing the game of college athletics," Adidas president Mark King stated in a press release announcing the deal that ended Nike's historic relationship with the 'Canes.[42]

Today, all-sports apparel contracts like Miami's original deal are the norm for major-conference athletic departments. For Nike, Adidas, and Under Armour, these arrangements provide greater exposure for their corporate logos on uniformed athletes. The marketing of apparel and gear is particularly valuable in sports that receive significant television coverage, especially men's football and basketball. However, the rise of ESPN and the expansion of cable sports television means that NCAA sports including women's basketball, men's baseball, women's softball, men's hockey, women's field hockey, plus volleyball and track and field for both genders are also broadcast on television, albeit to smaller and more targeted audiences. Athletic departments and universities, meanwhile, benefit from millions of dollars in sponsorship revenues, not to mention the ability to outfit for free the hundreds of athletes who compete in sports generating little or no revenue.

In the early days of the sports apparel revolution, team gear was primarily available for sale locally at a university's stadium, arena, or campus bookstore. Clothing and sneakers were also available by mail order, but in the pre-internet era fans did not enjoy the ease and speed of online ordering and delivery. Young African American fans of Georgetown or Miami in the 1980s who lived in New York, Chicago, Los Angeles, and other far-flung places therefore had to make an effort to secure a pair of trademark Hoyas sneakers or a 'Canes jersey in their size. As Todd Boyd pointed out, the limited availability of coveted team garb thus conferred a special—and perhaps risky—status upon those wearing the black and gray or the green and orange. "Sneakers and jackets became signs of success. It's cool, but the stakes were high," Boyd, who grew up in Detroit and coveted Georgetown gear, remembered. "If you had a Starter jacket on you could get a lot of compliments. You could also get robbed. That added to the cache of having it. Now, you can buy anything representing any team regardless of where you live." Boyd admitted that his own apparel choices on the intramural basketball courts at the University of Florida in the 1980s were heavily influenced by the

Black coaches he revered. He slung a white towel over his shoulder and wore track suits in tribute, respectively, John Thompson and another of that era's most prominent Black college coaches, George Raveling.[43]

Nike has been criticized frequently for its corporate behavior, especially the company's foreign labor practices. On the other hand, Nike has repeatedly shown leadership on racial matters. Given the millions of nonwhite customers who buy their shoes and apparel, cynics might dismiss Nike's race consciousness as self-interested. But the company has a reputation for putting its money where its mouth is. Nike hired Colin Kaepernick as a spokesperson when no NFL team would sign him. Amid the Black Lives Matter protests in 2020 following George Floyd's murder by Minneapolis police officers, Nike and its Jordan Brands subdivision pledged to donate a combined $140 million to social justice organizations fighting against systemic racism and police brutality. "We know Black Lives Matter," CEO John Donahoe said in a statement accompanying the pledge. "We must educate ourselves more deeply on the issues faced by Black communities and understand the enormous suffering and senseless tragedy racial bigotry creates."[44]

Nike celebrated the enduring symbolism of its Hoyas basketball sneakers and apparel in the retail store it opened in 2012 on the famed M Street shopping strip in Georgetown. The store features tributes to the late John Thompson, the jerseys of many notable Hoyas players, and a display case that includes shoes from Nike's Georgetown sneaker line. Joining Nike executives and Thompson for the ribbon-cutting ceremony were his son, then Hoyas coach John Thompson III, and notable former players including Patrick Ewing, Michael Graham, Mark Tillmon, and Michael Jackson, who attended the store opening in a dual role (he was also a vice president for Nike). "We're continuing the story and paying homage to Coach Thompson's legacy, what he means to the community, what he means to the brand, the relationship between Coach Thompson and Georgetown and Nike," Jackson, who played point guard for the Hoyas in the

1980s, said. "I don't think he got enough credit for what he represented in basketball. Georgetown changed the game, merged culture with sports. Georgetown did that before anyone else in college basketball."[45]

The convergence of Georgetown's racial pride and its sporting apparel relationship with Nike was also immortalized in the team's kente cloth–inspired uniforms, first worn in the 1994–95 season. At the time guard Allen Iverson was the star of a Hoyas team that included Othella Harrington and Jahidi White. The cloth's pattern appeared as piping along both sides of the jersey and shorts. Ron Hampston of the *Sportsfan Journal* described kente's cultural and political meaning:

> The cloth is known as "nwentom" in Akan, Ghana. It is a type of silk and cotton fabric made of interwoven cloth strips and is native to the Akan ethnic group of South Ghana.
>
> The Kente cloth was originated with the Ashanti Kingdom and was adopted by the people in the Ivory Coast and many other West African countries. The cloth itself is an Akan royal and sacred cloth worn only in times of extreme importance and was the cloth of kings. Over time, the use of kente became more widespread. However, its importance has remained and it is held in high esteem with Akans. The cloth is the best known of all African textiles and has become widespread internationally.[46]

The uniforms were a hit and are remembered fondly by players like Jerome Williams who wore them during that inaugural season. "In the basketball swag world, we felt as though we had the best jerseys in the NCAA," Williams told the website *Casual Hoya* for a 2018 feature commemorating Georgetown's uniforms. "It meant something to wear that Georgetown jersey. We were the first team to rock the Jordan patent leathers and we had these new uniforms. It was our own identity. It was about the Georgetown brand and what it represented. . . . We definitely had a serious swag about us."[47]

Georgetown revived the kente theme in 2015. That year, the university announced the conclusion of a contest in which alumni, fans, and students were encouraged to submit their ideas for a new basketball-court design during home games played at the Verizon Center (now Capital One Arena) in downtown Washington. The winning submission featured kente patterns in the restricted areas under each basket universally known as "the paint." The university likewise repainted the court at McDonough Gym on Georgetown's main campus, where the men's varsity team played before moving to larger arenas in suburban Maryland and downtown Washington. Georgetown's athletic department also rolled out new football uniforms in 2015 that feature kente designs.[48]

To its credit, the University of Miami recently took sports apparel marketing to a new level. In August 2019 the 'Canes and Adidas announced that the football team would be wearing new Parley uniforms. Designed in conjunction with Parley for the Oceans, a nonprofit that works to keep oceans clean, the team's uniforms, gloves, and cleats are made partially of ECONYL yarn, a substance "repurposed from fishing nets and other nylon waste removed from the ocean." Miami became the first team to wear eco-conscious footwear during an NCAA football game.[49]

The Parley uniforms are the latest of many precedents set by either the Hoyas or the Hurricanes: first to have its team name supplant a sneaker's corporate logo; first to sign its entire athletic program to an apparel contract; first to weave African artwork into team uniforms. Such was the mutually reinforcing power of collegiate sports marketing and racial identity during the formative 1980s. By combining athletic excellence with proudly racial postures, Georgetown and Miami enticed corporate America to create signature products and contractual relationships that helped turn the two universities into national brands.

Georgetown's and Miami's sports apparel contracts have created controversies typical of major universities with prominent Division I athletic departments. Those controversies have generally stemmed from the global labor practices of apparel companies, especially the exploitation of workers in developing countries. In response to complaints by student activists as well as recommendations from the university's own Licensing Oversight Committee, in 2016 Georgetown president John J. DeGioia issued a public letter calling upon Nike to comply with the Worker Rights Consortium's standards for foreign labor.[50]

The tribalism of sports fans—their desire to adorn themselves in replica jerseys of the teams and players they love—has blossomed into a lucrative industry. In 2013 collegiate-licensed apparel generated $4.6 billion in revenues. More than two hundred schools are represented by Collegiate Licensing Company. Cory Moss, the company's marketing director, confirmed that the 190 million consumers for collegiate gear are a diverse group. "When you look at the demographics of the college sports fan . . . 80 million are females, over 60 million are minorities and over 30 million earn over $100,000 annually," Moss told ESPN.[51] A broad, inclusive set of consumer-fans suit up for every game, and their devotion generates millions of dollars annually for the NCAA, its member universities, and the sports apparel industry.

Around-the-Clock Sports

From its one-trailer studio in Bristol, Connecticut, the fledgling Entertainment and Sports Program Network cable network launched on September 7, 1979. Within six months ESPN was airing live NCAA basketball tournament games. Within a year it was broadcasting a mix of live and taped programs around the clock. By July 1984—a few months after ABC spent $227 million to buy a controlling share of the network—ESPN had inked a deal with the now defunct College Football Association (CFA) to broadcast live college football games.[52] In five short years, ESPN had changed televised sports, especially college sports, forever.

On June 27, 1984, the Supreme Court accelerated the broadcasting revolution in televised college sports and magnified ESPN's power with its ruling in NCAA v. Board of Regents of the University of Oklahoma and the University of Georgia.[53] The class-action suit was filed by the two schools on behalf of the sixty-two member universities of the CFA. The CFA claimed that the NCAA was exploiting its monopoly power to control television contracts. Deciding 7–2 in favor of the plaintiffs, the Court declared the NCAA's broadcast arrangement with ABC and CBS to be an illegal cartel that violated free-market principles established by the 1890 Sherman Antitrust Act. The ruling gave teams and conferences the power to negotiate television deals directly with networks without first gaining permission from the NCAA. "From ESPN's early days, its executives looked at college football, with its iconic place in American culture, and saw opportunity. Before the mid-1980s televised college football amounted to little more than one national game a week, along with a few regional telecasts, all controlled by the N.C.A.A.," wrote *New York Times* reporter James Andrew Miller. "Then a Supreme Court antitrust ruling freed universities and conferences to negotiate their own TV deals."[54] In effect, television broadcasting rules returned to the situation prior to 1951, when the NCAA began negotiating contracts on behalf of member universities.

The impact of the Supreme Court's ruling was immediate. With their newfound negotiating power, universities and conferences initially engaged in unhealthy competition for TV contracts. Prior to the ruling, the NCAA had deals with three networks to broadcast eighty-nine Division I football games—thirty-five each with broadcast networks ABC and CBS, and another nineteen with Ted Turner's Atlanta-based cable station then known as WTBS, forerunner to TBS. By time the 1984 season started, ten networks including Raycom, Jefferson Productions, Sports Time, and even PBS had each signed contracts with either conferences or individual schools to broadcast games. (One of those games turned out to be the classic Thanksgiving 1984 weekend "Hail Mary" game between Miami and Doug Flutie's Boston College.) Without the leverage of the NCAA's monopoly power, however, the total revenues schools reaped from their broadcasting rights dropped.[55] Universities traded collective leverage for more independent power.

The CFA had its own problems, the most obvious of which is that it was engaging in the same cartel behaviors that the Supreme

Court had found the NCAA guilty of practicing. With a Court-imposed March 1985 deadline looming before ABC lost its rights to negotiate exclusively with the CFA, ABC inked a deal with the CFA for the next two seasons, just as ESPN had done a few weeks earlier. The combined value of the two CFA deals was $55 million. They required more broadcast games and yielded less total revenue for the CFA.[56] "One thing is clear: the Supreme Court decisions reinstate Home Rule for institutions and conferences and created telecasting chaos for the next decade," wrote sports media historian Ronald A. Smith. "Nearly all participants, including CFA member institutions, became financial losers after having gained the freedom to further commercialize intercollegiate athletics."[57] The CFA's demise was only a matter of time.

Sure enough, in January 1985 the University of Miami became just the eleventh school—and the first football conference independent—to negotiate a direct TV deal to broadcast its games. Athletic director Sam Jankovich announced that the Hurricanes had signed a $2.05 million contract with CBS to broadcast two Miami games in the 1985 season and a third the following year.[58] The NCAA responded to CFA's lawsuit in kind, suing the CFA in federal court and winning. "Not content with the ruling, the CFA petitioned an appeals court and lost again, with the court deciding that the CFA was doing what the NCAA had done for the previous thirty years, employing a group boycott and price-fixing. The CFA had learned little from the three years of litigation it had helped fund for its own members, Oklahoma and Georgia," Smith explained.[59] Founded in 1977, the CFA limped through the rest of the 1980s and into the early 1990s, but was more or less defunct by 1995. The organization officially shut its doors in 1997.

The free-market effects that initially squeezed universities and conferences were alleviated once ESPN and the other networks simply increased the supply by broadcasting more and more college games. Increased live-game broadcasts meant that, to avoid time conflicts, universities and conferences had to relax their scheduling rules so teams could play on different days and at different times.

"Beginning in the 1970s, television rights fees replaced ticket sales as principal sources of bowl game revenue, and currently, the networks that broadcast the games exercise considerable control over when those events take place," explained sports historian Howard Chudacoff. Ditto for basketball, where top conferences inked deals for weeknight game-of-the-week regular-season games. "Cheaper to produce than football games, basketball telecasts fit neatly into two-hour time slots. Consequently, ESPN worked out relatively inexpensive deals with major conferences in the late 1970s and began airing games during weekday evenings, giving the Big Ten and Big East a regular time block on Monday nights." Chudacoff noted that in 1983 a Chicagoan could watch only four regular-season NCAA basketball games on two local networks per week, mostly on Saturdays. By 2009 a Chicagoan could watch as many as thirty-seven games across eighteen regional, national, and cable networks scattered across the week.[60]

For college basketball's leadership, the rising demand to fill TV time triggered two related expansions. First, the number of live postseason tournament broadcasts steadily increased. Second, the NCAA tournament field expanded three times in just six years during the 1980s, from thirty-two teams to forty-eight in 1980, fifty-three teams in 1983, and sixty-four teams in 1985. The addition in 2011 of four play-in games eventually expanded the field to its current sixty-eight teams. The excitement of that 1989 opening round "game that saved March Madness" between Georgetown and the pesky Princeton Tigers, who nearly bounced the top-seeded Hoyas from the tournament, helped transform first-round games from untelevised afterthoughts into must-see TV. The confluence of these two developments led ineluctably to all sixty-seven games in the current format being broadcast live. Networks also televise most if not all major-conference tournament games live during championship week, held the week prior to the NCAA tournament.

For football, weekly games, traditionally played on Saturday, gradually spread out across the scheduling day. Kickoff times across multiple channels today are staggered from as early as 11 a.m. EST for East Coast matchups to 10 p.m. EST for Pac-10 and other West Coast games. To broadcast more games and reduce time conflicts, college football also liberated its regular season from the Saturday-only tradition. "In the chase for money and exposure, college football, once a quaint drama of regional rivalries played out on autumn Saturday afternoons, has become a national sport played throughout the week, intruding on class schedules and even on exams," wrote James Andrew Miller.[61]

Not surprisingly, profit-minded school presidents, conference leaders, and television executive were all too happy to ratchet up the number of postseason bowl games. The postseason bowl system steadily expanded beyond a few dozen teams playing during the traditional two-week window that ended on New Year's Day. At the conclusion of the 1979 football season, thirty teams played fifteen bowl games on eight different playing dates during an eighteen-day window from December 15 through January 1. Forty years later, after the 2019 season, eighty teams played forty bowl games on fifteen different dates spread across a twenty-five-day period that ended on January 13.[62] Television-driven bowl proliferation means more Division I teams now play in bowls than do not, which is why some teams with losing regular-season records nevertheless earn bowl bids. For student athletes the downside of the expanded bowl season is that it increasingly conflicts with the fall semester's period for final exams and term papers.

The biggest tradition sacrificed on the altar of the television gods was bowl game matchups like the Rose Bowl, which historically pitted the Pac-10 regular season champion against the Big 10 champion. The scuttling of that tradition at least freed teams at the top of the polls to play against each other in national championship bowl matchups. The first of those, of course, was the January 2, 1987, Miami–Penn State Fiesta Bowl game, which was also the first bowl game played after New Year's Day. The end of the two-week window bowl tradition was one of several reasons that in 2019, on the 150-year anniversary of college football, columnist Bill Bender ranked the 1987 Fiesta Bowl No. 1 on *The Sport-*

ing News' list of the 150 most important games in college football history: "Penn State may have won the game, but NBC won the night with a record 24.9 Nielsen rating, still the largest share for a college football game to this day. That game set the stage for conference realignment, the Bowl Alliance, Bowl Championship Series and, now, the College Football Playoff. The college football championship game is now big business, and this game opened the door for all that to happen."[63]

ESPN's rise during the 1980s compelled the broadcast networks to ramp up their coverage of Division I basketball and football. ABC went a step further, eliminating the threat ESPN posed by buying the sports channel. (Both are now owned by the Walt Disney Company, which bought ABC in 1995.) With teams and conferences able to sign their own television contracts, networks also created basketball tournaments hosted in places like Maui and New York City during the winter holidays, before the regular-season conference schedule began. Likewise, networks scheduled corporate-sponsored kickoff classics pitting major football powers against each other during the opening week of the fall season.

According to economists Allen Sanderson and John Siegfried, the increased demand for Division I men's basketball and football games clearly incentivized longer playing seasons in both sports. Expanding the schedule was a relatively low-cost change for NCAA conferences and teams because their athletes are uncompensated amateurs. "Broadcast revenues have grown rapidly as the number of sports broadcast networks that seek live-game content has increased faster than the supply of elite college athletic competition packages. To capture the increasingly attractive rents, the NCAA and its member institutions have expanded the lengths of their football and men's basketball seasons by about 25% . . . from the traditional 10-game football season (plus for a few teams a December bowl game), and 25-game regular-season schedule in basketball," Sanderson and Siegfried wrote. "The expanded schedules in college as opposed to their professional league counterparts are attributable to the low marginal cost of an extra game in the former because players are not compensated commensurately."[64] Simply put, universities and conferences can squeeze more labor out of their amateur athletes because those amateurs wield little to no power.

The launch and rise of ESPN created one more expansion—of ESPN itself. ESPN today is actually ten networks, including ESPN on ABC broadcast plus nine cable channels. The network created ESPN2 in 1993, ESPN News in 1996, ESPN Classic in 1997, and the Spanish-language ESPN Desportes in 2004. In 2005 the network launched ESPNU, a channel solely dedicated to college sports programming. Additional media ventures include ESPN Radio and ESPN+, the company's direct-to-consumer digital service. (After an eleven-year run, ESPN: *The Magazine* shut down in 2019.) Bristol's ESPN Plaza features eighteen buildings that contain 1.2 million square feet spread across 123 acres. Beyond its Connecticut headquarters, the network owns broadcast or administrative facilities in New York, Los Angeles, Charlotte, North Carolina, and a dozen foreign cities. ESPN even has its own annual award and companion show, the ESPY Awards, created in 1993.[65]

A lost part of the story of the televised cable sports explosion is the fact that ESPN almost failed. In its first few years, the all-sports channel struggled financially. It derived revenues solely from ad sales and was hemorrhaging money. McKinsey consultants hired by ESPN recommended that the channel demand cable networks pay per-subscriber fees for the right to broadcast ESPN programs. This financial arrangement contravened the historic practice in which cable channels provided their programs for free in the expectation that increased viewership would generate more income from higher ad rates. "It wasn't much, but it set a precedent," explained *Business Insider*'s Dashiell Bennett. "If your customers want sports, you'll have to pay us for it. Back then, nobody charged to carry their channel." Fast forward to today, and ESPN collects four dollars per cable subscriber in an industry where the average subscriber fee for other channels is twenty cents.[66]

Forty years ago, televised major-college basketball and football was a limited venture regulated by the NCAA and restricted to traditional networks broadcasting games mostly on weekends. Today, it is a multibillion-dollar industry that relies on both traditional and cable networks' broadcasts of regular and postseason tournament games throughout the week. The televised college sports explosion proceeded in stages, the first of which happened during the late 1970s and early 1980s. Triggered by the creation of an all-sports cable network and a pivotal Supreme Court ruling, the explosion in programming coincided with and also relied on the rapid increase of Black and other minority athletes on Division I basketball and football rosters. An almost perfect confluence of events helped transform college basketball and football from a series of mostly regional broadcasts into a national enterprise designed to rival the appeal of NBA and NFL programming. Not surprisingly, the Hoyas and Hurricanes participated in two of the most pivotal games in the history of major-college sports broadcasting: the opening-round near-upset of top-seed Georgetown by underdog Princeton in the 1989 NCAA tournament, and Penn State's surprise victory over Miami in college football's first true title game, the 1987 Fiesta Bowl.

Branded

Sports branding is important to professional and college sports organizations. Teams wear familiar and patented colors and logos. Universities and professional franchises employ full-time marketing and media specialists. Administrators, coaches, and athletes engage the community through charity sponsorships and outreach events. Although trades among professional teams and graduations at the college level produce regular roster turnover, a team closely connected to its supporters and fan base can establish itself as an enduring brand.

Historically, college teams were beloved (or hated) by alumni, conference rivals, and local fans. Over time, consistently great programs like UCLA basketball or Nebraska football gained national followings. However, for a college team to become a national *brand*—as Georgetown and Miami did in 1980s—was altogether unprecedented. "[Georgetown] was the first college sports team to become a brand—and it was a tremendously lucrative one," wrote *Slate* sports columnist Mike DeBonis. "By the early '90s, Georgetown apparel outsold even schools with powerhouse football programs. Georgetown Starter jackets sold well across the country, but the team's image was especially resonant in black America. Not only was this an all-black team with a black coach, the Hoyas also played in a majority-black city run by a black mayor. . . . Eventually, touchstones of black culture spread from Washington, D.C., to every corner of college hoops."[67] How enduring is the Hoyas brand? A Georgetown Starter jacket is enshrined in an exhibit about influential Black athletes at the National Museum of African American History and Culture, which opened in 2016 on the Mall in Washington DC.

Miami football created a national brand, too. In the 1980s the team refashioned itself to replace its failed identity with a new, winning attitude. The coaching hires, the recruits, the big plays and wins all mattered, but strategic marketing decisions by the team and university officials also solidified Miami's reputation. In 1973 Miami changed its logo to a split "U" with the left half of the letter orange and the right half green. By the early 1980s the program embraced the song "It's All about the U" to accompany the logo. Miami's two biggest in-state rivals used fan-favorite hand gestures every Sunshine Stater recognized: Florida's two-handed gator chomp and Florida State's one-armed tomahawk chop. So in 1992 Hurricanes fans and players developed their now-familiar "U" hand signal formed by holding both palms forward, with horizontal thumbs touching and the rest of the fingers pointing up. In 2017 Miami's defensive coaches started a link-chain tradition in which a gold, Cuban link-style chain is worn on the sideline by whichever Hurricanes player created the team's most recent defensive turnover. In a perfect fusion of on-field and off-field cultures, the practice inspired Miami rapper Solo D (Delonte Copeland) to write a link-chain song to accompany the tradition.[68] And has there ever been a better sports marketing campaign than having current and former Hurricanes identify their alma mater simply as "The U"? The names of hundreds of American colleges begin with "The University of." To assert that the University of Miami alone can call itself *the* U is branding at its most audacious.[69]

Because their athletes are amateurs, branding is different for universities. Despite rising corporate influence on campus in every realm, from sponsored academic programs to annual job fairs, universities are not for-profit ventures. The marketing of players and teams should in theory be connected to a university's academic mission of preparing young men and women for their careers, whether in athletics or not. Professional teams may develop the young athletes they draft, but they are under no obligation to do more than pay and manage their athlete-employees. Amateur athletes receive no direct remuneration for building a university's athletic program into a brand. Only the small subset of players talented enough to turn professional benefit financially, and their compensation comes after they leave campus. The value amateurs derive from commodifying their performance redounds almost entirely to their universities, their conferences, the NCAA, and their corporate sponsors. Universities thus profit from the performative draw of minority athletes and their racialized identities without having to share that windfall with the players who make major-college televised sports so entertaining and therefore so profitable.

In the 1980s, Georgetown and Miami proved that the first step in commodifying Black collegians was simply to recruit and play them. A phalanx of talented Black and other minority athletes began to flood the fields and hardcourts of Division I men's basketball and football. They excelled during games and expressed themselves between plays and off-the-field, too. College basketball and football viewership soared. Fans tuned in because Black athleticism sold well. By popularizing sneakers, jerseys, and other memorabilia, amateur Black and Latino athletes also contributed to the second-stage commodification of collegiate sports. Pop culture representations of college athletes in music and film increased apparel and merchandise sales, delivering millions of dollars in licensing revenues to universities, conferences, and the NCAA. Mix in the televised cable sports revolution accelerated by a key Supreme Court ruling, and major-college basketball and football rapidly morphed from a sleepy amateur enterprise into a multibillion-dollar industry.

The Hoyas and Hurricanes figured prominently in both stages of the commodification of amateur athletics. Love them or hate them, Georgetown and Miami made college sports more profitable by attracting new fans and consumers. The revolution the two programs started on college hardcourts and gridirons quickly spread to music, movies, and sports apparel stores. The teams were ubiquitous national brands easily recognized by their colors and logos.

[7]

Common Enemies

It's amazing, and damning, that we had a two-term black
President of the United States before we had a
black Power Five commissioner.

—PAT FORDE, *Yahoo* sportswriter

How can [the University of Mississippi] offer anything other than
empty words when they still have a Confederate monument right
in the center of campus? When they're named the Rebels?

—AMIRA ROSE DAVIS, Penn State professor of history
and African American studies

It is difficult to overstate how much African American athletes and coaches influenced major-college men's basketball
and football. They changed how teams compete on the hard
courts and gridirons. They changed the way universities recruit
and promote coaches and athletic directors. From television
broadcasting to team gear, they changed how networks and
apparel companies sell college athletics to consumers, spectators, and alumni. They changed the way fans root for athletes
and how the media covers them. They changed NCAA policies on issues ranging from academic standards to the licensing of players' images. None of these transformations happened

217

overnight, nor can any black athlete, coach, or administrator take sole credit.

In fact, it took the collective effort of an entire generation of pioneering minority athletes to puncture the overtly racist rules and practices of college sports. In the decades immediately following World War II, African Americans had little reason to root for college teams that featured few if any minorities on their rosters. Although most universities outside the South steadily integrated their varsity sports programs during the postwar decades, white athletes ruled the playing fields throughout the 1960s and into the early 1970s. Nonwhite players at most schools were few, and at some universities minorities were banned entirely. As for leadership, basketball and football programs in the postwar era at all but the HBCUs had almost exclusively white coaching staffs and athletic directors. The white lines chalked onto football gridirons and painted on basketball courts conferred both real and metaphorical meaning. As a predominantly white experience, major-college sports were mostly out of bounds for African Americans or other minority fans. Although certain vestiges of segregation endure and racism can never be wiped out entirely by legal fiat, that first generation of athletes toppled the racist pillars upon which college sports was built.

Yet college sports would not be what it is today absent the contributions of African Americans and other minorities of the generation that followed. In the late 1970s and early 1980s, the revolution led by this second wave of more fully integrated Black and minority collegians came to dominate Division I men's basketball and football. Sports began to look different because Black athletes made it different. Their impact was apparent in the competitive excellence they brought to playing fields, but also in the countless ways the so-called "Black style" turned sport into a performative art and entertainment spectacle. The long-term legacy of this second generation of minority athletes is both indisputable and readily quantifiable. Without them, the commercial value of the signature playoff events in NCAA Division I men's college basketball and football—the March Madness tournament and the

College Football Playoff—would not rival, as they do now, their NBA and NFL counterparts.

Along the way, the growth and professionalization of major-college sports has magnified the influence—and, for some, affluence—of tens of thousands of minority athletes. But the rising power and profitability of major-college basketball and football have also harmed student athletes, and especially Black, minority, and many underprivileged white athletes. Improvements in their student-athlete experience have been slow and incremental. Only a small fraction of the wealth these athletes help generate for their universities, corporate sponsors, athletic conferences, television networks and the NCAA trickles down to them. Their exploitation continues.

What are the lasting impacts of integrating major-college televised sports? The changes that Georgetown's and Miami's former sporting dynasties helped initiate led to important political and cultural transformations in college sports. The shared legacy of the Hoyas and Hurricanes includes reforms in academic eligibility standards for student athletes; efforts to diversify coaching staffs and administrative offices within college sports; the recent movement to compensate college athletes for their labor and commercial use of their likenesses; calls by amateur athletes who grew up with social media to change public attitudes on race. The spark ignited by these two programs still burns.

The Battle over Academic Standards

Georgetown's John Thompson and Miami's Howard Schnellenberger took the helm of their respective programs in the 1970s. During that decade a contentious argument began among university presidents, athletic directors, coaches, and the parents of student athletes about academic eligibility standards for incoming freshmen playing Division I sports on scholarship. This argument came to a head in 1983—the year Miami football and Georgetown basketball marched toward their first national championships—when the NCAA enacted Proposition (Prop) 48. Crafted by the American Council on Education, the DC-based trade association that represents university presidents, the new bylaw required scholarship athletes to enter college with at least a 2.0 high school grade point average and a minimum score of either 700 on the Scholastic Aptitude Test (SAT) or 15 on the American College Test (ACT) exams. After two hours of spirited debate at its January 1983 annual meeting in San Diego, the NCAA passed the measure with just 52 percent approval. Prop 48 took effect beginning in the 1986–87 academic year.

Opponents predicted that the new rules would disproportionately harm students from underprivileged backgrounds, particularly minorities. They warned that standardized exams like the SAT were faulty indicators of intelligence, poor predictors of student performance, and biased against nonwhites. The subset of HBCUs, represented by the National Association for Equal Opportunity (NAEO), issued a letter to the NCAA delegates opposing the new bylaw. "This proposal fails to discuss and to show the need for academic success to the student-athlete [and] fails to discuss and to show the need for a moral commitment on the part of the institution to high-risk students," the NAEO's letter stated.[1]

Five of the fifteen presidents who spoke in San Diego during the two-hour debate over Prop 48 were from HBCUs. Grambling's Joe Johnson and Tennessee State's Frederick Humphries complained about the proposal's racial bias and what they called its "hidden agenda" of making athletic teams whiter.[2] "Proposition 48 has been strongly criticized by members of the African-American community from its inception in 1983," wrote Kenneth Shropshire in *In Black And White: Race and Sports in America*. "The criticism is not only for the projected negative impact on African-American enrollment but also for the lack of inclusion of African-Americans in the original creation of the rule."[3] Indeed, of the 277 member institutions voting at the 1983 NCAA convention, only 17 were majority-Black universities.[4]

Penn State's Joe Paterno, who at the time was coach of the reigning national football champions, provided a key endorsement for Prop 48. Paterno rebuffed critics who claimed the new standards would have a disparate and unfair impact on minority student athletes. Only after the NCAA adopted Prop 48 were two 1983 reports issued that confirmed the likely racial impacts of the new standards, one by the Education Testing Service, which administers the SAT, and the other following an internal investigation by the Big Eight Conference. The Big Eight's report concluded that, had it already been in place, the NCAA's new regimen would have applied to from 60 to 80 percent of Black athletes from its member universities, compared to an estimated 10 to 27 percent of white athletes on Big Eight sports teams.[5] Data from the first three years after the new standards took effect validated the predictions from those preliminary studies. Of the student athletes ruled ineligible by Prop 48 from 1986 and 1988, more than 80 percent were Black, and in 1987 that share exceeded 90 percent.[6]

Prop 48 also included an exemption for what were known as "partial qualifiers," student athletes who failed initially to meet the high school academic standards. Partial qualifiers could still receive athletic scholarships but were barred from participating in intercollegiate sports during their freshman seasons. However, after just three years with the new academic standards in place, the NCAA in January 1989 adopted Proposal 42, an amendment to Prop 48 that removed the partial qualifier exemption, thereby depriving ineligible freshmen athletes of any scholarship support. After failing on the first ballot, Prop 42 passed with just 51 percent of the votes cast, 163–154.

Opposition to Prop 42 from coaches and administrators was swift, fierce, and led by none other than Georgetown's John Thompson. On Friday, January 13, 1989, Thompson said he would not coach in an NCAA-sanctioned game unless the NCAA did something to "provide these student-athletes with appropriate opportunity and hope for access to college."[7] The next night, moments before his Hoyas tipped off against Big East rival Boston College at the Capital Centre in Maryland, Thompson walked off the court in protest of Prop 42. (Led by Thompson's top assistant Craig Esherick, the Hoyas cruised to a 26-point victory over the Eagles that night.) Four nights later, Thompson refused to even attend the Hoyas' next game, which was against his alma mater, Providence.

After the Boston College game, Thompson proclaimed that the academic-standards debate was not exclusively a "black-white issue" because it affected all athletes from disadvantaged communities.[8] "He's making a statement that a lot of other coaches feel very strongly about," Boston College coach Jim O'Brien told the media during his postgame remarks. "He is one person who is in a position to make a little noise about this. We're talking about one of the most highly visible coaches in the country: the Olympic coach, coaching a team that's in the top five, one of the best programs in the country. So when he does [make noise] a lot of people sit up and take notice."[9] Other notable basketball coaches—both Black, like Temple's John Chaney, and white, like Notre Dame's Digger Phelps and Louisiana State's Dale Brown—also decried the new rule change. Thompson's Big East colleague Jim Boeheim of Syracuse rallied to his longtime rival's defense. "Because John did this, I guarantee the next time [Prop 42] comes up, it won't pass," Boeheim predicted.[10]

Boeheim's comment was more prescient then he imagined. After Thompson's no-show at the Providence game, NCAA officials set up an emergency meeting with Thompson and Georgetown administrators at the NCAA's headquarters in Kansas City. Following that meeting, the NCAA announced that it would recommend suspending Prop 42 until 1992, when a study of the effects of Prop 48 was due to be completed. Asked about the meeting, Thompson said, "No one had to be beaten over the head. It was a sensible, intelligent discussion in which we sat down and discussed the issues and came to a conclusion as a result of that, and came to an agreement."[11] Comparing his act to that of Rosa Parks refusing to give up her bus seat to a white passenger, *Newsweek*'s Jack Kroll wrote at the time: "The NCAA tried to downplay the significance of this meeting, but it was clearly a victory for Thompson, a victory that few other figures in American sports could have accomplished almost singlehandedly."[12] The debate over academic standards might have turned out very differently if John Thompson, rather than being the only living Black coach of an NCAA championship team, was still coaching at a Washington prep school.

In Coral Gables, Miami's Jimmy Johnson never seemed entirely sure how to respond to the new academic standards. Johnson complained that coaches at private universities, like his, would suffer disproportionately because of the higher tuition costs relative to public schools. "In state-supported schools, where the tuition is small, the coaches can sign these players and have them walk on, pay their own way [during freshman year] and then qualify and not lose any eligibility," said Johnson.[13] For the 1986 season, Miami accepted six Prop 42 partial qualifiers. The four who chose to enroll all met the freshmen-year criteria of a 1.8 minimum GPA for twenty-four completed credits and were eligible to play in 1987. "They will be behind, football-wise. They could be considered behind regular freshmen because they haven't even had a football uniform on in a year," Johnson said at the time.[14]

Unfortunately for Johnson, one of those four players was arrested for selling cocaine during the freshman year he sat out waiting to gain eligibility. The headache of a university investigation and the player's pending trial soured Johnson on Prop 42 players. By summer 1988 Johnson reversed himself and decided he would longer admit partial qualifiers. Johnson did not blame his Prop 42 recruits from that 1986 class, but instead pointed fingers at the media. "I see what these individuals go through. They're outcasts, and they have the stigma of not being able to make it academically," Johnson complained. "The media write down who they are, and it becomes a black cloud hanging over their heads."[15] A year later, Johnson reversed himself again and started admitting Prop 42 players.[16] A month after the Prop 42 controversy exploded in January 1989, Johnson packed his bags for Dallas.

In 1992 the NCAA set an even stricter standard with the passage of Proposition 16, which took effect in 1996. The new rule created a sliding-scale metric that rated test scores and grade point averages in tandem, with higher test scores offsetting lower GPAS or vice versa. Walter Byers, the NCAA's executive director from 1951 to 1988, defended the NCAA's position on academic standards for incoming freshman athletes. "It may be difficult to determine through academic studies the precise impact on blacks of Proposition 48/42, or what now is known as Proposition 16," Byers wrote in his book *Unsportsmanlike Conduct*. "In 1988, most black athletes were already meeting Prop. 48/42 standards—85 percent of those freshmen matriculating at Division I colleges. Opponents of Prop. 48/42 had argued that 90 percent of those who did not meet the rule were black." Byers cited 1988 data reported to the NCAA showing that only 65 percent of those who failed to meet the requirements were Black. He and other defenders of the standards regime argued that minority student athletes disqualified by the new rules would not necessarily be replaced by white athletes, but instead by other minorities with better academic records. The first and longest-serving executive director in NCAA history, Byers was a polarizing figure for much of his thirty-eight-year tenure.[17]

Setting aside the debate over racially disparate effects, Thompson and his fellow critics were correct about the class-based effects of eligibility standards. According to a report conducted by the U.S. Department of Education's National Center for Education Statistics in response to the passage of Prop 16, socioeconomic status (SES) was a potent determinant of whether high school seniors from the class of 1992 met the new eligibility criteria. "Students from higher SES groups were classified as being eligible to participate in sports in higher proportions than those from lower SES groups," the report stated. "For example, 73.4 percent of high SES college-bound seniors met the Proposition 16 eligibility requirement as compared to 60.9 percent for middle SES and 42.3 percent for low SES college-bound seniors."[18] Even if the impact of the standards was not explicitly racial, the effect of higher poverty rates within African American communities created an indirect racial bias in the form of class-based disparities. Poorer students, of whom a disproportionately large share were Black or belonged to other racial minorities, were less likely to meet the minimum thresholds for admittance.

The much larger problem with the standards debate, argued sportswriter and former Northwestern University football player Rick Telander, was the NCAA's monopoly power to define who qualified to be an amateur on campus. "An amateur student-athlete

Common Enemies

is whatever the colleges say he is. This is a wonderful situation for the universities because they can wash their hands of any problems that arise from their inherently corrupt and immoral amateur sports system just by saying that whatever happened was against the rules."[19] Restricting college athletes to amateur status is about more than not paying them. It is also about wielding near-total control over their athletic and academic lives by restricting their power to demand fair compensation.

The academic eligibility debates exposed the foundational lie about race, academics, and competitiveness in major-college televised basketball and football. The NCAA embraced integration to improve the talent on display, but also wanted to retain athletes' stature as unpaid amateurs. Classifying college athletics as an occupation was never an option, of course. Conferring on athletes the status of workers would give them the right to negotiate for fair compensation, thereby obliterating a business model that relies on the highly profitable fiction that athletes are students first, rather than underpaid professionals disguised as students. Indeed, the most cynical view of the admission standards and eligibility debates is that all the controversies kept the focus on test scores, grade point averages, and graduation rates to divert discussion away from paying athletes.

The controversies about academic integrity that began at that 1983 NCAA convention in San Diego continue to this day. Decades after those landmark fights of the 1980s, John Thompson made clear why he fought the NCAA so hard over academic standards. "Well, opportunity is what I fight for," Thompson explained. "See, we don't operate on a level playing field. You know, historically, we can go back and know that something occurred in this country— and I don't want to belabor it—that put people at a disadvantage. So now we start testing folks who've been put at a disadvantage, and then after we start testing them, we start labeling them."[20]

Diversifying College Sports Leadership

The racial integration of college sports proceeded in stages. In the decades before and especially after World War II, a small but critical cohort of pioneering athletes broke the color line at non-HBCUs outside the segregated South. In the 1970s a larger wave of Black and minority athletes flooded Division I programs. By the late 1980s and early 1990s, the racial mix on most Division I men's basketball and football rosters reached levels approaching those at most major-college programs today. In terms of sequencing—and perhaps only in that respect—the athletes came first.

The integration of coaching positions and athletic administrators occurred more slowly than the integration of rosters, and unfortunately, the share of minority coaches continues to be much lower than that of the minority athletes, and the share of minority administrators lower still. In fact, during the past decade the number of Black head coaches in major Division I men's basketball has *declined* slightly. According to an analysis conducted by Marcus Fuller for the Minneapolis *Star Tribune*, from 2004 to 2017 the share of Black head coaches at the seventy basketball programs in the major conferences dropped by almost half, from 33 percent to 17 percent. Consider the Big 10, founded in 1895. In 1976 the Minnesota Golden Gophers hired Clem Haskins, the conference's first Black basketball head coach. At one point the conference boasted four Black head coaches at the same time. By 2017, however, the misnamed conference that had expanded to fourteen schools suddenly had none. "As black coaches, we don't get to weather out the tough years," lamented Brian Ellerbe, the first Black coach hired by Big 10 powerhouse Michigan. "So guys like me, we don't resurface. Once you have that tough year, it's labeled such a bad thing."[21] Since leaving Michigan in 2001, Ellerbe has held several coaching positions, all of them as an assistant coach and none with teams in the power conferences.

The Wolverines have since hired Juwan Howard, the former "Fab Five" member and journeyman NBA forward. But Howard is the Big 10's lone minority coach, and the pattern of disappearing Black head coaches persists. By the end of the coronavirus-truncated 2019–20 season, only 29 percent of the 353 head or assistant coaches at the Division I level were Black. When HBCUs are removed, that share drops to 24 percent. Indeed, the more prestigious the school, the less likely that its program had a Black coach. In the so-called Power Five Leagues—the ACC, the Big 10, the Big 12, the SEC, and the Pac-10—the share of Black coaches, just 14 percent, was less than half the national average. One coach, who asked NBC Sports not to reveal his identity, said the problem was that "white presidents hire white search firms to hire white [athletic directors] who hire those same white search firms to hire white head coaches." It hardly helps that only 15 percent of athletic directors were Black, a figure that dropped to 10 percent at non-HBCUs. "People hire people that look like them," Patrick Ewing, Georgetown's head coach, told Ron Dauster of NBC Sports. "It's not necessarily racist. Most of the time you hire a person you can relate to."[22]

The unwritten rule in major-college basketball is that every four-member coaching staff should include at least one minority coach. That person is typically an African American and an assistant coach. Those assistants are more than mere window dressing to satisfy diversity officers, university leaders, students, and fans. The uncomfortable truth is that having a Black coach on the bench makes it easier for teams, especially those led by white head coaches, to recruit the talented minority players those programs need to compete. "I don't view any of the changes that have taken place through a lens that says these coaches are thinking in terms of progress, in terms of equal opportunity, in terms of racial equity," said sportswriter Dave Zirin. "I think on a very basic level the motivation was, 'How are we going to go into homes with white faces and recruit black players and fill our teams?' For this very post–civil rights generation, there's a value to diversity in terms of wins and losses in a way that speaks to the coaches' interests."[23]

Racial disparities between players and coaching pools are even greater at top football programs. Among Division I Football Bowl Subdivision (FBS) schools, where 65 percent of players during the 2018–19 academic year were minorities, only 15 percent of all head and assistant coaches were nonwhite. The number of minority head coaches at these 130 schools is even lower. Peaking at 17 percent in 2012, it has since oscillated between 12 and 13 percent. "If the voice [calling for diversity] is from the disparaged side, hardly people notice. But if the voice is unified from the oppressed as well as the majority then people listen," contended Floyd Keith, a veteran coach and former executive director of the Black Coaches and Administrators association. "People have to stop hiding from this and say it'll take care of itself."[24] About a decade ago, many universities began employing outside firms to conduct searches to fill coaching positions. Some welcomed this change, but critics believe that search firms merely provide a convenient scapegoat for university presidents and athletic directors when these firms recommend hiring white coaches.

Not all recent developments are bad. Annual hiring rates for minority head coaches in Division I basketball have rebounded lately, jumping from 28 percent of all open positions in 2016 to 34 percent in 2017 and to nearly half in 2018. But the overall share of minority head coaches continues to hover around 25 percent at Division I men's basketball programs, where roughly 60 percent of athletes are minorities. According to Richard Lapchick, director of the Institute for Diversity and Ethics in Sport (TIDES) at the University of Central Florida, progress in minority hiring has effectively stalled since the mid-2000s. "Sport can lead the way in a nation so divided by race," said Lapchick. "We need what I have been calling for since 2007—an Eddie Robinson rule requiring mandatory diverse pools of candidates similar to the Rooney Rule in the NFL. And we need to hold the search firms accountable also."[25] *Chicago Tribune* sportswriter Shannon Ryan agreed and put the NCAA's foot dragging into a larger historical context: "The NCAA's stance is that it can't make an overriding rule for the large swath of teams that are under different state laws. But the NCAA had no problem instituting the Academic Progress Rate and doling out consequences for teams that don't comply. Essentially, when it comes to diversity hiring, the NCAA tells teams to do their best. That's not good enough."[26]

If diversity within the coaching ranks remains "not good enough," the far less diverse set of university, conference, and NCAA administrators is an abomination. An enduring fact of major-college sports is that the most powerful and best-compensated executives are almost all white men. In 2019 Keith Gill finally became the first Black commissioner hired to lead an FBS conference, the Sun Belt. A few months later, Kevin Warren was appointed commissioner of the Big 10. "An African-American is now leading the oldest, most profitable and arguably most traditional of the Power Five conferences," *Yahoo Sports*' Pat Forde wrote upon learning of Warren's hire. "Selecting Warren to lead the Big Ten should do more than improve the bad optics of college sports (which, yes, extend to the media). It should herald the beginning of the end of a stubbornly enduring Old Boys Club. It's amazing, and damning, that we had a two-term black President of the United States before we had a black Power Five commissioner."[27]

Unfortunately, the diversification of coaching and administrative positions seems to have plateaued. Richard Lapchick and his TIDES team issue an annual report on diversity in college sports, entitled "Division I FBS Leadership College Racial and Gender Report" and informally known at the TIDES Report. In it Lapchick tracks all chancellors, presidents, athletic directors, and conference commissioners from the 130 FBS universities. White administrators account for 84 percent of the 400 total positions that TIDES monitors. The report provides annual grades for racial and gender diversity for each position, as well as overall. The overall grades for FBS schools in 2019 were "C" for racial diversity and F for gender diversity. "I challenge the leadership at all colleges and universities to mirror the heterogeneous makeup of their students and student-athletes," said Lapchick. "The people in these leadership positions hold a responsibility to adequately represent those who they lead. Unfortunately for collegiate sports, specifically the FBS institutions, the overrepresentation of white men has contributed to the lack of opportunities for women and people of color."[28] In a multibillion-dollar business highly dependent on the labor of Black and other minority athletes, racial parity in the leadership ranks of coaches, athletic directors, conference officials, and the NCAA remains a long-deferred dream.

In 2016 the NCAA's Board of Governors passed a resolution establishing three programs designed to promote diversity in college sports, including one to identify and train mid-level minority administrators for career advancement.[29] The board also drafted a 147-word "presidential pledge" for member universities to sign that declared a goal of "achieving ethnic and racial diversity, gender equity and inclusion, with a focus and emphasis on hiring practices in intercollegiate athletics, to reflect the diversity of" NCAA membership and the nation. As of August 2020, 78 percent of member universities and 73 percent of conferences in Divisions I, II, and III had signed it.[30] In April 2019, the Board of Governors, which had previously consisted solely of college and university presidents, was expanded to include five "independent" members. The inaugural class of independent board members includes two African American men—former American Express CEO Ken Chenault and Duke University legend and NBA star Grant Hill—plus former U.S. surgeon general Vivek Murthy and two female members.[31] It remains to be seen how much progress these NCAA initiatives and the increased diversity of its board will yield.

The histories of diversity in athletic leadership at Georgetown and Miami have some similarities. Neither school has had a minority president. Miami has had one female president, Donna Shalala, but Georgetown's religious tradition effectively limited its presidency to male Jesuit priests until 2001, when John DeGioia became the university's first lay president. Miami has not had a minority athletic director, but Bernard Muir served for four years as Georgetown's athletic director before taking similar positions at the University of Delaware and later Stanford University.

Reflecting the general disparities between Division I basketball and football coaching ranks, Georgetown boasts a more diverse coaching history than Miami. Three African Americans led the Hoyas for a combined forty-two of the past forty-seven seasons. Thompson's hire in 1972 was followed by a brief interregnum during which his top assistant, white coach Craig Esherick, led the program for five-plus years. After Esherick was fired in 2004, the Hoyas hired John Thompson III and Patrick Ewing as head coaches. All four coaches retained a number of Black assistants, as well. Minority football coaches at Miami have been fewer in number. Jimmy Johnson's assistants were almost exclusively white, with the notable exception of receivers coach Hubbard Alexander. Johnson was succeeded by three white head coaches—Dennis Erickson, Butch Davis, and Larry Coker—whose staffs had a number of minority coaches, including Mario Cristobal, Aubrey Hill, Clint Hurtt, and Tim Walton.

After Coker resigned in 2006, Miami promoted Hurricanes defensive coordinator Randy Shannon to become the program's first Black head coach. Erickson brought Shannon to Coral Gables in 1991 as a graduate assistant, and Shannon steadily climbed the coaching ladder to the top. After posting an underwhelming 34-29 record with no bowl victories in five seasons, Shannon was fired. In 2018 Miami set another precedent when it promoted defensive coordinator Manny Diaz Jr. to the top job. Diaz—a Cuban American whose father was born in Havana, emigrated to the United States in 1961, and eventually won two terms as mayor of Miami—thus joined a very small cohort of Latino American head coaches in Division I football history. "The University of Miami should reflect the city of Miami," said Diaz at the press conference in which the university announced his hire. "It should reflect it in our style of play. We should reflect it in the way we carry ourselves throughout the community. And we should hopefully reflect it in the way that we win."[32] The hiring of Shannon and Diaz made the Hurricanes only the second Division I program, after the University of Arizona, to boast both a Black and a Latino head coach.

The Players Take Ownership

Critics of major-college sports frequently invoke slavery and plantation metaphors to describe the treatment of student athletes. They characterize the NCAA and its member universities and conferences as exploitive regimes that extract billions of dollars annually from a cheap pool of mostly powerless laborers. Nor is this characterization limited to student athletes' undergraduate years. Former college athletes were, until a 2014 federal court ruling discussed below, uncompensated for the use and sale of their names and images in commercial products, most notably by the multibillion-dollar video-game industry.

College athletes are compensated in some ways, of course. They receive full scholarships that cover tuition, housing, and food, plus a number of small perks including athletic gear that nonathletes on campus do not get. But critics raise two related complaints about student athletes' compensation. The first is the myth that their educations are free, given the thousands of hours athletes spend training, traveling, playing in games, and making various public appearances on behalf of their universities. The second is that the billions of dollars that universities, conferences, and the NCAA generate from commercialized college sports dwarf the sums that trickle down to the players—especially when compared to what coaches, athletic administrators, and conference officials receive.

In a widely discussed 2011 essay, Pulitzer Prize–winning historian Taylor Branch blistered the NCAA for operating major-college sports as a highly unregulated, exploitive cartel. Branch avoids slavery metaphors because, he argued, despite the "unmistakable whiff of the plantation," college athletes are not slaves. Calling for wholesale reforms, including direct payments to college athletes, Branch preferred a different analogy:

> Perhaps a more apt metaphor is colonialism: college sports, as overseen by the NCAA, is a system imposed by well-meaning paternalists and rationalized with hoary sentiments about caring for the well-being of the colonized. But it is, nonetheless, unjust. The NCAA, in its zealous defense of bogus principles, sometimes destroys the dreams of innocent young athletes.
>
> The NCAA today is in many ways a classic cartel. Efforts to reform it—most notably by the three Knight Commissions over the course of 20 years—have, while making changes around the edges, been largely fruitless. The time has come for a major overhaul.[33]

Branch's sentiments echo those of a growing platoon of sportswriters and sports-and-society scholars who argue that the NCAA and its member conferences and universities care far more about profiting from these athletes than about how the athletes benefit, financially or otherwise, from their collegiate experiences. "Short of paying athletes, there must be greater measures applied to balancing the exchange between athletic participation and college education and degree completion," concluded Billy Hawkins, author of *The New Plantation: Black Athletes, College Sports, and Predominantly White NCAA Institutions*. "If these institutions expect four years of the very best running and jumping in the country, then these students should expect the very best educational assistance in the country."[34]

The Knight Commission on Intercollegiate Athletics is an ongoing panel that reports to the NCAA on a number of issues. It has issued three major reports, in 1991, 2001, and 2010. The first report focused on academic standards, financial integrity of athletic programs, and university presidents' oversight of athletics. *Washington Post* columnist Jonathan Yardley lambasted the 1991 Knight Commission report as a little more than a slick corporate justification for making a few marginal changes but largely validating most of the NCAA's practices, including separate standards for admitting athletes, use of scholarships as a pay-for-play mechanism, and permissive attitudes toward the behaviors of wealthy boosters. "In the world of the Knight Commission, college sport still exists as a machine to produce money and publicity; the only real changes it calls for have to do with who collects the money and who spends it," wrote Yardley in reaction to the 1991 report's release.[35] The topics and focus of the next two Knight Commission reports shifted and led to some notable changes. But critics generally dismiss these insider-led studies as designed to justify NCAA policies rather than overhaul them.

In 2020, Ramogi Huma, executive director of National College Players Association (NCPA), and Ellen Staurowsky, a professor at Drexel University's LeBow College of Business, published an NCPA study that estimated the overall and per-player value of scholarship athletes in major-college men's basketball and football. Values varied by conference, but the study pegged the "average fair market value" for football players at FBS schools for the academic year 2018–19 at $208,208, or more than $800,00 during a four-year playing career. For basketball players, who are far fewer in number per team, the estimates were $370,085 per year and nearly $1.5 million for a four-year career. For the so-called "Power Five" conferences, the four-year values for football and basketball players jumped to $1.4 million and $2.2 million, respectively. Huma and Staurowsky estimated these values for the four-year period ending in 2020:

> After accounting for the value of college athletes' athletic scholarships between 2017–2020, approximately $10 billion in generational wealth will have been transferred from college football and men's basketball players, the majority of whom are athletes of color, to coaches, athletics administrators, and college administrators who are predominantly White or to institutions and programs that serve majority White constituencies. This transfer of wealth takes the form of lucrative salaries for athletic directors, conference commissioners, college sport leaders and bowl championship directors, and coaches. This wealth transfer has significant consequences for the athletes who are deprived of their fair share of the revenues they produce for the college sport industry.[36]

A four-year, $10 billion wealth redistribution from the players to universities and athletic conferences—and, indirectly, to apparel companies—puts a tangible price tag on the extractive and exploitative practices in Division I college basketball and football. Even if the NCPA's estimates are discounted slightly because the organization represents players, there's little doubt that universities and the NCAA profit handsomely from their undercompensated pool of laborers.

Some critics are encouraging minority athletes to take aggressive action to spur change. One idea gaining steam is for elite minority athletes to deprive majority-white colleges of their talents. Sportswriter Jemele Hill called for top Black athletes to abandon the major-conference teams and instead play for HBCUs. As Hill explained in a 2019 article for the *Atlantic*, thirty universities—

most of them members of the Power Five athletic conferences—each derive about $100 million in annual revenues from sports. Clemson's football complex, Hill noted, is alone worth about the same as North Carolina A&T's entire endowment. Even more stark is the racial imbalance between athletes on the revenue-generating teams at the Power Five's sixty-five universities and their student bodies; 55 percent of football players and 56 percent of basketball players are Black men, compared to fewer than 3 percent of all undergraduates. Given how much these universities profit from the athletic talents of Black and other minority athletes, Hill argued, that wealth would be better channeled into financially strapped HBCUs: "But what if a group of elite athletes *collectively* made the choice to attend HBCUs? Black athletes overall have never had as much power and influence as they do now.... They are essential to the massive amount of revenue generated by college football and basketball. This gives them leverage, if only they could be moved to use it."[37]

Nine months after Hill's article appeared, one of the nation's top prep basketball prospects, Makur Maker of Phoenix, announced that he was spurning offers from national powerhouses including Kentucky and UCLA to commit instead to Howard University, coached by former Duke University star Kenny Blakeney. "I need to make the HBCU movement real so that others will follow," Maker, who encouraged other top prospects to join him, tweeted on the day of his announcement.[38] If other star Black athletes follow Maker's lead, teams like Howard from the Mid-Eastern Athletic Conference and the other three HBCU conferences could draw bigger crowds and negotiate better media and apparel deals. Presumably, development officers at these HBCUs could parlay sporting excellence into donations that would grow their schools' endowments, as majority-white universities have done for decades.

Former college athletes are also flexing their legal muscles to reclaim the proprietary value of their names, images, and athletic likenesses, or "NIL." In a 2014 class-action case filed by former UCLA basketball star Ed O'Bannon, a federal appeals court upheld most of a lower court's ruling that the NCAA, EA Sports, and the Collegiate Licensing Corporation violated anti-trust law by using images of O'Bannon and other collegians in EA's basketball video game. EA Sports and the Collegiate Licensing Corporation reached a $40 million out-of-court settlement to compensate former college athletes for the previous use of their images.[39] In a similar class-action lawsuit filed by former Clemson defensive back Martin Jenkins, a federal judge in 2019 ruled that universities can limit their scholarship compensation to student athletes but may not collude with other universities to cap the value of those scholarships.[40] These two rulings still grant NCAA member schools significant power to regulate and profit from amateur athletics, but athletes have gained new leverage in their fight to share in the profits they help generate.

In September 2019 California set a powerful precedent when its state legislature passed and Governor Gavin Newsom signed the Fair Pay to Play Act. The law empowers California's amateur athletes to control and therefore profit from their NIL without fear of legal recrimination by the NCAA; in effect, the new law codifies the rights won by litigants like Ed O'Bannon. According to *California Black Media* reporter Antonio Ray Harvey, only two percent of the 2,400 male students admitted to the 2013–14 freshman class at O'Bannon's alma mater, UCLA, were Black—and a stunning 65 percent of those Black male freshmen were varsity athletes. "The majority of college basketball and football players are Black and most head coaches are White," Newsom told Harvey. "The financial imbalance is hiding in plain sight."[41]

Surely the leaders of California's higher education system immediately lined up behind the politicians in Sacramento to prevent the ongoing exploitation of their student athletes, right? Wrong. The University of California system, the California State University schools, private universities Stanford and USC, and the Pac-12 Conference instead joined NCAA president Mark Emmert in denouncing the legislation. But the NCAA felt immediate and intense pressure to relent. The month after California passed its law the NCAA's Board of Governors voted unanimously to order all three NCAA divisions to establish by January 2021 new rules and bylaws that allow players to benefit from the commercial use of their names, images, and likenesses. However, the NCAA's resolution stipulates that players can only benefit "in a manner consistent with the collegiate model." The stipulation's ambiguous language will likely trigger future controversies and further NIL lawsuits in California and elsewhere. "As the train they should've been engineering years ago came barreling toward them in the here and now, the NCAA saw the most 'existential threat' to its existence realized late last month when California Governor Gavin Newsome signed the Fair Pay to Play Act," scoffed John Taylor of NBC Sports.[42] Within two months of California's new law, legislators in eighteen states introduced similar bills to protect their state's current and former student athletes.[43]

At Georgetown, John Thompson was always sensitive to the financial hazards and depredations his athletes endured. When offered the job in 1972, Thompson insisted on having a dedicated tutor for the team—an unusual request for that time, particularly by one of what was then just a handful of Black men's coaches in Division I. As his first hire, Thompson brought Mary Fenlon, a nun and teacher he knew from St. Anthony's, to serve as Georgetown's academic mentor. Fenlon sat on the Hoyas bench alongside the coaches, graduate assistants, and players. By the time she retired in 1999, a few months after Thompson did, she was a fixture of the program almost as recognizable as Thompson himself.

In her role, Fenlon got an up-close look at how Thompson schooled his players not only about basketball but about the economics of major-college sports. "We travel first-class, stay in nice places, order whatever we want in dining rooms, but John always brings the boys together at the end of a trip and goes over the bills with them, shows them how much those rooms and meals and plane tickets cost," she told *Sports Illustrated* in 1980. "A lot of them never lived that way before—I know I didn't—and he wants them to know what it takes to go first-class. It's one of his ways of reminding them that it's important for them to get an education so that they can amount to something, be first-class on their own."[44]

By 1991 Thompson's salary and his Nike endorsement deals netted him about $1 million annually. He always advocated for better treatment for minority athletes, but never apologized about his own personal ambitions. "I want to be a winner," he said. "I want my players to graduate, and I want to get rich. . . . The biggest con in education is kids saying they were exploited. If the kid doesn't get an education, it's his fault. . . . The world is not black or white as much as it is green."[45]

Jimmy Johnson likewise forced the young men in his charge at the University of Miami to think ahead about their lives after football. His preferred method was weekly career-themed meetings. "We'd have these Thursday-night meetings where he would go around the room to each individual, and you had to tell him what you planned on doing in 10 years," recalled Michael Irvin, his star wide receiver on those dominant mid-1980s teams. "He wouldn't let you say football. And you had to tell him what you were doing toward that goal."[46]

Thompson and Johnson understood that most of their players would not play professionally once their college careers ended. The talented few who did turn pro often enjoyed only short careers and many retired with lifetime injuries. Football's special violence also includes the risk of suffering long-term brain injuries like chronic traumatic encephalopathy, which medical experts link to depression, anti-social tendencies, violence, and self-harm. Graduating, learning employable skills, and understanding how to manage money are valuable assets for student athletes once their playing careers end.

To call them slaves or colonial subjects may be a metaphorical stretch, but there's no doubt that modern student athletes—especially major-college basketball and football players—are unfairly compensated. The NCAA's exploitive practices are under increasing attack, but the power of universities to extract profits from amateur performers remains largely intact. Greater structural reform is needed, but that will likely happen only when a new generation of minority athletes advocates and agitates for change.

Amateur Athletes, Professional Advocacy

The video appalled Americans and citizens around the world. For almost nine minutes, Minneapolis police officer Derek Chauvin kneeled on the neck of George Floyd. Floyd begged for his life, desperately pleaded for help from his already deceased mother, and then suffocated to death. The protests that erupted in hundreds of American cities in spring and summer 2020 after Floyd's murder provided Black college athletes a unique opportunity to express their opinions about structural racism. Hundreds of players shared discomfiting episodes from their own experiences. Dozens of players and coaches spoke out forcefully, protested or marched in defense of Black Lives Matter.

Some university coaches and administrators attracted scrutiny for their behaviors. Liberty University and its president, Jerry Falwell Jr., came under fire for racist practices in the university's athletic programs and on campus generally. In early June 2020 Falwell removed a tweet in which he analogized wearing coronavirus masks to donning Ku Klux Klan hoods. The tweet generated backlash from several Black alumni and led three African American staffers, including the school's director of diversity, to resign.[47] Two weeks later, Black sophomore defensive backs Tayvion Land and Kei'Trel Clark for Liberty's football team—which had just earned its first-ever bowl bid the previous season—announced they intended to transfer to another school and football program. Although Land said that most of his interactions with athletic department officials and faculty were positive, via tweet he explained the reason for his decision: "Unfortunately, due to the racial insensitivity displayed by leadership at Liberty University, I have decided to enter my name into the transfer portal and no longer be a student-athlete at Liberty University."[48] (Falwell later resigned the presidency following unrelated personal and marital scandals.)

Amid the Black Lives Matter protests, a number of white football coaches were criticized for their treatment of Black players. Five dozen current and former Iowa football players complained that head coach Kirk Ferentz and his staff demeaned certain minorities on the team. In public statements Hawkeyes players including Derrell Johnson-Koulianos, LeBron Daniel, James Daniels, and Marvin McNutt specifically cited Ferentz—the longest tenured FBS coach—and conditioning coach Chris Doyle for discriminatory behaviors. One ugly incident reported by ESPN involved Doyle's humiliation of Johnson-Koulianos. With parents and fans watching practice from the stands, Doyle made Johnson-Koulianos run around the field with a giant yellow garbage can on his head. Doyle apparently kept a photo of the incident on his office wall as a cherished keepsake. In 2019, before George Floyd's death, Iowa conducted an internal investigation of racist incidents within its football program. When former Hawkeyes players went public with their grievances following the Floyd protests, pressure on Ferentz and his staff increased anew. The university has since hired a law firm to conduct a second, external investigation of its football program, yet still had to pay Doyle $1.3 million in separation benefits after dismissing him.[49]

Oklahoma State University head football coach Mike Gundy also became a lightning rod for criticism. Gundy shared on social media a photo of himself wearing a One America News Network T-shirt. OANN, which presents itself as a conservative news alternative to Fox News, has produced some questionably sourced, even conspiratorial reports. The network is a favorite of Donald Trump, who at times has signaled his preference for OANN reporters over Fox correspondents whom Trump considers insufficiently supportive of his agenda. After Gundy posted the photo, OSU star running back Chuba Hubbard tweeted an objection. Linking a copy of the photo, Hubbard wrote: "I will not stand for this. This is completely insensitive to everything going on in society, and it's unacceptable. I will not be doing anything with Oklahoma State until things CHANGE." The tweet attracted national headlines. Arguably the Cowboys' best player after finishing eighth in the Heisman Trophy balloting the previous year, Hubbard forced Gundy to respond. The two spoke and then issued a joint video in which Gundy promised changes to come. OSU president Burns

Hargis and athletic director Mike Holden also spoke up in defense of the team's student athletes.[50]

Some of the scrutiny facing major-college white head coaches is coming from their minority peers. North Carolina Central University head men's basketball coach LeVelle Moton expressed his disappointment with white coaches at major programs in the Power Five conferences.[51] "The reality is a lot of these coaches have been able to create generational wealth," Moton said on ESPN Radio's *Sunday Morning* program. "Their grandkids' kids are gonna be able to live a prosperous life because athletes who were the complexion of George Floyd were able to run a football, throw a football, shoot a basketball. . . . But whenever people the complexion of George Floyd are killed, assassinated, murdered in the street in broad daylight, they're silent." Moton speaks from personal experience: He was stopped and held at gunpoint along with University of North Carolina star Raymond Felton just days after Felton led the Tar Heels to the 2005 NCAA basketball title. Placing four chairs on the basketball court in a rectangle to simulate an automobile, Moton takes time during practices with his players to role-play being pulled over by the police so they know what to do and not do in such situations.[52] His technique bears a striking similarity to John Thompson's "mental practice" tradition at Georgetown and Jimmy Johnson's Thursday-night career sessions in Coral Gables.

Several white Division I coaches spoke out or took action in the wake of George Floyd's police murder. A notable example is Tom Herman, then the head football coach at the University of Texas. According to *Austin American-Statesman* sportswriter Brian Davis, Herman rated among the more progressive Division I coaches. As the protests grew, Herman conducted a three-hour virtual meeting with his players and coaches to discuss racial issues and the public response. Herman reminded his team that white citizens often take for granted their interactions with police, and that he and other white Americans need to understand how their experiences with might differ from encounters African Americans have with law enforcement. "When I make an illegal U-turn and get pulled over, I fear about what the cost of the ticket is going to be," Herman told Davis. "I don't fear that I'm going to get dragged out of my car and maybe killed because of something I said or did." Herman went further, raising some uncomfortable questions for white fans and boosters: "We're gonna cheer when they score touchdowns, and we're gonna hug our buddy when they get sacks or an interception. But we gonna let them date our daughter? Are we going to hire them in a position of power in our company? That's the question I have for America. You can't have it both ways."[53]

In Mississippi, the state with the nation's highest Black population share, the continued depiction of the Confederate battle flag in the top-left corner of the state flag again became a hot-button issue in 2020 during the Black Lives Matter protests. When Georgia voted in 2001 to change its state flag, Mississippi became the last state with a flag that includes the Confederate battle standard. (Georgia and some other states still include versions of other Confederate symbols, but not the battle flag.) Making all too clear their defense of the state's Confederate pride, in response to Georgia's change Mississippians in 2001 voted 2 to 1—a margin curiously similar to the state's white-Black population split—to reaffirm its status as the lone Confederate holdout.

In June 2020, however, the Republican-controlled Mississippi legislature passed and Republican governor Tate Reeves promptly signed into law an order for the state to replace its flag. In a 2020 referendum, 72 percent of Mississippi voters approved a new flag featuring the state's flower, the magnolia. Did a wave of racial inclusivity suddenly wash over Mississippi's almost all-white cohort of Republican state legislators? Not quite. The more likely motivation was the NCAA's decision to ban championship games from being held in states where the confederate flag had "a prominent presence," coupled with SEC commissioner Greg Sankey's announcement that the SEC would no longer hold conference sporting tournaments in Mississippi if the state refused to change its flag. "It is past time for change to be made to the flag of the State of Mississippi," Sankey said. "Our students deserve an opportunity to learn and compete in environments that are inclusive and welcoming to all."[54] The good news is that the financial power of college sports forced the state's hand. The bad news is that the state's white citizens and the politicians who represent them refused to budge for decades until they faced the specter of lost revenues.

Amira Rose Davis, professor of history and African American studies at Penn State, was unimpressed by the University of Mississippi's response to the flag controversy. Davis draws a straight line between the Black Lives Matter protests and those by college players in the late 1960s and early 1970s at schools like Wyoming. Today's coaches know better than to respond by kicking students who protest off the team like Cowboys head coach Lloyd Eaton did in 1969. Even if coaches issue statements supporting equality for the most cynical of reasons—to protect their jobs or to keep top players from leaving—few dare chastise a player for speaking out in opposition to systemic racism. Still, Davis wonders if the actions are mere window dressing. "So like, Ole Miss Athletics. They went on a march and they talked and they spoke out. . . . But how can that university offer anything other than empty words when they still have a Confederate monument right in the center of campus? When they're named the Rebels?"[55]

From the civil rights movement to the Black Lives Matters protests, for more than half a century Black and other minority athletes have used their outsized platforms to demand racial and social justice. For a number of reasons, today's student athletes wield more power than their predecessors. Politicians, university leaders, and conference officials are much more sensitive to issues of equality and social justice. Student athletes also have powerful social-media tools at their fingertips that allow them to speak directly to broad audiences without having to filter their messages through sports information directors or university spokespeople.

Greater agency and bigger platforms notwithstanding, the situation facing student athletes remains fraught. The profitability of college sports provides few incentives for NCAA executives, conferences officials, or university presidents to tinker with a business model that delivers billions of dollars in revenues to member schools. Amateur athletes have won new legal rights, but on many issues they still wield little to no legal or political power. Nor do they receive much public sympathy. The same fans who dismiss professional athletes who dare to speak out as a bunch of whiny, overpaid millionaires tend to also view student athletes as ungrateful complainers who fail to appreciate the "free" education they receive from top-tier colleges. The public's pervasive shut-up-and-play attitude only reinforces the NCAA's strong grip on power.

Athletes as Provocateurs

In the 1980s Georgetown basketball and Miami football gained parallel reputations as programs that broke the rules and flaunted traditional norms for intercollegiate sports. They played the game differently on the field and challenged long-held assumptions and stereotypes about race and athleticism. "It was Thompson's all-black, Ewing-led teams a decade before the Fab Five that shook the foundation of college basketball, changed the complexion of starting lineups across the country, opened coaching doors that had previously been closed to blacks and paved the way for black sportswriters at major newspapers," sportswriter Jason Whitlock wrote.[56] Miami-based television and radio sports talk host Dan Le Batard credited his hometown Hurricanes with a similarly profound impact: "They were a fun mix of swagger, rebellion and freedom. They felt dangerous on the field, like a vibrating power line humming with electricity. But they were not only dangerous to sportsmanship and largely white ideas of how responsibly or cordially and politely we should play our games—a flimsy conceit—but the amount of trouble they found off the field made it so people could feel actually endangered by the team."[57]

Georgetown and Miami are no longer the dominant programs they were four decades ago. Coached by John Thompson III and led by star forward Jeff Green, the Hoyas reached the Final Four in 2007. The younger Thompson's bid to join his namesake as the first father-son coaching tandem to win national titles ended when the Hoyas lost to Ohio State in the semifinal round. That 2007 squad is also the only Georgetown team to claim a Big East title in twenty-one seasons between John Thompson's retirement and his death in 2020. Miami football has suffered through a similar downturn. In the twenty-three years beginning with their storybook 1983–84 championship season, the 'Canes won 82 percent of all games, including fourteen seasons with at least ten wins, thirteen bowl victories, and five national titles. In the fourteen seasons since, Miami has won just 58 percent of its games, two bowls, and zero national championships.

The two programs' recent fortunes cannot erase their far-reaching impact on college sports, however. Georgetown Hoyas basketball and Miami Hurricanes football were vanguards for the racial transformation of Division I men's televised college sports during the pivotal decade of the 1980s. They forced university, conference, and NCAA officials   not to mention competing programs and fans   to respond to the changes they wrought both on and off the fields and courts of play. This second wave of African American and other minority athletes at both universities set an example for other players and programs. Many of these changes no doubt would have happened in due course absent the rise of these two programs at these two universities located in two cities with checkered racial histories. But Georgetown basketball and Miami football sometimes precipitated and almost always accelerated these transformations. Wittingly or not, these two programs worked in common cause to promote and defend equality for Black and other minority athletes, their legion of common enemies be damned.

NOTES

1. Rise of the Black Style

1. William C. Rhoden, *Forty Million Dollar Slaves: The Rise, Fall, and Redemption of the Black Athlete* (New York: Three Rivers, 2006), 164.

2. As recently as 2012, nearly 90 percent of athletic directors and roughly 95 percent of sports information directors at Football Bowl Subdivision (FBS) universities were white. See Richard Lapchick, "The 2012 Racial and Gender Report Card: College Sport," ncaa .org, July 10, 2013, https://www.ncaa.org/sites/default/files/Final%2B2012%2BCollege %2BRGRC.pdf.

3. Curry Kirkpatrick, "Why the Game Is on the Level," *Sports Illustrated*, March 3, 1980, 30–35, https://vault.si.com/vault/1980/03/03/why-the-game-is-on-the-level-whos-no 1 depaul right-now-but-when-the-ncaas-start-anytime-could-be-so-evenly-distributed -is-the-talent.

4. Richard Pennington, *Breaking the Ice. The Racial Integration of Southwest Conference Football* (Jefferson NC: McFarland, 1987), 157.

5. Rhoden, *Forty Million Dollar Slaves*, 142.

6. George Vecsey, "Sports People; Should Pat Ewing Leave Georgetown?," *New York Times*, January 14, 1983, http://www.nytimes.com/1983/01/14/sports/sports-people -should-pat-ewing-leave-georgetown.html.

7. Quoted in *The U*, directed by Billy Corben, ESPN 30 for 30 documentary, originally aired December 12, 2009.

8. Georgetown Hoyas AP Poll History, https://www.sports-reference.com/cbb/schools /georgetown/polls.html.

9. Georgetown Basketball History Project, "Georgetown All-Americans" entry, http:// www.hoyabasketball.com/players/allamerica.htm, retrieved April 20, 2021.

10. Throughout the book the 1980s are defined as including the 1979–80 through the 1988–89 basketball seasons, and the 1980 through 1989 regular football seasons. Obviously,

the bowl games for those football seasons often happen after the new year; thus, Miami's 1980 bowl game is not considered part of the decade, whereas its 1990 Sugar Bowl victory ending its 1989 national championship season is included.

11. "Hurricanes Football: All-Americans (1980–89)" (Coral Gables FL: Hurricane Club, July 28, 2011), https://hurricanesports.com/news/2011/7/28/205539114.aspx.

12. Quoted in Ed Hinton, "Deep into His Job," *Sports Illustrated*, September 7, 1992, https://www.si.com/vault/1992/09/07/127090/deep-into-his-job-jimmy-johnson-dived-headfirst-into-coaching-the-cowboys-and-he-wont-come-up-for-air-until-he-wins-a-super-bowl.

13. Quoted in George Vecsey, "John Thompson's Wall," *New York Times*, March 26, 1984, http://www.nytimes.com/1984/03/26/sports/john-thompson-s-wall.html.

14. Quoted in Alan Siegel, "Hoya Euphoria: Georgetown Basketball, the Big East, Syracuse, John Thompson Jr., and D.C.; An Oral History," *Washington City Paper*, March 8, 2013, http://www.washingtoncitypaper.com/news/article/13043798/hoya-euphoria-georgetown-basketball-the-big-east-syracuse-john-thompson.

15. Vecsey, "John Thompson's Wall."

16. Quoted in *The U*.

17. Derek Thompson, "Which Sports Have the Whitest/Richest/Oldest Fans?," *Atlantic*, February 10, 2014, http://www.theatlantic.com/business/archive/2014/02/which-sports-have-the-whitest-richest-oldest-fans/283626/.

18. "Fast Facts" (Washington DC: National Center for Education Statistics, U.S. Department of Education, n.d.), https://nces.ed.gov/fastfacts/display.asp?id=72.

19. Ken Fang, "ESPN's John Skipper Talks about Streaming and Hiring African-Americans," AwfulAnnouncing.com, February 18, 2016, http://awfulannouncing.com/2016/espns-john-skipper-talks-about-streaming-and-hiring-african-americans.html.

20. Interview by phone with author, April 30, 2020.

21. Peter Alfano, "John Thompson's Way," *New York Times*, March 8, 1985, http://www.nytimes.com/1985/03/08/sports/sports-of-the-times-john-thompson-s-way.html.

22. Malcom Moran, "St. John's Sets Back Georgetown, 76–67," *New York Times*, January 9, 1983, http://www.nytimes.com/1983/01/09/sports/st-john-s-sets-back-georgetown-76-67.html.

23. Interview with author via email, April 23, 2020.

24. Gary Pomerantz, "Ewing under Siege," *Washington Post*, February 9, 1983, https://www.washingtonpost.com/archive/sports/1983/02/09/ewing-under-siege/a17fe474-6ec8-42a9-8ad6-19880d4d9990/?utm_term=.78f05c01f143.

25. Quoted in *Requiem for the Big East*, directed by Ezra Edelman, ESPN 30 for 30 documentary, originally broadcast March 16, 2014.

26. Curtis Bunn, "We May Never See Another Team Like John Thompson's 1980s Hoyas, Which Captured Black America's Heart," *Atlanta Black Star*, March 11, 2015, http://atlantablackstar.com/2015/03/11/march-madness-reflection-georgetown-black-americas-team-30-years-ago/.

27. Quoted in Tom Callahan, "A Banner Year for Meanness," *Time*, March 14, 1983.

28. Vecsey, "Sports People."

29. John Feinstein, "On Court and Off, Critics Say Hoyas Walk a Hard Line," *Washington Post*, March 20, 1984, https://www.washingtonpost.com/archive/sports/1984/03/20/on-court-and-off-critics-say-hoyas-walk-a-hard-line/2fa1cd9b-0278-4043-a60b-584ff5f86ab8/.

30. Mike Wise, "Big John Is Still Big John," *Washington Post*, February 10, 2007, http://www
.washingtonpost.com/wp-dyn/content/article/2007/02/09/AR2007020902184_3.html.

31. Quoted in Bil Gilbert, "The Gospel According to John," *Sports Illustrated*, December 1, 1980, https://www.si.com/vault/1980/12/01/825202/the-gospel-according-to-john
-georgetown-basketball-was-white-and-wan-before-john-thompson-came-in-to-recruit
-blacks-and-to-preach-discipline-and-education.

32. Quoted in Mark Heisler, "When Michael Graham Gets Excited, Watch Out," *Los Angeles Times*, April 2, 1984, 49.

33. Eve Zibart and Mark Asher, "Hoyas Honored by City, White House," *Washington Post*, April 8, 1984, https://www.washingtonpost.com/archive/sports/1984/04/08
/hoyas-honored-by-city-white-house/2760b4da-2580-425c-9d80-7b58f42484a3/?utm
_term=.511f57b5d686.

34. Curry Kirkpatrick, "Hang On to Your Hats . . . and Heads," *Sports Illustrated*, March 19, 1984, http://www.si.com/vault/1984/03/19/569018/hang-on-to-your-hatsand-heads.

35. "Visual Identity" (Washington DC: Georgetown University, n.d.), https://
visualidentity.georgetown.edu/colors.

36. Anakin Cane, "Miami Hurricanes: Is Hatred for the U Justified?," *Bleacher Report*, July 20, 2010, http://bleacherreport.com/articles/422450-the-hatred-for-the-u-justified
-or-unjustified.

37. Jimmy Johnson, *Turning the Thing Around: Pulling America's Team out of the Dumps—and Myself out of the Doghouse*, with Ed Hinton (New York: Hyperion, 1993), 130.

38. Quoted in *Catholics v. Convicts*, directed by Patrick Creadon, ESPN 30 for 30 documentary, originally aired December 10, 2016.

39. Dan Le Batard, "Miami's Dan Le Batard Reflects on Hurricanes Football Program, Featured in Next 30 for 30," interview by Jennifer Cingari, ESPN *Front Row*, December 2014, http://www.espnfrontrow.com/2014/12/miamis-dan-le-batard-reflects-hurricanes
-football-program-featured-next-30-30/.

40. At the time, neither PSU nor UM were members of a conference, and therefore both were unbound to play in any particular bowl game. The Fiesta Bowl was thus able to sign the two highest ranked and undefeated teams to decide the championship head to head.

41. Michael Weinreb, "The Night College Football Went to Hell," ESPN: *The Magazine*, January 2007, http://www.espn.com/espn/eticket/story?page=fiesta87.

42. Rick Reilly, "The Battle for No. 1," *Sports Illustrated*, December 22, 1986, https://vault
.si.com/vault/1986/12/22/the-battle-for-no-1-using-a-unique-and-highly-sophisticated
-rating-system-which-considers-everything-from-shoes-to-safeties-the-author-explains
-why-miami-will-beat-penn-state-by-85-points.

43. "Greatest Penn State Upsets of All Time—The 1987 Fiesta Bowl," *Black Shoe Diaries*, September 9, 2010, http://www.blackshoediaries.com/2010/9/9/1677482/greatest
-penn-state-upsets-of-all.

44. Irvin and Brown comments quoted in Michael Weinreb, *Bigger Than the Game: Bo, Boz, the Punky QB and How the '80s Created the Celebrity Athlete* (West Hollywood CA: Gotham, 2010), 264.

45. Herschel Nissenson, "Trying to Change Miami Vice to Miami Nice," Associated Press, August 29, 1987, http://www.apnewsarchive.com/1987/Trying-to-Change-Miami
-Vice-to-Miami-Nice/id-17a7234bf5a4c6791730e7725577fcf6.

46. "The 25 Most Hated Teams," *Sports Illustrated,* July 29, 2010, https://www.si.com/more-sports/2013/12/13/most-hatedteams.

47. "Fiesta Bowl Sets Record for TV," *New York Times,* January 6, 1987, http://www.nytimes.com/1987/01/06/sports/fiesta-bowl-sets-record-for-tv.html.

48. Rhoden, *Forty Million Dollar Slaves,* 164–66.

49. Malcom Moran, "Life in the Eye of the Hurricanes," *New York Times,* August 25, 1991, http://www.nytimes.com/1991/08/25/sports/college-football-life-in-the-eye-of-the-hurricanes.html?pagewanted=all.

50. Bruce Feldman, *'Cane Mutiny: How the Miami Hurricanes Overturned the Football Establishment* (New York: New American Library, 2005), 108–12.

51. Moran, "Life in the Eye."

2. Campus Color Barriers

1. Zach Osterman, "IU Reconciles with 1969 Football Players Who Boycotted over Racism," *Indianapolis Star,* May 29, 2015, http://www.indystar.com/story/sports/college/indiana/2015/05/28/indiana-university-announces-reconciliation-1969-iu-10/28089015/.

2. Ian Powers, "The Triumph and Tragedy of the 1950 City College Grand Slam," *New York Daily News,* n.d., http://creative.nydailynews.com/grandslam.

3. Gregory J. Kaliss, *Men's College Athletics and the Politics of Racial Equality* (Philadelphia PA: Temple University Press, 2012), 90–92.

4. Richard Pennington, "Racial Integration of College Football," November 6, 2010, https://richardpennington.com/2010/11/racial-integration-college-football/.

5. Patrick B. Miller and David Kenneth Wiggins, eds., *Sport and the Color Line: Black Athletes and Race Relations in Twentieth-Century America* (London: Routledge, 2004).

6. Charles H. Martin, *Benching Jim Crow: The Rise and Fall of the Color Line in Southern College Sports, 1890–1980* (Champagne: University of Illinois Press, 2010), 294.

7. Phil White, "The Black 14: Race, Politics, Religion and Wyoming Football" (Wheatland: Wyoming State Historical Society, n.d.), WyoHistory.org, http://www.wyohistory.org/essays/black-14-race-politics-religion-and-wyoming-football.

8. Eric Winkler, "Why NCAA Once Banned Slam Dunk?" *DunkorThree.com,* May 14, 2020, https://dunkorthree.com/ncaa-once-banned-slam-dunk/.

9. In 1970 the statewide black population was 1.4 million; California's total population was 19.9 million. Frank Hobbs and Nicole Stoops, *Demographic Trends in the 20th Century: Census 2000 Special Reports* (Washington DC: U.S. Census Bureau, November 2002), https://www.census.gov/prod/2002pubs/censr-4.pdf.

10. Lane Demas, "Integrating the Gridiron," interview by Serena Golden, *Insider HigherEd,* June 23, 2010, https://www.insidehighered.com/news/2010/06/23/demas.

11. Bob Carlton, "Historic 1970 Alabama-USC Football Game Is Subject of Showtime Documentary 'Against the Tide,'" Alabama.com, November 5, 2013, http://www.al.com/entertainment/index.ssf/2013/11/historic_1970_alabama-usc_foot.html.

12. Michael Oriard, *Bowled Over: Big-Time College Football from the Sixties to the BCS Era* (Chapel Hill: University of North Carolina Press, 2009), 39–44.

13. Harry Edwards, *The Revolt of the Black Athlete* (New York: Free Press, 1969), http://www.blackpast.org/aah/harry-edwards-1942.

14. Edwards, *The Revolt*, xxvii.

15. Oriard, *Bowled Over*, 54.

16. Michael Oriard, "College Football's Season of Discontent," *Slate*, September 3, 2009, http://www.slate.com/articles/sports/sports_nut/2009/09/college_footballs _season_of_discontent.html.

17. Dave Zirin, "Race, Power & American Sports," interview with Sut Jhally, Media Education Foundation, 2013, transcript available at http://www.mediaed.org/transcripts /Race-Power-and-American-Sports-Transcript.pdf.

18. Richard O. Davies, *Sports in American Life: A History*, second ed. (Hoboken NJ: Wiley-Blackwell, 2012), 291.

19. David Maraniss, *Clemente: The Passion and Grace of Baseball's Last Hero* (New York: Simon & Schuster, 2006).

20. Ryan Basen, "Fifty Years Ago, Last Outpost of Segregation in N.F.L. Fell," *New York Times*, October 6, 2012, http://www.nytimes.com/2012/10/07/sports/football/50-years -ago-redskins-were-last-nfl-team-to-integrate.html.

21. Dean Anderson, "Cultural Diversity on Campus: A Look at Intercollegiate Football Coaches," *Journal of Sport and Social Issues* 17, no. 1 (April 1993): 61–66.

22. Barry Bozeman and Daniel Fay, "Minority Football Coaches' Diminished Careers: Why Is the 'Pipeline' Closed?," *Social Science Quarterly* 94, no. 1 (March 2013): 29–58, https://www.jstor.org/stable/42864456?seq=1.

23. Jon Entine, *Taboo: Why Black Athletes Dominate Sports and Why We're Afraid to Talk about It* (New York: Public Affairs, 2000), 74.

24. Quoted in Alan Siegel, "Hoya Euphoria: Georgetown Basketball, the Big East, Syracuse, John Thompson Jr., and D.C.; an Oral History," *Washington City Paper*, March 8, 2013, https://www.washingtoncitypaper.com/news/article/13043798/hoya-euphoria -georgetown-basketball-the-big-east-syracuse-john-thompson.

25. Entine, *Taboo*, 72–73.

26. Michael Wilbon, "The Greek's Apology Is Difficult to Accept," *Washington Post*, January 17, 1988

27. Derrick Z. Jackson, "Calling the Plays in Black and White," *Boston Globe*, January 22, 1989. The earlier study was Raymond E. Rainville, Al Roberts, and Andrew Sweet, "Recognition of Covert Racial Prejudice," *Journalism Quarterly* 55, no. 2 (1978): 256–59.

28. John Hoberman, *Darwin's Athletes: How Sport Has Damaged Black America and Preserved the Myth of Race* (Boston MA: Mariner, 1997), 221.

29. Phillip M. House, *Necessities: Racial Barriers in American Sports* (New York: Random House, 1989), 22–23.

30. David J. Leonard, *Playing While White: Privilege and Power on and off the Field* (Seattle: University of Washington Press, 2017), 79; cf. chap. 3.

31. Michael Weinreb, *Bigger Than the Game: Bo, Boz, the Punky QB and How the '80s Created the Celebrity Athlete* (London: Penguin, 2010), 123–26.

32. Princess Gabbara, "The History of the Fade," *Ebony*, December 27, 2016, https:// www.ebony.com/style/history-fade-haircut.

33. Robbie Andreu, "Bosworth: 'I Hate Miami's Football Program,'" *South Florida Sun Sentinel*, September 24, 1986, http://articles.sun-sentinel.com/1986-09-24/sports /8602270285_1_football-program-miami-players-miami-hurricanes.

34. Jimmy Johnson, *Turning the Thing Around: Pulling America's Team out of the Dumps—and Myself out of the Doghouse*, with Ed Hinton (New York: Hyperion, 1993), 131–32.

35. Seth Davis, *When March Went Mad: The Game That Transformed Basketball* (New York: Times, 2009).

36. Zorich and Pierce statements quoted in *Catholics v. Convicts*, directed by Patrick Creadon, ESPN 30 for 30 documentary, originally aired December 10, 2016.

37. Randall Mell, "Notre Defame Getting Gold Welcome to South Bend," *South Florida Sun Sentinel*, October 14, 1988, https://www.sun-sentinel.com/news/fl-xpm-1988-10-14-8802290677-story.html.

38. Rick Telander, "Pluck of the Irish," *Sports Illustrated*, October 24, 1988, https://www.si.com/vault/1988/10/24/118722/pluck-of-the-irish-spunky-notre-dame-laid-claim-to-the-top-spot-in-the-national-rankings-by-outlasting-no-1-miami-31-30.

39. C. Richard King and Charles Fruehling Springwood, *Beyond the Cheers: Race as Spectacle in College Sport* (Albany: SUNY Press, 2001), 152–53.

40. Johnson, *Turning the Thing Around*, 132.

41. Ivan Maisel, "Why 'Catholics vs. Convicts' Is Such a Memorable Game," ESPN.com, December 10, 2016, http://www.espn.com/college-football/story/_/id/18246606/why-catholics-vs-convicts-miami-hurricanes-notre-dame-fighting-irish-such-memorable-game.

42. "What Was the Greatest Fighting Irish Football Game in the History of Notre Dame Stadium?," August 29, 2005, University of Notre Dame website, https://web.archive.org/web/20170619224140/http://www.und.com/sports/m-footbl/spec-rel/082905aaf.html.

43. Matt Fortuna, "The Legacy of the Infamous 'Catholics vs. Convicts' T-shirts," ESPN.com, December 9, 2016, http://www.espn.com/blog/acc/post/_/id/97264/the-story-of-what-happened-after-catholics-vs-convicts.

44. Justin Tinsley, "The Notre Dame vs. Miami Rivalry Is the Most Relevant in This Monstrous Weekend of College Football," *Undefeated*, November 9, 2017, https://theundefeated.com/features/college-football-notre-dame-vs-miami-rivalry-is-the-most-relevant-in-this-monstrous-weekend-of-college-football/.

45. For Princeton and Georgetown lineups and statistics, see Sports Reference College Basketball, "1988–89 Princeton Tigers Roster and Stats" entry, https://www.sports-reference.com/cbb/schools/princeton/1989.html, retrieved April 10, 2021; Sports Reference College Basketball, "1988–89 Georgetown Hoyas Roster and Stats" entry, https://www.sports-reference.com/cbb/schools/georgetown/1989.html, retrieved April 10, 2021.

46. Sean Gregory, "The Game That Saved March Madness," *Sports Illustrated*, March 17, 2014, https://www.si.com/vault/2014/03/17/106443314/the-game-that-saved-march-madness.

47. Alonzo Mourning, "Waking Up," *Players' Tribune*, April 7, 2015, https://www.theplayerstribune.com/en-us/articles/alonzo-mourning-princeton-georgetown-ncaa-tournament-march-madness.

48. Gregory, "The Game That Saved."

49. Gregory, "The Game That Saved."

50. Gregory, "The Game That Saved." Crowd booing clearly audible in *Sports Illustrated*'s companion video segment: https://www.youtube.com/watch?v=5yHlOwFFsyY.

51. Game box score: Sports Reference College Basketball, "Princeton vs. Georgetown Box Score, March 17, 1989" entry, https://www.sports-reference.com/cbb/boxscores/1989-03-17-georgetown.html.

52. Gregory, "The Game That Saved."

53. Patrick B. Miller, "The Anatomy of Scientific Racism," in Miller and Wiggins, *Sport and the Color Line*, 329–30.

54. Matthew Frye Jacobsen, "'Richie' Allen, Whitey's Ways and Me: A Political Education in the 1960s," in *In the Game: Race, Identity, and Sports in the Twentieth Century*, ed. Amy Bass, 19–46 (New York: Palgrave, 2005).

55. Richard Lapchick, *Smashing Barriers: Race and Sport in the New Millennium* (New York: Madison, 2000), 268.

56. Edwards, *The Revolt*, 9.

3. Unlikely Incubators

1. "Traditions," sublink of the "About UM" homepage of the University of Miami, https://welcome.miami.edu/about-um/traditions/index.html, retrieved April 10, 2021.

2. Alex Kellogg, "D.C., Long 'Chocolate City,' Becoming More Vanilla," NPR *Morning Edition*, February 15, 2011, https://www.npr.org/2011/02/15/133754531/d-c-long-chocolate-city-becoming-more-vanilla.

3. For compelling and detailed histories of the Washington DC riots, consult J. Samuel Walker, *Most of 14th Street is Gone: The Washington, DC Riots of 1968* (Oxford UK: Oxford University Press, 2018); and Clay Risen, *A Nation on Fire: America in the Wake of the King Assassination* (Hoboken NJ: Wiley, 2009).

4. Walker, *Most of 14th Street*, chaps. 3–5.

5. Walker, *Most of 14th Street*. 100–101.

6. Risen, *A Nation on Fire*, 4–5.

7. David Maraniss, "The Cloud That Burst on the Class of '68," *Washington Post*, June 5, 1993, https://www.washingtonpost.com/archive/lifestyle/1993/06/05/the-cloud-that-burst-on-the-class-of-68/5850d63e-9ef8-4f04-9005-ddb11ccb9ec6/?utm_term=.3f8d21ed4510.

8. Nelson George, *Elevating the Game: Black Men and Basketball* (Lincoln: University of Nebraska Press, 1999), 207.

9. "DC Never Stood for Dodge City," *Economist, Prospero* blog, February 28, 2013, https://www.economist.com/prospero/2013/02/28/dc-never-stood-for-dodge-city.

10. Mikaela Lefrak, "40 Years Ago Terrorists Took Over the D.C. Council and Shot Marion Barry," WAMU, March 9, 2017, https://wamu.org/story/17/03/09/40-years-ago-today-terrorists-took-d-c-council-shot-marion-barry/.

11. Charles, Howard, and Montgomery counties in Maryland, plus Arlington, Fairfax, and Loudoun counties in Virginia.

12. See table 10.1 in Marvin Dunn, *Black Miami in the Twentieth Century* (Gainesville: University Press of Florida, 1997), 335.

13. Janis Johnson, "Anti-Latin Rage: A War of Words Waged in Miami," *Washington Post*, August 30, 1980, https://www.washingtonpost.com/archive/politics/1980/08/30/anti-latin-rage-a-war-of-words-waged-in-miami/189a4f60-5742-42a0-be3a-7f5d3feca1c5/.

14. Alfred Spellman, "Griselda Blanco's Other Favorite Hitman Dies in Prison," ExtraNewsFeed.com, March 17, 2016, https://extranewsfeed.com/griselda-blanco-s-other-favorite-hitman-dies-in-prison-e13744e0fd89; "Murder Verdicts in Drug Ring Case," *New York Times*, May 14, 1987, https://www.nytimes.com/1987/05/14/us/murder-verdicts-in-drug-ring-case.html.

15. Francisco Alvarado, "1981: Miami's Deadliest Summer," *Miami New Times*, August 10, 2011, https://www.miaminewtimes.com/news/1981-miamis-deadliest-summer-6565290.

16. James Kelly, "South Florida: Trouble in Paradise," *Time*, November 23, 1981, http://www.miamiasis.com/paradise-lost/.

17. Katt Shea, "On Scarface," TrailersFromHell.com, http://trailersfromhell.com/scarface/, retrieved April 10, 2021.

18. Larry Getlen, "Miami's Legendary Club Makes Studio 54 Look Tame," *New York Post*, October 19, 2017, https://nypost.com/2017/10/19/inside-the-mutiny-club-the-1980s-home-to-every-miami-vice/.

19. Bruce Porter and Marvin Dunn, *The Miami Riot of 1980: Crossing the Bounds* (New York: Lexington, 1984).

20. Porter and Dunn, *Miami Riot of 1980*, 56.

21. WTVJ newscast with host Bob Mayer, May 18, 1980, https://www.youtube.com/watch?v=XyXVA7RahMc.

22. Porter and Dunn, *Miami Riot of 1980*, xiii.

23. "Cops Freed in McDuffie Case: Rage at Verdict Erupts into Violence," *Miami Herald*, May 18, 1980, https://www.miamiherald.com/news/local/community/miami-dade/article77769522.html.

24. Quoted in Amy Driscoll, "The McDuffie Riots 25 Years Later," *Miami Herald*, May 15, 2005. See also David Smiley, "McDuffie Riots: Revisiting, Retelling Story—35 Years later," *Miami Herald*, May 16, 2015, https://www.miamiherald.com/news/local/community/miami-dade/article21178995.html.

25. Roshan Nebhrajani, "Liberty City: From a Middle-Class Black Mecca to Forgotten," *New Tropic*, March 13, 2017, https://thenewtropic.com/liberty-city-history-moonlight/.

26. Interview with author by phone, July 8, 2020.

27. *Hip Hop Evolution*, original Netflix series, 2016–, https://www.netflix.com/title/80141782.

28. Interview with author via email, June 20, 2020.

29. María Cristina García, *Havana USA: Cuban Exiles and Cuban Americans in South Florida, 1959–1994* (Berkeley: University of California Press, 1996), see especially chap. 3.

30. Julio Capó Jr., "The White House Used This Moment as Proof the U.S. Should Cut Immigration; Its Real History Is More Complicated," *Time*, August 4, 2017, http://time.com/4888381/immigration-act-mariel-boatlift-history/.

31. García, *Havana USA*, 118.

32. Kelly, "South Florida."

33. Charles Rabin, "Miami Was Once a Murder Capital; the Gunfire Deaths This Year Tell a New Story," *Miami Herald*, July 21, 2017, https://www.miamiherald.com/news/local/crime/article162757543.html#storylink=cpyhttps://www.miamiherald.com/news/local/crime/article162757543.html; Jerry Iannelli, "Crime in Miami-Dade Drops to One-Third of Cocaine-Era Peak, New Data Show," *Miami New Times*, June 14, 2017 https://www.miaminewtimes.com/news/miami-dade-county-crime-rate-drops-to-one-third-the-peak-of-1980s-cocaine-era-new-data-show-9420663.

34. The GU272 Memory Project, https://gu272.americanancestors.org/history/timeline.

35. Noel King, "Georgetown, Louisiana, Part One," *Planet Money*, episode 766, NPR, April 21, 2017, https://www.npr.org/sections/money/2017/04/21/525058118/episode-766-georgetown-louisiana-part-one.

36. The GU272 Memory Project.

37. Rachel L. Swarns, "272 Slaves Were Sold to Save Georgetown; What Does It Owe Their Descendants?" April 16, 2016, https://www.nytimes.com/2016/04/17/us/georgetown-university-search-for-slave-descendants.html.

38. Swarns, "272 Slaves."

39. The GU272 Memory Project.

40. Charlton Tebeau, *The University of Miami: A Golden Anniversary History, 1926–1976* (Miami FL: University of Miami Press, 1976) chap.11, p. 1 emphasis added, https://scholar.library.miami.edu/umdesegregation/pdfs/dlp00190000030001001.pdf.

41. Tebeau, *The University of Miami*, 6.

42. Tebeau, *The University of Miami*, 7–8.

43. Meredith Camel, "Bringing History to Life," *News@TheU*, February 27, 2017, https://news.miami.edu/stories/2017/02/bringing-history-to-life.html.

44. Leonard Shapiro, *Big Man on Campus: John Thompson and the Georgetown Hoyas* (New York: Henry Holt, 1991).

45. Quoted in John Feinstein, "Georgetown: In the Big Time," *Washington Post*, December 2, 1981, https://www.washingtonpost.com/archive/sports/1981/12/02/georgetown-in-the-big-time/c5257b6c-ff59-4203-8ca9-c855e5fee24f/?utm_term=.770a0cd76e2a.

46. Shapiro, *Big Man on Campus*, 80.

47. Statistics courtesy of Basketball Reference, https://www.basketball-reference.com/players/t/thompjo01.html.

48. Quoted in Bil Gilbert, "The Gospel According to John," *Sports Illustrated*, December 1, 1980, https://www.si.com/vault/1980/12/01/825202/the-gospel-according-to-john-georgetown-basketball-was-white-and-wan-before-john-thompson-came-in-to-recruit-blacks-and-to-preach-discipline-and-education.

49. Dave McKenna, "The Power Struggle at Georgetown Goes Back to a Petty, 50-Year Old D.C. High School Hoops Feud," Deadspin.com, March 27, 2017, https://deadspin.com/the-power-struggle-at-georgetown-goes-back-to-a-petty-1793666837. The only school with more NBA alums is Virginia's Oak Hill Academy which, unlike DeMatha, accepts senior-year transfers from schools around the country.

50. Feinstein, "Georgetown."

51. Josh Zumbrun, "The Lingering Legacy of the 60s," *Hoya*, November 9, 2004, http://www.thehoya.com/the-lingering-legacy-of-the-60s/.

52. Braden McDonald and Molly Simio, "Marching On," *Hoya*, March 21, 2014, http://www.thehoya.com/marching-on/.

53. Quoted in Gilbert, "The Gospel."

54. Feinstein, "Georgetown."

55. Quoted in Juan Williams, "John Thompson's Olympic Trial," *Washington Post*, August 28, 1988.

56. Georgetown Basketball History Project, "Scoring Leaders" entry, https://www.hoyabasketball.com/records/scoring_leaders_19.htm, retrieved April 10, 2021.

57. Georgetown Basketball History Project, "Bernard White" entry, http://www.hoyabasketball.com/players/b_white.htm, retrieved April 10, 2021.

58. Gilbert, "The Gospel."

59. Zack J. Tupper, "Hoya Paranoia: How Georgetown Found Its Swagger during the Reagan Years" (senior undergraduate thesis, Georgetown University, May 4, 2009), https://repository.library.georgetown.edu/bitstream/handle/10822/555517/TupperZacharyThesis.pdf?sequence=2.

60. Shapiro, *Big Man on Campus*, 143.

61. Sports Reference College Basketball, "Craig Shelton" entry, https://www.sports-reference.com/cbb/players/craig-shelton-1.html, retrieved April 10, 2021.

62. Mark Asher, "Shelton Keeps On Hustling," *Washington Post*, March 8, 1979, https://www.washingtonpost.com/archive/sports/1979/03/08/shelton-keeps-on-hustling/9d849a5b-fd2e-43e0-8c09-4b54c80a1a31/; Georgetown Basketball History Project, "Craig Shelton" entry.

63. Sports Reference College Basketball, "John Duren" entry, https://www.sports-reference.com/cbb/players/john-duren-1.html, retrieved April 10, 2021.

64. Alejandro Danois, *The Boys of Dunbar: A Story of Love, Hope and Basketball* (New York: Simon & Schuster, 2016), 95–97.

65. Georgetown Basketball History Project, "Records v. Opponents, 1980s" entry, http://www.hoyabasketball.com/records/bb-1980.htm, retrieved April 10, 2021; Georgetown Basketball History Project, "Records v. Opponents, 1990s" entry, http://www.hoyabasketball.com/records/bb-1990.htm, retrieved April 10, 2021.

66. Feinstein, "Georgetown."

67. Feinstein, "Georgetown."

68. Craig T. Smith, *Game of My Life* (New York: Sports Publishing, 2014).

69. Quoted in Bruce Feldman, *'Cane Mutiny: How the Miami Hurricanes Overturned the Football Establishment* (New York: New American Library, 2005), 13.

70. Marc Tracy, "Howard Schnellenberger's Legacy Gets a Shine This Postseason," *New York Times*, December 28, 2017, https://www.nytimes.com/2017/12/28/sports/ncaafootball/howard-schnellenberger-miami-louisville-fau.html.

71. Howard Schnellenberger, *Passing the Torch: Building Winning Football Programs . . . with a Dose of Swagger along the Way*, with Ron Smith (Overland Park KS: Ascend, 2014).

72. Mark Story, "Howard Schnellenberger Offers Assessment of What Has Held Back UK Football Program," *Lexington Herald-Leader*, August 30, 2014, https://account.kentucky.com/paywall/subscriber-only?resume=44507823&intcid=ab_archive.

73. "Teams Laud Howard Schnellenberger," ESPN.com news service, August 27, 2013, http://espn.go.com/college-football/story/_/id/9605253/miami-florida-atlantic-honor-icon-howard-schnellenberger-season-opener.

74. Dirk Chatelain, "Calhoun Foiling NU's Two-Point Try in 1984 Orange Bowl Elevated Miami's Program," *Omaha World-Herald*, September 17, 2015, http://www.omaha.com/huskers/chatelain-calhoun-foiling-nu-s-two-point-try-in-orange/article_9b01a17f-7472-576a-925a-ac5d9190a44f.html.

75. Quoted in *The U*, directed by Billy Corben, ESPN 30 for 30 documentary, originally aired December 12, 2009.

76. Interview with author via email, April 22, 2020.

77. "Black Hoyas Too: A Collection of Voices," *Georgetown Voice*, March 21, 2002, https://georgetownvoice.com/2002/03/21/black-hoyas-too-a-collection-of-voices/.

78. Interview with author by phone, July 8, 2020.

4. Title Town

1. Quoted in Jon Nyatawa, "Miami Notes: 1984 Orange Bowl a Fond Memory for Assistant Coach Art Kehoe," *Omaha World-Herald Bureau*, September 17, 2014, https://www.omaha.com/huskers/miami-notes-orange-bowl-a-fond-memory-for-assistant-coach/article_5fed411e-cfe1-5521-9661-0068aecfcf3b.html.

2. John Feinstein, "Georgetown's Pressure Cooks Up a Title," *Washington Post*, April 3, 1984, https://www.washingtonpost.com/wp-srv/sports/longterm/memories/final4/articles/gtown84.htm.

3. Sports Reference College Football, "1982 Miami (FL) Hurricanes Stats," https://www.sports-reference.com/cfb/schools/miami-fl/1982.html.

4. Andrea Adelson, "Miami Dynasty Born out of '83 Defeat," ESPN.com, September 4, 2013, http://www.espn.com/college-football/story/_/id/9630381/miami-hurricanes-football-dynasty-began-loss-florida-gators-1983-national-championship-season

5. Sports Reference College Football, "1983 Miami (FL) Hurricanes Stats," https://www.sports-reference.com/cfb/schools/miami-fl/1983.html.

6. Michael Wilbon, "Nebraska Falls, 31–30, on Day of Upsets," *Washington Post*, January 3, 1984, https://www.washingtonpost.com/archive/sports/1984/01/03/nebraska-falls-31-30-on-day-of-upsets/7de9a6bd-04ce-424b-a860-4ec5fdc30e55/?utm_term=.6d5ca506ffff.

7. Wilbon, "Nebraska Falls."

8. John Underwood, "No Team Was Ever Higher," *Sports Illustrated*, January 9, 1984, https://www.si.com/vault/1984/01/09/569867/no-team-was-ever-higher.

9. Quoted in Kristen Spillane, "Hurricane Achievement Started with Schnellenberger," *Miami Hurricane*, August 9–September 4, 2013, 13, https://issuu.com/miamihurricane/docs/082913.

10. Mark Asher, "1984 NCAA Basketball Championship," *Washington Post*, April 4, 1984, https://www.washingtonpost.com/archive/sports/1984/04/04/1984-ncaa-basketball-championship/bbff452c-a3fc-4c59-b01e-a43aba1995f1/.

11. Gary Pomerantz, "Georgetown Stretches, but Comes Up Short," *Washington Post*, March 21, 1983, https://www.washingtonpost.com/archive/sports/1983/03/21/georgetown-stretches-but-comes-up-short/c14103a0-1cf2-46b5-b6c2-6cf374e35164/.

12. Thomas Boswell, "Boeheim Cries Foul without Much Sympathy," *Washington Post*, March 11, 1984, https://www.washingtonpost.com/archive/sports/1984/03/11/boeheim-cries-foul-without-much-sympathy/6fe62281-a0a2-4996-92fa-d3b619d8bc13/.

13. Curry Kirkpatrick, "Hang On to Your Hats . . . and Heads," *Sports Illustrated*, March 19, 1984, http://www.si.com/vault/1984/03/19/569018/hang-on-to-your-hatsand-heads.

14. Curry Kirkpatrick, "Who'll Be Destiny's Darling?," *Sports Illustrated*, March 26, 1984, https://www.si.com/vault/1984/03/26/569043/wholl-be-destinys-darling.

15. Quoted in "SMU Loses by 37–36," *New York Times*, March 19, 1984, C1, https://timesmachine.nytimes.com/timesmachine/1984/03/19/issue.html.

16. Mark Asher, "Dayton Out, 61–49," *Washington Post*, March 26, 1984, https://www.washingtonpost.com/archive/sports/1984/03/26/dayton-out-61-49/bfa5d57d-5821-4d06-9b64-10dc14f5a23e/?utm_term=.ba9ee12892c0.

17. Kirkpatrick, "Hang On to Your Hats."

18. Malcom Moran, "Georgetown, Led by Freshmen, Wins Title," *New York Times*, April 3, 1984, http://www.nytimes.com/1984/04/03/sports/georgetown-led-by-freshmen-wins-title-georgetown-84-houston-75.html.

19. Eve Zibart and Mark Asher, "Hoyas Honored by City, White House," *Washington Post*, April 8, 1984, https://www.washingtonpost.com/archive/sports/1984/04/08/hoyas-honored-by-city-white-house/2760b4da-2580-425c-9d80-7b58f42484a3/?utm_term=.511f57b5d686.

20. "1983 Nebraska Football Roster," HuskerMax.com, https://www.huskermax.com/rosters/1983-roster/, retrieved April 11, 2021.

21. Joel Dinerstein, "Backfield in Motion," in *In the Game: Race, Identity and Sports in the Twentieth Century*, ed. Amy Bass, 169–90 (New York: Palgrave Macmillan, 2005).

22. Interview with author by phone, February 20, 2020.

23. Dinerstein, "Backfield in Motion."

24. Racial identities for players in the 1984 Orange Bowl inferred from images displayed on screen by NBC during the first quarter of its televised broadcast (see: https://www.youtube.com/watch?v=XvNHfzitK0U). Racial identities for the 2017 Nebraska defense inferred from player photos, using the depth chart announced by the football team prior to its opening game against Arkansas State. See Michael Bruntz, "Huskers Release First Depth Chart," 247Sports.com, August 28, 2017, https://247sports.com/college/nebraska/Article/Nebraska-football-releases-opening-depth-chart-106585515/; the two white starters were tackle Mick Stoltenberg and linebacker Chris Weber.

25. George Vecsey, "Nebraska Also Won," *New York Times*, January 4, 1984, B9, https://www.nytimes.com/1984/01/04/sports/sports-of-the-times-nebraska-also-won.html.

26. Adam Rittenberg, "Miami, FSU Felt the Need for Speed, and Changed the Game in the Process," ESPN.com, July 1, 2015, http://www.espn.com/college-football/story/_/id/13174840/how-jimmy-johnson-bobby-bowden-changed-college-football.

27. Interview with author by email, May 18, 2020.

28. Jimmy Johnson, *Turning the Thing Around: Pulling America's Team out of the Dumps—and Myself out of the Doghouse*, with Ed Hinton (New York: Hyperion, 1993), 129–30.

29. Video: John Thompson interview with Gary Miller, ESPN *Up Close*, February 14, 2001, http://www.espn.com/page2/tvlistings/upclosearchive2001.html; transcript: "Hoy History Maker," ESPN.com, February 25, 2001, http://a.espncdn.com/ncb/s/johnthompson.html. Thompson said similar things in 2014: "How John Thompson and Nolan Richardson Broke through the Championship Color Barrier," *Yahoo Sports*, March 13, 2014 https://sports.yahoo.com/news/how-john-thompson-and-nolan-richardson-broke-through-the-championship-color-barrier-083032327-ncaab.html.

30. "Year-by-Year Statistics/Final Release," Cuse.com, https://cuse.com/sports/2009/2/3/sidebar_52.aspx, retrieved April 11, 2021.

31. Jamal Murphy, "Big East Leads the Way in Hiring Black Men's Basketball Head Coaches," *Undefeated*, February 14, 2020, https://theundefeated.com/features/big-east-leads-the-way-in-hiring-black-mens-basketball-head-coaches/.

32. Adam Zagoria, "The 14-Team Big Ten Had 14 White Basketball Coaches: Michigan AD Warde Manuel Can Change That," *Forbes*, May 20, 2019, https://www.forbes.com/sites/adamzagoria/2019/05/20/the-14-team-big-ten-had-14-white-basketball-coaches-michigan-ad-warde-manuel-can-change-that/#475bac4f74e4.

33. Shane Mettlen, "We Are Georgetown: John Thompson Jr. Reflects on Coaching the Hoyas to an NCAA Title," *Washingtonian*, March 12, 2014 https://www.washingtonian.com/2014/03/12/we-are-georgetown-john-thompson-jr-reflects-on-coaching/.

34. Quoted in Alan Siegel, "Hoya Euphoria: Georgetown Basketball, the Big East, Syracuse, John Thompson Jr., and D.C.; an Oral History," *Washington City Paper*, March 8, 2013, https://www.washingtoncitypaper.com/news/article/13043798/hoya-euphoria-georgetown-basketball-the-big-east-syracuse-john-thompson.

35. Brandon Edler, "The 20 Greatest Sneakers in Georgetown Basketball History," *Complex*, February 9, 2012, https://www.complex.com/sneakers/2012/02/the-20-greatest-sneakers-in-georgetown-basketball-history/8.

36. Quoted in Mike Bianchi, "Pipe Dream: FAU Coach Schnellenberger Says Program Will Rise to Top," *Orlando Sentinel*, August 16, 2001, http://articles.orlandosentinel.com/2001-08-16/sports/0108160254 1 boca-raton-slippery-rock-schnellenberger.

37. Michael Janofsky, "Miami Doesn't Seem Upset by the Loss of Its Coach," *New York Times*, August 26, 1984, S9, https://www.nytimes.com/1984/08/26/sports/miami-doesn-t-seem-upset-by-the-loss-of-its-coach.html.

38. Sports Reference College Football, "1984 Miami (FL) Hurricanes Schedule and Results" entry, https://www.sports-reference.com/cfb/schools/miami-fl/1984-schedule.html, retrieved April 11, 2021.

39. Sports Reference College Football, "1984 Miami (FL) Hurricanes Stats" entry, https://www.sports-reference.com/cfb/schools/miami-fl/1984.html, retrieved April 11, 2021.

40. Quoted in Dave Sell, "Terps Still Remember College Football's Greatest Comeback," *Register-Guard* (Eugene OR), October 10, 1987, 16.

41. Tony Kornheiser, "'Hail Mary' Preys on Miami's Mind," *Washington Post*, November 25, 1984, https://www.washingtonpost.com/archive/sports/1984/11/25/hail-mary-preys-on-miamis-mind/cc24030c-fe89-4aa9-a451-946e521fbdb9/.

42. Greg Garber, "No Matching the Talent of 1986 Miami Hurricanes," *Hartford Courant*, December 27, 1992, https://www.latimes.com/archives/la-xpm-1992-12-27-sp-5064-story.html.

43. Brian Goff, "The Rise and Fall of University of Miami Football," *Forbes*, October 28, 2015, https://www.forbes.com/sites/briangoff/2015/10/28/the-rise-and-fall-of-university-of-miami-football/.

44. The Cleveland Browns drafted FAU tight end Harrison Bryant with pick No. 115 and the New York Jets took FIU quarterback James Morgan with pick No. 125, before the Jacksonville Jaguars finally selected Miami linebacker Shaquille Quarterman with the No. 140 pick. According to lists compiled by 247Sports.com, from the 1981 to 2020 drafts only Hurricanes defensive back Brandon McGee, chosen at No. 149 in 2013, was selected later than Quarterman. "Miami Hurricanes Draft History," 247Sports.com, https://247sports.com/Team/Miami-Hurricanes-Football-13/DraftPicks/?year=alltime, retrieved April 11, 2021.

45. Mike Waters, "Patrick Ewing Q&A: On Pearl Washington, The Punch and the Syracuse-Georgetown Rivalry," *Syracuse Post-Standard*, December 15, 2016, http://www

.syracuse.com/orangebasketball/index.ssf/2016/12/patrick_ewing_qa_on_pearl
_washington_the_punch_and_the_syracuse-georgetown_rival.html.

46. Frank Fitzpatrick, *The Perfect Game: How Villanova's Shocking 1985 Upset of Mighty Georgetown Changed the Landscape of College Hoops Forever*. New York: Thomas Dunne, 2013; Kyle Keiderling, *The Perfect Game: Villanova vs. Georgetown for the National Championship*. New York: Morning Star Communications, 2012.

47. Alan Siegel, "The Troubled, Tormented, Surprisingly Lucky Life of Michael Graham," *Washingtonian*, March 22, 2015, https://www.washingtonian.com/2015/03/22/the -troubled-wasted-surprisingly-lucky-life-of-michael-graham/.

48. Tony Kornheiser, "Reggie and Miracles," *Washington Post*, March 20, 1987, https:// www.washingtonpost.com/archive/sports/1987/03/20/reggie-and-miracles/02cf2913 -0600-47be-a42a-21b90fb14707/.

49. Roy S. Johnson, "Williams Is Going Out in Style," *New York Times*, March 2, 1987, https://www.nytimes.com/1987/03/02/sports/the-big-east-tournament-williams-is -going-out-in-style.html.

5. John and Jimmy, Patrick and Michael

1. Juan Williams, "John Thompson's Olympic Trial," *Washington Post*, August 28, 1988, https://www.washingtonpost.com/archive/lifestyle/magazine/1988/08/28/john -thompsons-olympic-trial/ca40dadd-5ca1-4a0e-a8fd-566e80525262/; Tom Callahan, "A Banner Year for Meanness," *Time*, March 14, 1983 http://content.time.com/time/subscriber /article/0,33009,951986-1,00.html.

2. Bruce Lowitt and Ira Rosenfeld, "John Thompson: A Firm Hand at the Helm," *Free Lance-Star*, March 16, 1985, 11–12, https://news.google.com/newspapers?id=uOJLAAAAIBAJ &sjid=9osDAAAAIBAJ&pg=800,2451944&hl=en.

3. Wikipedia, "1976 United States Men's Olympic Basketball Team" entry, https://en .wikipedia.org/wiki/1976_United_States_men%27s_Olympic_basketball_team, retrieved April 11, 2021.

4. Quoted in Bil Gilbert, "The Gospel According to John," *Sports Illustrated*, December 1, 1980, https://www.si.com/vault/1980/12/01/825202/the-gospel-according-to-john -georgetown-basketball-was-white-and-wan-before-john-thompson-came-in-to-recruit -blacks-and-to-preach-discipline-and-education.

5. Larry Keith, "Homebodies Rule in D.C.," *Sports Illustrated*, February 16, 1976.

6. Quoted in Curry Kirkpatrick, "Why the Game Is on the Level," *Sports Illustrated*, March 3, 1980, 30–35.

7. Mark Asher, "Iowa Trips Georgetown, 81–80," *Washington Post*, March 17, 1980, https:// www.washingtonpost.com/archive/sports/1980/03/17/iowa-trips-georgetown-81-80 /31a5f6d3-c5d6-42ed-8ca5-e8ccdb68c9a7/.

8. Leonard Shapiro, *Big Man on Campus: John Thompson and the Georgetown Hoyas* (New York: Henry Holt, 1991), 154–57.

9. Ralph Wiley, "The Master of the Key: After Years of Relying on Others to Unlock Doors for Him, Georgetown's Center Patrick Ewing Will Soon Go Off on His Own," *Sports Illustrated*, January 7, 1985, https://www.si.com/vault/1985/01/07/627663/the -master-of-the-key.

10. Michael Wilbon and Leonard Shapiro, "Thompson: Letter on Ewing 'Backfired,'" *Washington Post*, April 15, 1981, https://www.washingtonpost.com/archive/sports/1981 /04/15/thompson-letter-on-ewing-backfired/b366943b-2f07-40f9-a44e-0444f7c8860f /?utm_term=.07ffa795ff67.

11. Michael Wilbon, "Georgetown Basketball: In the Bonus Situation," *Washington Post*, May 17, 1982, https://www.washingtonpost.com/archive/sports/1982/05/17/georgetown -basketball-in-the-bonus-situation/67af6cb7-cd24-4b74-8771-99bcdc30361c/.

12. Williams, "John Thompson's Olympic Trial."

13. Richard E. Lapchick, *Sport and Society: Equal Opportunity or Business as Usual?* (Thousand Oaks CA: Sage, 1996), 16.

14. Mike Wise, "Big John Is Still Big John," *Washington Post*, February 10, 2007, http:// www.washingtonpost.com/wp-dyn/content/article/2007/02/09/AR2007020902184 .html.

15. Dom Amore, "Ollie Proud to Be Role Model for African American Coaches," *Hartford Courant*, March 31, 2014, https://www.courant.com/sports/uconn-mens-basketball /hc-uconn-men-notes-0401-20140331-story.html.

16. Alan Siegel, "Hoya Euphoria: Georgetown Basketball, the Big East, Syracuse, John Thompson Jr., and D.C.; an Oral History," *Washington City Paper*, March 8, 2013, https:// www.washingtoncitypaper.com/news/article/13043798/hoya-euphoria-georgetown -basketball-the-big-east-syracuse-john-thompson.

17. Sports Reference College Football, "Oklahoma State Cowboys School History" entry, https://www.sports-reference.com/cfb/schools/oklahoma-state/index.html, retrieved April 11, 2021.

18. Wikipedia, "1983 Oklahoma State Cowboys Football Team" entry, https://en .wikipedia.org/wiki/1983_Oklahoma_State_Cowboys_football_team, retrieved April 11, 2021.

19. "Johnson Heads for Miami's Beaches," *Oklahoman*, June 6, 1984, https://oklahoman .com/article/2070583/johnson-heads-for-miamis-beaches.

20. Bill Haisten, "How Limited Was OSU Financially in 1983? Jimmy Johnson Interviewed with Rice," *Tulsa World*, July 11, 2018, https://www.tulsaworld.com/sportsextra /osusportsextra/bill-haisten-how-limited-was-osu-financially-in-jimmy-johnson/article _179357ab-2153-5b39-a918-edcfa475602f.amp.html.

21. Quoted in "Jimmy Johnson: A Football Life," an NFL Films production, season 12, episode 9, originally aired on NFL Network, November 14, 2012.

22. "Johnson Heads for Miami's Beaches"; and Michael Janofsky, "Miami Doesn't Seem Upset by the Loss of Its Coach," *New York Times*, August 26, 1984, S9, https://www.nytimes .com/1984/08/26/sports/miami-doesn-t-seem-upset-by-the-loss-of-its-coach.html.

23. Interview with author by phone, February 20, 2020.

24. Wikipedia, "Bedlam Series" entry, https://en.wikipedia.org/wiki/Bedlam_Series, retrieved April 11, 2021.

25. Interview with author by phone, February 20, 2020.

26. Ross Dellenger, "Pete and Jimmy: LSU's Ed Orgeron Draws from His Mentors to Build a Champion," *Advocate* (Baton Rouge LA), August 17, 2017, https://www.theadvocate .com/baton_rouge/sports/lsu/article_2d9f626c-7e5c-11e7-953c-03fabd24cea5.html.

27. "LSU Football Coach Ed Orgeron Previews Spring Practice," by Glen West, *Sports Illustrated* (online), February 18, 2020, https://www.si.com/college/lsu/football/expectations-leading-into-spring.

28. Jimmy Johnson, *Turning the Thing Around: Pulling America's Team out of the Dumps—and Myself out of the Doghouse*, with Ed Hinton (New York: Hyperion, 1993).

29. Phil Hersh, "Irish Eyes Aren't Smiling," *Chicago Tribune*, December 2, 1985, https://www.chicagotribune.com/news/ct-xpm-1985-12-02-8503230680-story.html.

30. Peter Alfano, "Miami Coach Ignores Critics and Remains Successful," *New York Times*, January 4, 1989, https://www.nytimes.com/1989/01/04/sports/football-miami-coach-ignores-critics-and-remains-successful.html.

31. Alfano, "Miami Coach Ignores Critics."

32. Quoted in Peter Alfano, "Talk Is Cheap at Showdown," *New York Times*, December 31, 1986, https://www.nytimes.com/1986/12/31/sports/fiesta-bowl-talk-is-cheap-at-showdown.html.

33. Malcolm Moran, "Hurricanes Overwhelm the Sooners to Claim No. 1," *New York Times*, January 2, 1988, https://www.nytimes.com/1988/01/02/sports/orange-bowl-hurricanes-overwhelm-the-sooners-to-claim-no-1.html.

34. "Longtime Cowboys and NFL Assistant Coach Hubbard Alexander Passes Away," DallasCowboys.com, August 29, 2016, https://www.dallascowboys.com/news/longtime-cowboys-and-nfl-assistant-coach-hubbard-alexander-passes-away-411596.

35. Jeff Legwold, "Jimmy Johnson to Be Part of Hall of Fame's Centennial Class," ESPN.com, January 12, 2020, https://www.espn.com/nfl/story/_/id/28472454/jimmy-johnson-part-hall-fame-centennial-class.

36. IMDB, "Jimmy Johnson" entry, https://www.imdb.com/name/nm0425384/?ref_=nv_sr_srsg_3, retrieved April 11, 2021.

37. Sports Reference College Basketball, "Patrick Ewing" entry, https://www.sports-reference.com/cbb/players/patrick-ewing-1.html, retrieved April 11, 2021; Georgetown Basketball History Project, "Records" entry, https://www.hoyabasketball.com/records.htm, retrieved April 11, 2021.

38. Mike Richard, "State Boys' Basketball Championship History," *Telegram* (Worcester MA), March 17, 2017, https://www.telegram.com/news/20170317/state-boys-basketball-championship-history; Ronnie Flores, "Ranking McDonald's Top 35," ESPN.com, January 30, 2012, http://www.espn.com/high-school/boys-basketball/story/_/id/7521370/ranking-mcdonald-top-35; Wikipedia, "Mr. Basketball USA" entry, https://en.wikipedia.org/wiki/Mr._Basketball_USA#Winners, retrieved April 11, 2021.

39. As fate would have it, the 1980 Olympic team was coached by Dave Gavitt, who had just stepped down after eleven years coaching at Boston College to become the first commissioner of the new Big East conference that would include his former and Ewing's future programs. The 1980 team never got to participate because of the U.S. boycott of the Moscow games.

40. John Conceison, "Cambridge Rindge & Latin's Pat Ewing Visits," *Heights*, November 17, 1980, https://newspapers.bc.edu/?a=d&d=bcheights19801117.2.67.

41. John Feinstein, "Georgetown: In the Big Time," *Washington Post*, December 2, 1981, https://www.washingtonpost.com/archive/sports/1981/12/02/georgetown-in-the-big-time/c5257b6c-ff59-4203-8ca9-c855e5fee24f/?utm_term=.0b964a38e773.

42. Michael Wilbon, "Ewing," *Washington Post*, January 1, 1982, https://www
.washingtonpost.com/archive/sports/1982/01/01/ewing/dcd0e6a8-a477-4d35-a19c
-c6b9d1dea5b0/.

43. Malcolm Moran, "The Protection of Pat Ewing," *New York Times*, January 12, 1982,
https://www.nytimes.com/1982/01/12/sports/the-protection-of-pat-ewing.html.

44. Sports Reference College Basketball, "Patrick Ewing" entry.

45. Roy S. Johnson, "Patrick Ewing and the Art of Defense," *New York Times*, September 29, 1985, https://www.nytimes.com/1985/09/29/magazine/patrick-ewing-and-the
-art-of-defense.html.

46. Sports Reference College Basketball, "Patrick Ewing" entry.

47. George Vecsey, "Sports People; Should Pat Ewing Leave Georgetown?," *New York
Times*, January 14, 1983, https://www.nytimes.com/1983/01/14/sports/sports-people
-should-pat-ewing-leave-georgetown.html.

48. Scott Henry, "Ranking the 20 Greatest Players in Big East Basketball History," *Bleacher
Report*, December 17, 2012, https://syndication.bleacherreport.com/amp/1447386-the
-20-greatest-players-in-big-east-history.amp.html.

49. Sports Reference College Basketball, "Patrick Ewing" entry.

50. Basketball Reference, "1994 NBA Finals Knicks vs. Rockets" entry, https://www
.basketball-reference.com/playoffs/1994-nba-finals-knicks-vs-rockets.html, retrieved April
11, 2021.

51. "Patrick Ewing's Basketball Hall of Fame Enshrinement Speech," YouTube.com,
https://www.youtube.com/watch?v=47IcYphP6ZE, retrieved April 11, 2021.

52. Roy S. Johnson, "Thompson-Ewing's Rite of Passage," *New York Times*, April 1, 1985,
https://www.nytimes.com/1985/04/01/sports/thompson-ewing-s-rite-of-passage.html.

53. "Michael Irvin Returns to St. Thomas Aquinas High School," NFL.com, January
27, 2016, https://www.nfl.com/news/michael-irvin-returns-to-st-thomas-aquinas-high
-school-0ap3000000629268.

54. A. J. Mada, "Cowboys' Michael Irvin Opens Up to Joe Buck on Infamous 'White
House,'" *USA Today*, June 6, 2018, https://cowboyswire.usatoday.com/2018/06/06/dallas
-cowboys-michael-irvin-joe-buck-undeniable-att-directv/.

55. Sports Reference College Football, "Michael Irvin" entry, https://www.sports
-reference.com/cfb/players/michael-irvin-1.html, retrieved April 11, 2021.

56. Christy Cabrera Chirinos, "Richards Passes Irvin to Set UM Freshman Receiving Record," *Capital Gazette*, November 19, 2016, https://www.capitalgazette.com/fl-um
-hurricanes-notes-1120-20161119-story.html.

57. "Michael Irvin University of Miami Sports Hall of Fame," YouTube.com, https://
www.youtube.com/watch?v=7-xFaJa5eNw, retrieved April 11, 2021.

58. Interview with author by phone, July 8, 2020.

59. Jim Martz, *Tales from the Hurricane Sideline: A Collection of the Greatest Hurricane
Stories Ever Told* (New York: Sports Publishing, 2012).

60. "1987 Miami Hurricanes: Undefeated National Champions," 3 Penny Films, https://
www.youtube.com/watch?v=eEDVBJECWWE.

61. Sports Reference College Football, "Michael Irvin" entry.

62. Michael Irvin interview with *The Joe Show*, WQAM Miami, August 23, 2019, https://
wqam.radio.com/media/audio-channel/8-23-19-best-joe-show-podcast.

63. Bruce Feldman, *'Cane Mutiny: How the Miami Hurricanes Overturned the Football Establishment* (New York: New American Library, 2005), 92–94.

64. Richard Hoffer, "The Party's Over," *Sports Illustrated*, July 8, 1996, https://vault.si.com/vault/1996/07/08/the-partys-over-the-drug-case-of-michael-irvin-took-a-dark-turn-when-a-dallas-cop-allegedly-tried-to-have-him-killed.

65. Michael Irvin, speech at Pro Football Hall of Fame, August 4, 2007, transcript, https://www.profootballhof.com/players/michael-irvin/.

66. Cyd Zeigler, "Michael Irvin: The Playmaker Preaches," *Out*, July 11 2011, https://www.out.com/entertainment/sports/2011/07/10/michael-irvin-playmaker-preaches.

67. Dancing with the Stars Wiki, "Michael Irvin" entry, https://dancingwiththestars.fandom.com/wiki/Michael_Irvin, retrieved April 11, 2021.

68. Quoted in Peter Walsh, "The Playmaker," SLAM (online), April 27, 2017, https://www.slamonline.com/archives/the-playmaker-michael-irvin-interview/.

6. Commodifying Color

1. Richard Sandomir, "College Football Championship Game TV Viewership Drops 23 Percent," *New York Times*, January 12, 2016, http://www.nytimes.com/2016/01/13/sports/ncaafootball/college-football-championship-game-tv-ratings-drop-23-percent.html.

2. "College Bowl Payouts Surpass $500 Million," Associated Press, April 14, 2005, http://espn.go.com/college-football/story/_/id/12688517/college-bowl-game-payouts-surpass-500-million-first-year-college-football-playoff.

3. Allen R. Sanderson and John J. Siegfried, "The Role of Broadcasting in National Collegiate Athletic Association Sports," *Review of Industrial Organization* 52, iss. 2, no. 8 (2018): 305–21, https://home.uchicago.edu/arsx/The%20Role%20of%20Broadcasting%20in%20National%20Collegiate%20Athletic%20Association%20Sports.pdf.

4. Oriana Schwindt, "March Madness 2016: How CBS and Turner Made the NCAA's Basketball Playoffs Bigger Than NBA Playoffs," *International Business Times*, March 16, 2016, http://www.ibtimes.com/march-madness-2016-how-cbs-turner-made-ncaas-basketball-playoffs-bigger-nba-playoffs-2337504.

5. "1981 National Championship Season," Clemson SC: Clemson University, 2006, https://clemsontigers.com/wp-content/uploads/2018/07/1981_national_championship-1.pdf.

6. "2016 Clemson Football Roster," Tigernet.com, https://www.tigernet.com/2016-Clemson-Football-Roster, retrieved April 11, 2021.

7. Interview with author by phone, April 30, 2020.

8. Interview with author by email, May 18, 2020.

9. Michael Weinreb, *Season of Saturdays: A History of College Football in 14 Games* (New York: Scribner, 2014), 142–50.

10. Dennis Dodd, "The Birth of Swag: 30 Years into the Launch of College Football's New Era," CBSSports.com, August 17, 2016, https://www.cbssports.com/college-football/news/the-birth-of-swag-30-years-into-the-launch-of-college-footballs-new-era/.

11. Rick Reilly, "Miami Vice Twice," *Sports Illustrated*, October 6, 1986, https://vault.si.com/vault/1986/10/06/miami-vice-twice-of-dubious-reputation-off-the-field-but-a-fearsome-force-on-it-the-hurricanes-blew-away-oklahoma-again-and-took-over-no-1-.

12. Michael Weinreb, "The Night College Football Went to Hell," ESPN: The Magazine, January 2007, http://www.espn.com/espn/eticket/story?page=fiesta87&redirected=true.

13. John Kunda, "'Good Guy' Vinny Wins Maxwell Honor," *Morning Call* (Lehigh Valley and Allentown PA), December 3, 1986, https://www.mcall.com/news/mc-xpm-1986 -12-03-2548334-story.html.

14. Interview with author via email, June 20, 2020.

15. Linda Robertson, "Hatred for Notre Dame Was Just Part of the 'U' Brand," *Miami Herald*, October 27, 2016, https://www.miamiherald.com/sports/spt-columns-blogs/linda -robertson/article110973737.html.

16. Interview with author by phone, July 8, 2020.

17. Nelson George, *Elevating the Game: Black Men and Basketball* (Lincoln: University of Nebraska Press, 1999), 211.

18. Jalen Rose, "Man of The People: Jalen Rose on New Book *Got To Give The People What They Want* and the Art of Trash Talking," interview by Adelle Platon, Vibe.com, October 9, 2015, http://www.vibe.com/2015/10/jalen-rose-got-to-give-the-people-what -they-want-interview/.

19. Grant Hill, "Grant Hill's Response to Jalen Rose," *New York Times*, March 16, 2011, https://thequad.blogs.nytimes.com/2011/03/16/grant-hills-response-to-jalen-rose/.

20. Patrick Hruby, "The Passion of Patrick Ewing," *Washingtonian*, January 14, 2018, https://www.washingtonian.com/2018/01/14/the-passion-of-patrick-ewing-georgetown -basketball-ncaa/.

21. The other four college teams were Notre Dame football 1993, USC football 2005, Duke basketball 1991–92, and UNLV basketball 1989–90, https://www.si.com/more-sports /2011/06/17/17most-hated-teams-of-all-time.

22. Theresa A. Martinez, "Popular Culture as Oppositional Culture: Rap as Resistance," *Sociological Perspectives* 40, no. 2 (1997): 265–86, quote at 279, https://www.jstor .org/stable/1389525.

23. Ken McLeod, "The Construction of Masculinity in African American Music and Sports," *American Music* 27, no. 2 (Summer 2009): 204–26, quote at 223, https://www .jstor.org/stable/25602271.

24. Officially, the colors are Pantone Blue 282 and Cool Gray 10: https://www.georgetown .edu/color-guide/.

25. Jonny Amon, "More Than Coaches: Looking Back on the Thompson Era," *Georgetown Voice*, April 28, 2017, https://georgetownvoice.com/2017/04/28/more-than-coaches -looking-back-on-the-thompson-era/.

26. *Hip Hop Evolution*, season 2, episode 1, directed by Darby Wheeler, October 19, 2018.

27. "2 Live Crew," Hip Hop Golden Age, http://hiphopgoldenage.com/artists/2-live-crew/.

28. *Hip Hop Evolution*, season 2, episode 1.

29. Quote from email interview with author, April 26, 2020.

30. Steven Godfrey, "2 Live Crew's Uncle Luke Brought Swagger to Miami," SBNation. com, October 7, 2015, http://www.sbnation.com/college-football/2015/10/7/9411057 /luther-campbell-uncle-luke-coach-miami-hurricanes.

31. Interview with author by email, May 18, 2020.

32. "Warriors of Liberty City," series page, Starz.com, retrieved April 11, 2021, https:// www.starz.com/us/en/series/39040/episodes?season=1.

33. Dan Wetzel and Don Yaeger, *Sole Influence: Basketball, Corporate Greed, and the Corruption of America's Youth* (New York: Grand Central, 2000), 24–26.

34. "Nike Profits Increase 84%," Associated Press, July 10, 1990, https://www.nytimes.com/1990/07/10/business/nike-profits-increase-84.html.

35. Matthew Kish, "Longtime Nike Board Member John Thompson to Retire," *Portland Business Journal*, May 28, 2020, https://www.bizjournals.com/portland/news/2020/05/28/longtime-nike-board-member-john-thompson-to-retire.amp.html.

36. At first glance, the sneaker version Blackmon wears during his first appearance on screen in the movie appears to be the famed Nike "Terminator" Hoyas shoe (see this youtube: https://www.youtube.com/watch?v=koRKdhiF1Tw). However, thanks to the thorough accounting of the 20 greatest Hoyas sneakers by Complex.com's Brandon Edler, the color pattern of the Blackmon version clearly reveals it to be the Dynasty model. Brandon Edler, "The 20 Greatest Sneakers in Georgetown Basketball History," Complex.com, February 9, 2012, https://www.complex.com/sneakers/2012/02/the-20-greatest-sneakers-in-georgetown-basketball-history/8. Edler ranks the Terminator and the Dynasty, respectively, as the first- and fifth-ranked sneakers in the program's history.

37. Edler, "20 Greatest Sneakers."

38. Edler, "20 Greatest Sneakers."

39. Zac Dubasik, "Why the Nike Terminator Was the Perfect Shoe for the Hoyas: Remembering the Hoya's '80s Classic, the Terminator," SoleCollector.com, March 24, 2014, https://solecollector.com/news/2014/03/why-the-nike-terminator-was-the-perfect-shoe-for-the-hoyas.

40. Todd Boyd, "The Day the Niggaz Took Over," in *Out of Bounds: Sports, Media and the Politics of Identity*, ed. Aaron Baker and Todd Boyd (Bloomington: Indiana University Press, 1997), 138–39.

41. Matthew Kish, "Sonny Vaccaro, the University of Miami and the $250 Million NCAA Shoe Business," *Portland Business Journal*, December 18, 2014, https://www.bizjournals.com/portland/blog/threads_and_laces/2014/12/sonny-vaccaro-the-university-of-miami-nike-adidas.html.

42. Matthew Kish, "Miami Hurricanes, the Original Nike School, Sign a 12-year Deal with Adidas," *Portland Business Journal*, January 8, 2015, https://www.bizjournals.com/portland/blog/threads_and_laces/2015/01/miami-hurricanes-the-original-nike-school-sign-a.html.

43. Phone interview with author, February 12, 2020.

44. Reggie Wade, "Nike, Michael Jordan Commit $140 Million to Support the Black Community," Yahoo.com, June 5, 2020 https://finance.yahoo.com/news/nike-commits-40-million-to-support-the-black-community-135747947.html.

45. Dan Steinberg, "John Thompson, Georgetown and Nike," *Washington Post*, October 26, 2012, https://www.washingtonpost.com/news/dc-sports-bog/wp/2012/10/26/john-thompson-georgetown-and-nike/.

46. Ron Hampston, "Black History Month: Remember When the Georgetown Hoyas Wore Kente Cloth?" *Sportsfan Journal*, February 18, 2016, http://www.thesportsfanjournal.com/sports/basketball/black-history-month-remember-georgetown-hoyas-wore-kente-cloth/.

47. "Make Georgetown Kente Again: The Saga of Georgetown's Failed New Court Design Contest," CasualHoya.com, June 9, 2016, https://www.casualhoya.com/2016/6/9/11878160/georgetown-hoyas-basketball-court-kente-cloth-make-georgetown-kente-again.

48. "Here Is Georgetown's New Basketball Court," CasualHoya.com, June 9, 2015, https://www.casualhoya.com/2015/6/9/8744759/georgetown-hoyas-new-basketball-court-verizon-center; "Make Georgetown Kente Again."

49. Kevin Allen, "Miami Hurricanes Will Wear Uniforms and Cleats Made from Ocean Garbage," *USA Today*, August 20, 2018, https://www.usatoday.com/story/sports/2018/08/20/miami-hurricanes-wear-uniforms-made-ocean-garbage/1045237002/.

50. Madison Ashley, "President DeGioia Addresses Nike Labor Disputes," *Hoya*, April 19, 2016, https://thehoya.com/president-degioia-addresses-nike-labor-disputes/.

51. Kristi Dosh, "Significant Growth in College Apparel," ESPN.com, September 16, 2013, https://www.espn.com/blog/ncfnation/post/_/id/82927/significant-growth-in-college-apparel.

52. Jack Doyle, "All Sports, All the Time, 1978–2008," PopHistoryDig.com, April 2, 2008. https://www.pophistorydig.com/topics/tag/espn-1980s/.

53. National Collegiate Athletic Association v. Board of Regents of the University of Oklahoma, 468 U.S. 85 (1984), https://www.oyez.org/cases/1983/83-271.

54. James Andrew Miller, Steve Eder, and Richard Sandomir, "College Football's Most Dominant Player? It's ESPN," *New York Times*, August 24, 2013, https://www.nytimes.com/2013/08/25/sports/ncaafootball/college-footballs-most-dominant-player-its-espn.html.

55. Ronald A. Smith, *Play-by-Play: Radio, Television, and Big-Time College Sport* (Baltimore MD: Johns Hopkins University Press, 2001), see chap. 23.

56. Jerry McConnell, "CFA Reaches $31 Million, 2-Year TV Deal with ABC," *Oklahoman*, March 7, 1985, https://oklahoman.com/article/2100774/cfa-reaches-31-million-2-year-tv-deal-with-abc.

57. Smith, *Play-by-Play*, 168.

58. Dave Joseph, "UM Signs Contract with CBS in '85–86, CBS to Air at Least Three Games," *South Florida Sun-Sentinel*, January 25, 1985, https://www.sun-sentinel.com/news/fl-xpm-1985-01-25-8501030189-story.html.

59. Smith, *Play-by-Play*, 170.

60. Howard P. Chudacoff, *Changing the Play: How Power, Profit, and Politics Transformed College Sports Book* (Champagne: University of Illinois Press, 2015), 128–29.

61. Miller, Eder, and Sandomir, "College Football's."

62. Bowl game schedules for 1979 and 2019 seasons, respectively: Sports Reference College Football, "1979 College Football Bowl Games," https://www.sports-reference.com/cfb/years/1979-bowls.html, and "2019 College Football Bowl Games," https://www.sports-reference.com/cfb/years/2019-bowls.html, retrieved April 28, 2021.

63. Bill Bender, "CFB 150: Top 10 Most Impactful Games in College Football History," *The Sporting News*, November 6, 2019, https://www.sportingnews.com/us/ncaa-football/news/cfb-150-top-10-most-impactful-games-in-college-football-history/obqtalymtvi914i3xj76ktozn.

64. Sanderson and Siegfried, "The Role of Broadcasting."

65. "ESPN, Inc. Fact Sheet," https://espnpressroom.com/us/espn-inc-fact-sheet/, retrieved April 11, 2021.

66. Norman Chad, "ESPN Rises from the Dust with Diamond Schedule," *Washington Post*, September 7, 1989 https://www.washingtonpost.com/archive/sports/1989/09/07

/espn-rises-from-dust-with-diamond-schedule/f990bcef-f3f7-42d5-9561-8834960fc204/;
Dashiell Bennett, "The Revolutionary Strategy That Made ESPN an $8 Billion Company,"
Business Insider, May 24, 2011, https://www.businessinsider.com/espn-an-8-billion-company
-2011-5.

67. Mike DeBonis, "The World's Most Dangerous Basketball Team," *Slate*, March 29,
2007, http://www.slate.com/articles/sports/sports_nut/2007/03/the_worlds_most
_dangerous_basketball_team.html.

68. Nihal Kolur, "Everything You Need to Know about Miami's Turnover Chain,"
Sports Illustrated, November 24, 2017, https://www.si.com/college/2017/11/24/miami
-hurricanes-gold-turnover-chain; David Furones, "Turnover Chain Song by Miami Rapper SoLo D a Hit among Hurricanes Fans," *South Florida Sun-Sentinel*, November 17, 2017,
https://www.sun-sentinel.com/sports/miami-hurricanes/fl-sp-um-turnover-chain-song
-20171117-story.html.

69. Lyssa Goldberg, "History Reveals Iconic 'U' Logo's Meaning," *Miami Hurricane*,
April 26, 2012, http://www.themiamihurricane.com/2012/04/26/history-reveals-iconic
-%E2%80%98u%E2%80%99-logo%E2%80%99s-meaning-2/.

7. Common Enemies

1. Quoted in Walter Byers, with Charless Hammer, *Unsportsmanlike Conduct: Exploiting College Athletes* (Ann Arbor: University of Michigan Press, 1995), 311n18.

2. Joseph N. Crowley, *The NCAA's First Century in the Arena*, digital edition (Indianapolis: National Collegiate Athletic Association, 2006), 65, http://citeseerx.ist.psu.edu
/viewdoc/download?doi=10.1.1.119.6843&rep=rep1&type=pdf.

3. Kenneth Shropshire, *In Black And White: Race and Sports in America* (New York:
New York University Press, 1996), 108.

4. Ray Yasser, "The Black Athletes' Equal Protection Case against the NCAA's New
Academic Standards," *Gonzaga Law Review* 19 (1983): 83–103, https://digitalcommons
.law.utulsa.edu/cgi/viewcontent.cgi?article=1038&context=fac_pub.

5. Yasser, "Black Athletes' Equal Protection Case."

6. The respective percentages for the first three years, in order, were 81 percent, 90 percent, and 87 percent. "Blacks Hit Hard by Proposition 48, Survey Shows," Associated Press,
September 9, 1988, https://www.nytimes.com/1988/09/09/sports/blacks-hit-hard-by
-proposition-48-survey-shows.html.

7. William C. Rhoden, "Thompson's Protest Intensifies Debate," *New York Times*, January 16, 1989, https://www.nytimes.com/1989/01/16/sports/big-east-thompson-s-protest
-intensifies-debate.html.

8. William F. Reed, "A New Proposition: An NCAA Rule Deemed Unfair to Minorities
Drew Angry Reactions, and a Walkout," *Sports Illustrated*, January 23, 1989, https://www
.si.com/vault/1989/01/23/119260/a-new-proposition-an-ncaa-rule-deemed-unfair-to
-minorities-drew-angry-reactions-and-a-walkout.

9. Rhoden, "Thompson's Protest Intensifies Debate."

10. Reed, "A New Proposition."

11. William C. Rhoden, "Thompson Returns as N.C.A.A. Acts to Delay Rule," *New
York Times*, January 21, 1989, https://www.nytimes.com/1989/01/21/sports/thompson
-returns-as-ncaa-acts-to-delay-rule.html.

12. Jack Kroll, "Race Becomes the Game: A Defiant Coach Challenges the NCAA's Rule Book," *Newsweek*, January 30, 1989, 56–59.

13. Reed, "A New Proposition."

14. Randall Mell, "Most State Recruits Have Made the Grade," *South Florida Sun-Sentinel*, July 19, 1987, http://articles.sun-sentinel.com/1987-07-19/sports/8703010188 _1_recruits-requirements-test-score.

15. Randall Mell, "UM Coach Vows to Take No Prop 48s," *South Florida Sun-Sentinel*, August 5, 1988, http://articles.sun-sentinel.com/1988-08-05/sports/8802150239_1 _standards-proposition-qualifiers.

16. "Miami Eases Policy on Proposition 48," *Los Angeles Times*, August 6, 1989, http:// articles.latimes.com/1989-08-06/sports/sp-395_1_miami-hurricanes.

17. Byers, *Unsportsmanlike Conduct*, 317.

18. "Who Can Play? An Examination of NCAA's Proposition 16," Statistics in Brief (Washington DC: National Center for Education Statistics, U.S. Department of Education, August 1995), https://nces.ed.gov/pubs/web/95763.asp.

19. Rick Telander, *Hundred Yard Lie: The Corruption of College Football and What We Can Do to Stop It* (Champagne: University of Illinois Press, 1996), 99.

20. "A D.C. Story: Georgetown's John Thompson Jr.," interview, *Kojo Nnamdi Show*, April 26, 2012, https://thekojonnamdishow.org/shows/2012-04-26/dc-story-georgetowns -john-thompson-jr.

21. Marcus Fuller, "Black Coaches Vanish from Big Ten Basketball, Once a Model for Diversity," *Star Tribune*, March 4, 2017, https://www.startribune.com/black-coaches-vanish -from-big-ten-once-a-model-for-diversity-in-college-basketball/415396354/.

22. Rob Dauster, "'It's Very Disappointing': The Number of Black Head Coaches Continues to Fall at College Hoops' Highest Level," March 3, 2020, https://collegebasketball .nbcsports.com/2020/03/03/its-very-disappointing-the-number-of-black-head-coaches -continues-to-fall-at-college-hoops-highest-level/. Percentages cited in the text are rounded to the nearest whole number.

23. Interview with author by phone, April 30, 2020.

24. Chris Hummer, "College Football Still Has a Diversity Problem among Its Coaches," 247Sports.com, June 4, 2020, https://247sports.com/college/stanford/Article/College -football-coaches-diversity-minority-head-coach-numbers--147843640/.

25. Adam Zagoria, "On Hiring of African-American Coaches in Division 1 Basketball, 'Progress Is a Process,'" Zagsblog.com, April 26, 2018, http://www.zagsblog.com/2018/04 /16/on-hiring-of-african-american-coaches-in-division-1-basketball-progress-is-a-process/.

26. Shannon Ryan, "With Number of Black Head Coaches Down, NCAA Needs Its Own Rooney Rule," *Chicago Tribune*, January 18, 2016, https://www.chicagotribune.com /sports/ct-ncaa-black-coaches-ryan-column-spt-0118-20160117-column.html.

27. Pat Forde, "Why Big Ten's Hiring of Kevin Warren Is So Significant," *Yahoo Sports*, June 4, 2019, https://sports.yahoo.com/why-big-tens-hiring-of-kevin-warren-is-so-significant -185412233.html.

28. Brock Fritz, "Report Finds College Sports Leaders Lacking Diversity," *Athletic Business*, December 2019, https://www.athleticbusiness.com/college/report-finds-college -sports-leaders-lacking-diversity.html; Richard Lapchick, "College Sports Continue to Fall Short When It Comes to Hiring Diversely," ESPN.com, December 18, 2019, https://

www.espn.com/college-football/story/_/id/28325924/college-sports-continue-fall-short
-comes-hiring-diversely.

29. Kelsey Boyd, "Board of Governors Diversity and Inclusion Programming Impact,"
NCAA press release, April 22, 2019, http://www.ncaa.org/about/resources/media-center
/news/board-governors-diversity-and-inclusion-programming-impact.

30. "Presidential Pledge: The Pledge and Commitment to Promoting Diversity and Gender Equity in Intercollegiate Athletics," http://www.ncaa.org/about/resources/inclusion
/ncaa-presidential-pledge, statistics as of August 1, 2020.

31. "NCAA Elects Independent Leaders to Top Board," NCAA press release, April 30,
2019, http://www.ncaa.org/about/resources/media-center/news/ncaa-elects-independent
-leaders-top-board.

32. Tom D'Angelo, "Manny Diaz Achieved Dream Job as Miami's Head Coach
That Started When Family Fled Cuba," *Palm Beach Post*, January 11, 2019, https://www
.palmbeachpost.com/sports/20190111/manny-diaz-achieved-dream-job-as-miamis-head
-coach-that-started-when-family-fled-cuba.

33. Taylor Branch, "The Shame of College Sports," *Atlantic*, October 2011, https://
www.theatlantic.com/magazine/archive/2011/10/the-shame-of-college-sports/308643/.

34. Billy Hawkins, *The New Plantation: Black Athletes, College Sports, and Predominantly
White NCAA Institutions* (New York: Palgrave Macmillan, 2010), 131.

35. Jonathan Yardley, "Crying Foul over the Knight Report," *Washington Post*, March
25, 1991, https://www.washingtonpost.com/archive/lifestyle/1991/03/25/crying-foul
-over-the-knight-report/edf7323e-3787-467e-8372-aa2eda84275f/.

36. Ramogi Huma and Ellen J. Staurowsky, "How the NCAA's Empire Robs Predominantly Black Athletes of Billions in Generational Wealth" (Riverside CA: National College
Players Association, 2020), https://www.ncpanow.org/news/releases-advisories/study
-how-the-ncaas-empire-robs-predominantly-black-athletes-of-generational-wealth. Four-
year estimates rounded by author to the nearest $100,000 increment.

37. Jemele Hill, "Why Black Athletes Should Leave White Colleges," *Atlantic*, October 2019, 11–14.

38. Tramel Raggs, "Five-Star Makur Maker Picks Howard over Blue Bloods Kentucky
and UCLA," *Washington Post*, July 3, 2020.

39. Michael McCann, "In Denying O'Bannon Case, Supreme Court Leaves Future of
Amateurism in Limbo," *Sports Illustrated*, October 3, 2016, https://www.si.com/college
/2016/10/03/ed-obannon-ncaa-lawsuit-supreme-court; the ruling is O'Bannon v. NCAA,
et al., No. 14-16601 (9th Cir. 2015).

40. Michael McCann, "Why the NCAA Lost Its Latest Landmark Case in the Battle
over What Schools Can Offer Athletes," *Sports Illustrated*, March 8, 2019, https://www.si
.com/college/2019/03/09/ncaa-antitrust-lawsuit-claudia-wilken-alston-jenkins; the ruling is Jenkins v. NCAA, No. 14-md-2541 CW (N.D. Cal. 2016).

41. Antonio Ray Harvey, "Black Student Athletes in California Can Now Say, 'Show
Me the Money,'" *L.A. Watts Times*, October 10, 2019, http://www.lawattstimes.com/index
.php?option=com_content&view=article&id=6157:black-student-athletes-in-california
-can-now-say-show-me-the-money&catid=12&Itemid=110.

42. John Taylor, "NCAA Board of Governors Gives Unanimous Go-Ahead for Athletes
to Benefit off Their Names, Images, Likenesses," by NBCsports.com, October 29, 2019,

https://collegefootballtalk.nbcsports.com/2019/10/29/ncaa-board-of-governors-gives
-unanimous-go-ahead-for-athletes-to-profit-off-their-names-images-likenesses/; "Board
of Governors Starts Process to Enhance Name, Image and Likeness Opportunities," NCAA
press release, http://www.ncaa.org/about/resources/media-center/news/board-governors
-starts-process-enhance-name-image-and-likeness-opportunities.

43. "The State(s) of NIL Legislation," *Sports Business Daily*, December 2, 2019, https://
www.sportsbusinessdaily.com/Journal/Issues/2019/12/02/In-Depth/NIL-map.aspx.

44. Bil Gilbert, "The Gospel According to John," *Sports Illustrated*, December 1, 1980,
https://www.si.com/vault/1980/12/01/825202/the-gospel-according-to-john-georgetown
-basketball-was-white-and-wan-before-john-thompson-came-in-to-recruit-blacks-and-to
-preach-discipline-and-education.

45. Ron Fimrite, "The Head Hoya—a Revealing Look," *Sports Illustrated*, February 18,
1991, https://www.si.com/vault/1991/02/18/106782431/the-head-hoyaa-revealing-look.

46. Quoted in Ed Hinton, "Deep into His Job," *Sports Illustrated*, September 7, 1992, https://
www.si.com/vault/1992/09/07/127090/deep-into-his-job-jimmy-johnson-dived-headfirst
-into-coaching-the-cowboys-and-he-wont-come-up-for-air-until-he-wins-a-super-bowl.

47. Sarah Pulliam Bailey, "Liberty's Jerry Falwell Jr. Apologizes for Tweet; Director
of Diversity Resigns," *Washington Post*, June 8, 2020, https://www.washingtonpost.com
/religion/2020/06/08/liberty-falwell-blackface-tweet/.

48. Barrett Sallee, "Liberty DBs Tayvion Land, Kei'Trel Clark Enter Transfer Portal
Because of 'Racial Insensitivity,'" CBSsports.com, June 22, 2020, https://www.cbssports
.com/college-football/news/liberty-dbs-tayvion-land-keitrel-clark-enter-transfer-portal
-because-of-racial-insensitivity/.

49. Adam Rittenberg and Michelle Steele, "Iowa Football and Kirk Ferentz See Black
Players Speak Out on Program's Racial Inequities," ESPN.com, July 27, 2020, https://www
.espn.com/college-football/story/_/id/29517486/iowa-football-kirk-ferentz-see-black
-players-speak-program-racial-inequities; John Steppe, "Former Iowa Football Strength
Coach Chris Doyle to Receive over $200,000 in Benefits," *Gazette* (Cedar Rapids IA),
June 19, 2020, https://www.thegazette.com/former-iowa-hawkeyes-assistant-chris-doyle
-to-receive-over-200000-in-benefits-20200619.

50. Jill Martin, Alicia Lee, and Saba Hamedy, "Oklahoma State Football Coach Responds
after Star Running Back Chuba Hubbard Calls for Change," CNN.com, June 16, 2020, https://
edition.cnn.com/2020/06/15/sport/mike-gundy-osu-chuba-hubbard-trnd/index.html.

51. Myron Medcalf, "LeVelle Moton, NCCU Men's Basketball Coach, Bothered by
Silence of White Power 5 Coaches," ESPN.com, May 31, 2020, https://www.espn.com
/mens-college-basketball/story/_/id/29248680/levelle-moton-nccu-men-basketball
-coach-bothered-silence-white-power-five-coaches.

52. Medcalf, "LeVelle Moton."

53. Brian Davis, "Texas Coach Tom Herman Opens Up on Race Relations as His Longhorns Speak Up in Team Meetings," *Austin American Statesman*, June 1, 2020, https://www
.hookem.com/story/20200601/texas-coach-tom-herman-opens-race-relations-longhorns
-speak-team-meeting/.

54. Matt Bonesteel, "NCAA Bans Championship Events in Mississippi Because of Its
Flag," *Washington Post*, June 19, 2020, https://www.washingtonpost.com/sports/2020/06
/19/sec-issues-ultimatum-mississippi-over-state-flag-that-features-confederate-symbol/.

55. Amira Rose Davis, "College Athletes Are, Once Again, Protesting Racism: Could This Time Be Different?," interview by Emma Pettit, *Chronicle of Higher Education*, June 15, 2020.

56. Jason Whitlock, "Fab Five Film Fantasy, Not Documentary," FoxNews.com, March 15, 2011, https://www.foxsports.com/stories/college-basketball/fab-five-film-fantasy-not-documentary.

57. Interview with author via email, June 20, 2020.

INDEX